# My Turn

A Memoir

# My Turn

## When Caregiving Roles Reverse

*To Debbie,
With deep appreciation
for the gifts of love that bind us
one generation to another
time without end,
Linda Wright*

# Linda Wright

Graywood Press

Tallahassee, Florida

Paperback ISBN: 978-1-945505-33-1
Kindle ISBN: 978-1-945505-34-8

Library of Congress Control Number: 2017960512
Cataloging in Publication Data on file with publisher.

Graywood Press
c/o CMI
4822 South 133rd Street
Omaha, NE 68137


Production, Distribution and Marketing: Concierge Marketing Inc.


Cover photos: The author; her father, Horace, in the US Navy during WWII; and mother, Daisy, 1940s. Back cover paintings, Robin F. Gray.


Printed in the United States
10 9 8 7 6 5 4 3 2 1

*To Robin, the love of my life.*

# *Part 1*

# In the Soup

An osprey circled high above the inlet, scanning the water for fish under the surface, then swooping down, dipping its talons into the sea with a splash, surprising the prey. Rising up from the water and into the air, the powerful bird seized the flapping fish in its claws, carrying it back to the top of a tall tree to feed its chicks. Mesmerized by the accuracy, power, and grace of the bird and the vulnerability of the fish, I watched in awe the dance of survival and death.

Death had once terrified me. I woke from sleep realizing that someday I would not exist. Emergency trips to a hospital wrenched me away from holiday celebrations, school days, picnics, appointments. Everything was secondary to managing my disorder. Each time the medical intervention restored me, my joy in the ordinary soared. Doctors had readjusted their predictions as I lived past my tenth birthday, then my twentieth. In less than a year I would be fifty.

While many of my friends lamented the loss of their youth, I celebrated a victory with each new gray hair and every wrinkle on my face. I had escaped capture. My bleeding disorder caused less disruption in my routine than it had during my childhood and adolescence. Over time I no longer feared my own death. I could see myself, not solely in the vulnerable fish but also in the tenacious bird.

I shivered from the chilly night air. "Let's go inside," I said to Robin. "I need to get up early tomorrow and call my parents."

It had become my habit to telephone my parents every Sunday morning. When I called them from our vacation cottage, my mother's voice was thready.

"Are you all right?" I asked.

"Linda, enjoy yourself. Don't worry about us. Just relax on your vacation. You deserve the time off." Then she changed the subject. "I hope it is cooler there than it is here. Have you been bird watching?"

The call ended with my usual, "I love you, and tell Dad I love him too."

Unsettled by my mother's evasion, I turned to Robin. We had lived together for twenty-five years by then. To my eyes, Robin was as young as she had been when we first met in college. We had become friends, then roommates, and later realized that we wanted to spend the rest of our lives with each other. We acknowledged that our bond was more than a friendship. We loved each other. During that time, Robin's parents and my parents had joined us for most holidays and special occasions. In the past few years we had watched our parents become elderly.

"You think we should go check on them after we leave?" I asked her.

"Sure," she replied.

We were only midway through our two-week vacation in Maine and there seemed to be no immediate need to leave earlier than planned. The lobster boat engines woke us at dawn. As we ate our breakfast at the oak cabin table, we watched the fishermen stopping at each of their color-coded buoys, pulling up their traps. By midmorning we were out on the cabin deck. Robin with her head tilted over her watercolor paints and paper, capturing the egg-yolk yellow day lilies, sapphire hydrangea blossoms, and scarlet geraniums with each meticulous stroke of her brush. Sitting beside her, I worked on a piece of needlework. Each of us stopped occasionally to pick up the binoculars and watch a seabird bobbing along on a wave.

Ending each day with the same routine I had done in the morning, I lay my yoga mat on the wood floor. My back pain no longer limited my walking and standing now that I practiced the gentle stretches. By early evening we read in bed and slept to the lapping tide.

On the Saturday we left Maine, we hurried to pack the car before checkout time. Our dog Penny, part Beagle and part Brittany spaniel, scampered to her favorite spot in the car by the rear window. The calm pace of vacation was beginning to pick up speed.

The next morning, Robin and I drove the two hours to my parents' home in Western Massachusetts. As I opened the back door to their house, I heard Kay's voice.

"What else does Daisy put in the soup? She must use something other than chicken and green beans!"

"I don't know," Dad answered with a shrug.

Kay leaned over a simmering pot on the stove. Her gray hair in tight permanent wave curls had frizzed in the steam. She looked unsure about what to do next.

"Mom's in bed," Dad announced before I had closed the door behind me. His weariness, confusion, and fear wrapped itself around me with his hug. "We are trying to make soup and not disturb her," he whispered.

Something must be wrong. Why is mother in bed? My father depended on Mom to prepare his meals. He considered it his job to wash the dishes after a meal, using only a trickle of hot water to conserve. When he finished washing and rinsing the dishes, he set each plate on the rack, tilting them precisely. Then he scoured the enamel sink until it glistened. If no one else was around to cook for him, he would boil an egg or fry a ground beef patty, but that was it. Without my mother to give step-by-step instructions, he looked helpless. He had removed all the spice jars from the cabinet, placed them on the counter, and stood staring at them in bewilderment.

"Oh my," Kay said, "we were supposed to finish this before you two arrived!" She wiped her brow, then smiled, "It's so good to see you."

Kay lived down the street from my parents. She was not related by blood, although she would joke, "We don't know this for a fact. I was adopted." She was eight years younger than my mother, and they were more like sisters than friends. Kay didn't cook in her own kitchen. She preferred sliding a frozen dinner into the microwave oven.

"This isn't how it smells when Daisy makes it," I heard Kay say to Robin.

"Let's see if I can help." Robin stepped toward the sink.

I kept walking through the kitchen and down the hallway eager to see my mother. In four footsteps I passed the bathroom. I could detect the faint smell of urine in the house. My mother would never have allowed that if she were able to clean.

I entered my parents' bedroom. Hesitating at the door, I focused my eyes on the small lump under the quilt that looked like a rag doll with only a head and hands visible. Over the past few years osteoporosis had shrunk Mom's height, inch by inch. Now at eighty-five years of age her spine was misshaped into a frozen forward bend.

Years ago, Mom had been diagnosed with Parkinson's disease. Her medications were less effective now in controlling the tremors. As she lifted her hands to reach out to me, it looked as if a puppeteer controlled her hands and head, twisting and jerking them with strings.

"Don't look so worried," she said as I approached the bedside. "My own mother died when she was eighty-six. I probably will too." Her eighty-sixth birthday would be in three months.

Without thinking, I blurted out, "No!" I struggled to keep my voice free of despair. I swallowed. "You've always said you wanted to live to be one hundred."

Mom appeared as weak as the hot water and skim milk she now called tea. I sat down on the lid of the bedside commode, reaching out my hand and stroking her white hair. I had not imagined such a radical change in her mobility in one month.

I wanted to cry, but instead I scanned my parents' bedroom, attempting to regain some composure. In the forty-seven years my parents had lived in this house, the bedroom had been re-wallpapered only once, shortly after we had moved into the house. The wallpaper had faded to a dusty gray with pale pink flowers. Five small pieces of furniture were wedged into the room. I stood by her side since there was no room for a chair.

A few years ago twin beds replaced their double bed. "Neither of us sleeps well anymore," explained my mother at the time. "We toss and turn and kick each other."

The space between the foot of my mother's bed and the dresser was so narrow you could not open the drawers fully. No two pieces of furniture matched and each looked battered and worn with age.

Mom squeezed my hand. "I have some hairline fractures in my back, the doctor says."

"Can I get you anything?" I asked.

"I need to use the commode." She paused, "Your father has difficulty emptying it without spilling."

She shifted one leg and then the other leg. It took several seconds for her to roll onto her side. As she struggled to sit up, she winced. She looked so fragile. I worried that I could break one of her brittle bones if I helped her stand. Her delicate skin reminded me of rice paper, puckered and flecked with age. "Hold onto my arm, Mom," I said.

She tried to smile, "It's not as bad as what you have had to deal with in your life," she said when she caught me looking at her with concern. She had used this phrase often, exaggerating any pain I had and belittling her own.

I flinched at the comparison. Suffering is not a competitive sport. Why does she need to compare her pain to what I experienced? She was not the only one who had said, "At least I don't have what you do." It annoyed me when people called me courageous. It may have given them a way to distance themselves from their own fear, but it provided me with no comfort.

I silenced my internal ranting and refocused on helping Mom to the commode, pulling down her underpants before she sat. I left her sitting on the commode and reached into the dresser drawer for a clean pair of underwear. "There's a pair I rinsed out hanging in the bathroom," I heard her say. It must have been some time since she had been able to walk down the basement stairs to use the washing machine. I couldn't imagine how she had made it to the bathroom before soiling her pants.

It took several minutes for me to help her back onto the bed and into a position where she could rest. She looked exhausted by the effort. The sunlight from the window highlighted the soft wrinkles on her pale face.

How could I not have known about the severity of her condition? Had I chosen not to notice or had she hidden things the way I had withheld bad news from her? During the past few years, we had established a routine. Once a month I would drive the hour and a half to my parents' home, usually with Robin. We would arrive in the early afternoon and leave before suppertime, so my mother would have no obligation to serve us a meal.

During our visits, Mom would often sit in her rocking chair knitting mittens. My father would slump into his recliner as we all searched for things to talk about. Dad had always been a good listener. There had been a time when my mother talked politics, religion, science, life, and death. As the spaces in her spinal column narrowed, so did the things that mattered to her.

Had there been times when she positioned herself in her rocking chair before my arrival, propped up her back by leaning on the chair's arms, and assumed the posture for receiving guests?

"It's the most comfortable chair for my back," my mother explained. "Just like President Kennedy used to say after he injured his back." The question I asked myself now was did she return to bed exhausted, as soon as we drove away?

Being honest with myself, I remembered how I covered up my pain from her. Living away from my mother's sight made it easier. I rarely told her the whole truth anymore, leaving out details about my latest injury or omitting the details of a trip to the hospital for an infusion. Why make them worry, I had told myself when there is nothing they can do?

Now we had switched roles. I understood my mother's pretense. "Did the doctor give you anything for the pain?" I asked knowing in advance what the answer would be.

"You know pain medications upset my stomach, so I don't take them," she said.

"How about just one Tylenol, Mom?"

"Oh, all right," she said wrinkling her nose. She sounded too weary to argue.

While emptying the urine from the commode into the toilet bowl, I realized all the things Mom had been unable to do anymore. Did she take the prescriptions her doctor ordered? Had my father remembered to take his medications without my mother to remind him? I doubted it; he seemed more forgetful. Had Dad been able to hear her if she called to him? He missed many of my words, even when I shouted.

The implications of my parents' situation spilled out in a stream.

After Mom swallowed the capsule, I sat with her for a few minutes until she dozed off, and then I went back to the kitchen. The sink was now cluttered with dirty dishes. With Robin's help the soup was cooling in the plastic tubs spread out in rows. Kay's shoulders drooped. At my suggestion, she went home for a rest.

"Is your mother asleep?" Dad asked. "I can always tell when she's asleep. Her hands stop shaking."

I nodded. "Why don't you sit down awhile, Dad? We'll clean up."

Soon I could hear my father snoring. With my parents napping, Robin and I did some housecleaning and laundry.

"I wish I could stay overnight with them, but I absolutely must go to work tomorrow morning," I whispered to Robin.

When Dad woke up, he announced he was going for a walk. "Have to get my walk in before we eat."

Robin reheated enough soup for the four of us. I set the table and put out the crackers. I put Mom's serving in a mug and brought it to her in the bedroom.

Before leaving, I kissed my mother and promised to return soon. "We'll be fine dear," Mom said. "Kay checks on us every day."

As much as I wanted to pretend that they were still able to care for themselves and each other, I knew they needed me to help. Their lives depended on my care as my well-being had once depended on them. When I backed our car out of my parents' driveway, I said to Robin, "I don't know how I will manage it. I have to make time to come back here soon. They need me."

# Do No Harm

From my parents I learned that during the first months of my life in 1949, I seemed like any other child. When I began to crawl and stand, bruises appeared on my pudgy arms and legs. "I'm so careful with Linda, but she still has black and blue marks. Aren't you worried?" Mom said to Dad. He shrugged and turned to feed me another spoonful of mashed squash.

One of the stories my parents told became embedded in my own memory, as if I could actually remember it myself.

As a toddler, I loved taking a bath. I played with the floating Ivory soap, splashing and giggling. It had a pungent smell and made bubbles as Mom lathered my hair. I wiggled as she scrubbed my back with the washcloth.

One evening, in a hurry to get to the bath, I slipped and hit the bridge of my nose on the edge of the porcelain tub. It was something that could happen to any toddler still learning how to walk. By the next morning, a deep blue sac appeared under my tongue. It hurt when I tried to eat or drink. My mother rushed to a neighbor's apartment. "Can you take me to the hospital? Something's wrong with Linda."

Noises from metal instruments clanked as they dropped onto trays in the emergency room. The unfamiliar smells of disinfectant and isopropyl alcohol filled the air. The bright lights erased all the shadows.

The on-call physician bent over me and put his fingers on the pressure points under my chin. He squeezed hard.

My mother gasped, "Don't do that. She bruises easily."

The man in the white coat glared at her. "Let me do my job or I'll have you removed from the room," he snarled. He left welts around my tiny neck where his fingers had pressed. Even when he saw what he had done, he didn't apologize for accusing my concerned mother of being a hysterical woman.

The doctor ordered a blood transfusion. He stuck a needle into my arm and pulled it out. Then he stuck a needle into my other arm. "It's hard to find a vein on a child this young," he said more to himself than as an explanation to my mother. By this time I was wailing and struggling to get away. The nurse held me down while the doctor took a scalpel and cut a line on my ankle, inserting a tube into the vein so the blood could flow from the glass bottle and into me.

"I want to keep her here overnight for observation," he said, removing the IV line and wrapping a bandage over the wounds he had made. Then he admitted me to the pediatric ward. Dad had come to the hospital on the city bus. After he got out of work, he found a note from my mother on the kitchen table explaining where we were. The nurse was trying to put me in a crib with cold, slippery bars. I stood up raising my arms toward Dad. He shook his head sadly.

My mother took the charge nurse aside. "My daughter will climb right out of that crib."

"Don't worry, we have many children in cribs. They don't get out," replied the nurse.

The lights flickered. Visiting hours ended. My parents looked at each other and then at me.

"We have to go now." Dad kissed my fingers.

"I'll be back to get you in the morning," Mom sniffled.

By the time my parents reached the elevator door, they turned to see me tottering as fast as I could behind them. I had climbed to the top of the bars and shimmied down to the polished linoleum floor, running to catch up with Mom and Dad.

What my parents did next, I don't know. They didn't say. My parents recalled the details from their different perspectives. My father told the story with pride, like the story he told about purchasing one guaranteed-to-be-spill-proof baby dish after another, only to watch me overcome the newest foil within minutes. I have no memory of ever sitting in a high chair spilling pureed vegetables onto the floor for my dad's entertainment, but he seemed pleased by my reaction. His daughter could problem solve. She was intelligent, gutsy too. Of course I could get out of that crib and free myself.

My mother told the story of my first hospitalization with remorse. Mom expected that another woman would understand a mother knew her own child better than anyone else. Each time my mother told me this memory, she would end with, "I was afraid of that doctor. I couldn't stand up to him."

She had done everything she could to make a safe home for me. Frustrated that she could not make the doctor or the nurse understand, I could hear her anger and fear each time she told me the story. Her baby had been mistreated while she stood powerless. She vowed she would never let that happen again. It was an impossible promise to keep.

# *Baby Goes to Boston*

"Stop your fidgeting and sit still," my mother said as she shampooed my hair and then wrapped it in rags while it was still damp. When the hair was dry and the rags untied, blond ringlets cascaded down my head.

At two years of age, strangers would coo, "What a pretty little girl." If they noticed the ever-present blue marks on my skin, they would glance at my mother and step away in disgust. Unlike the chameleon that changes color as a camouflage, my colors only drew attention. When people noticed them, they no longer saw all the other parts of me.

Every childhood photo showed at least one bruise on my forehead, arm, or leg. Other children's bruises from bumps or scrapes were small; mine only got bigger each day. When my mother told the doctor about how large the bruises were after each vaccination, he apologized. "I'm so sorry. I am as gentle as I can be," he would say as he handed me back to my mother. "I can't understand why she has such a big bruise from the shot."

By the third round of injections, the family doctor knew that the bruises were a symptom of an underlying problem. Like my parents, he did not have an answer.

The elderly doctor practiced medicine in a way that had been common in the nineteenth century. He made house calls carrying his large black leather bag filled with a stethoscope, small surgical tools, and bottles of assorted pills. "I don't know what her problem is, but I recommend you make an appointment with Dr. William Dameshek. He's a hematologist in Boston. I'm sure if anyone can determine the problem, it's him."

"I hope so," my mother said.

My parents didn't own a car, and my father could not afford to take a day off from work. Mom and I would travel by train. The night before, Dad read one of my favorite nursery rhymes, "Baby Goes to Boston."

I laughed every time I heard the repeated phrase, "Jiggle-joggle-jiggle-joggle…Jiggle-joggle-jee."

Mom packed a lunch for us. "You can take your Raggedy Ann doll," Mom said, "and stop jumping up and down." Mom had hand sewn the doll, after she realized that I got bruises from a doll made of hard plastic. My mother cautioned, "Don't let go of my hand, no matter what." I nodded. I was so excited about going on a train, I was unaware of her concern.

With her other hand, my mother gripped her purse. It contained more than a month's pay for my father. The doctor would not see me if she didn't have cash to pay. My father's health insurance plan covered only hospitalizations, not doctors' appointments.

Mom also had cash to pay for a taxi or trolley. We had to get from the train station to the red-brick building where the doctor had his office near the New England Medical Center.

The granite steps of the office building were steep. Afraid I might trip and fall, Mom carried me up the stairs. Mom filled out the forms the receptionist handed her, and I glanced around the room, noticing that there were several other children waiting to be seen by the doctor. Once we were inside, Dr. Dameshek explained that he would order some blood samples to be drawn after we talked. He asked my mother, "Did anyone in your family or your husband's family have trouble with bruises or bleeding that didn't stop?"

"No one," Mom said.

As they talked, I looked around the small office. Books overflowed from the shelves and desk and onto the floor. There was a large map on the wall with pushpins scattered in different spots.

Then Dr. Dameshek performed a physical examination. He looked at my arms, legs, back, and belly. He touched my skin gently. From the first, I liked this man with the round face and ears that stuck out. He looked at me and smiled. Best of all he talked to me, explaining what he was going to do next, although I was only a little over two years of age at the time.

On the train going home, I took a nap curled up next to Mom, cuddling my Raggedy Ann doll. Mom no doubt stared out the window wondering what life would be like for her daughter.

Dr. Dameshek determined that I had congenital afibrinogenemia, a rare bleeding disorder like hemophilia. The problem now had a name. My blood did not clot. At that time, there were only a few cases in the medical journals of people who had the same diagnosis. He wrote a letter to my parents with the details and requested that we come back to see him again in three months. In the meantime he wrote, "I'll find her a pediatrician in your hometown who knows about hematology. He can consult with me if he needs to."

"Is there a treatment?" my mother asked when we met with Dr. Dameshek again.

"If she has a life-threatening injury, we can give her a blood transfusion. We now have a way to separate whole blood into its component parts including fibrinogen. We can inject fibrinogen into one of Linda's veins, but we don't want to do that unless there is no other way. We still don't know what the risks are," the doctor said. "It's very new."

Only later would I begin to understand how transforming that day was for me and for my parents. My mother and father no doubt discussed what this diagnosis would mean for them. From what I know of them, Dad would have deferred to my mother. She was the one who would make the decisions. In my earliest years of life she would make decisions for me and then she would teach me how to make wise decisions for myself. It was a good plan and to a large degree it worked. But completely avoiding injuries and hospitalizations proved to be impossible. I was already strong willed, showing signs of wanting to be independent.

When I told someone my blood did not clot, the question most people asked was, "Does that mean you will bleed to death from a cut?"

"No," I would respond. Initially I found this question silly; as I grew older I became more and more annoyed. Clearly if I died from a small cut, I would not still be alive. Throwing back my shoulders confidently, I'd answer, "It means sometimes I need a blood transfusion."

By nature I preferred to run, not walk. "Linda, slow down!" Mom would caution over and over again. Full of energy, I wanted to climb, jump, race like the other children. If I had not had a bleeding disorder, my rambunctious behavior would have had no consequences.

Mom's friends whispered, "If she was my child, I'd wrap her up in pillows." Their worries could be as contagious as chicken pox. I tried to build up immunity.

However, if I bumped against the chair seat when I stood up from the dinner table, it would leave a bruise on the back of my leg. Bruises came and went. They didn't worry me. If minor, the bruise would expand a little bit each day. I watched the blooming bud of a bruise develop from a small pink itchy spot. I learned not to scratch or it would only get worse. It would grow wider each day, turning to purple, blue, then become greenish-yellow, fading away in about a week. By the time it turned purple, it didn't hurt anymore, and I had forgotten about it until someone else noticed. That was when people began to comment. If I said, "I don't know where I got that bruise," no one believed me. When I tired of the odd questions, I gave a smart-aleck answer. "The canary kicked me," I'd say, trying to be funny.

When Dr. Dameshek diagnosed me as a person with a bleeding disorder, I was no longer a typical child. Having a diagnosis labeled me. I became a person with a rare form of hemophilia.

# Senior Discount

As I began traveling to my parents' home in Western Massachusetts on a more frequent basis in 1998, I saw my parents were the ones wearing degrading labels. Putting people into a category allows others to believe they know more about you than they actually do. It gives others permission to treat you differently. It detracts from your individuality and often highlights what you cannot do instead of recognizing your strengths.

When my father was sixty-five, he retired. For more than twenty years thereafter, my parents were labeled senior citizens. It did not bother them because it came with benefits. They drove outside the city limits to local farms and orchards when fruits and vegetables were in season. My mother clipped coupons and made her shopping list, based on the sale items in grocery stores. "We get a senior discount," my frugal mother exclaimed one day, and we go to free classes at the senior center."

In retirement my father could do all the things he had wanted to do before. Each Monday my father and his friend Joe would examine a woodland path, recording whatever was in season and identifying mushrooms, bird songs, and wildflowers. My mother would start the telephone tree, notifying more than twenty people where they would meet that week. On Wednesday, the walking group followed Dad and Joe, making notes or taking photos. The group ended each walk with a picnic. They walked every week of the year through all four seasons, unless the temperature dropped below zero. On bitter cold winter days, the Wednesday Walkers met in a church, and the photographers would share their best nature pictures.

My father constructed a wooden dollhouse each year. Each one was different from any of the previous ones. Before I was born, he made one for his niece. Later he constructed a different one for me. In his retirement Dad cut the scraps of wood to size, gluing the pieces into place for shingles, roof tiles, and shutters, while my mother cut fabric saved from garments she had once made. Mom hand stitched tiny curtains for each window and spreads for the beds. She stuffed tiny pillows with cotton. From lace-weight yarn she fashioned itty-bitty hooked rugs. The basement of their house transformed into a workshop for hundreds of two-inch tables, chairs, baby cribs, and rockers. My father painted the interior and exterior of the dollhouses, then stained and varnished the furniture.

Together my parents went to craft fairs where people would stand in awe, sucking in their breath as they admired the staircase banister or individual wooden books on the bookshelf. The most ardent admirers were children, both little boys and girls, who would ask, "May I rearrange the furniture?" While a parent often said no, my father always replied, "Of course."

Mom stuck price tags on each item that was sold singly, like a dining room chair or commode. She made tickets to purchase a chance at winning the house. They donated all of the proceeds to the local chapter of the Hemophilia Foundation.

During those years they had friends I didn't know. Each time I would go to visit them, their doorbell would chime three or four times each day.

When I heard someone shuffling on the back porch, a woman said, "Don't let me interrupt you. I'm dropping off these magazines for your parents to give away."

Over my shoulder I heard Mom sing out, "Thanks, Tina."

Later that morning, I opened my parents' back door to see a man putting some plastic bags by the garage. "I picked up these soda cans on a walk this morning," he explained to me. "I know your parents will be going to the recycle center on Monday."

In the early afternoon there was a soft knock. "Can yo' modder come out and play?" a little boy said with a smile.

"My daughter is here for a visit today, Danny," mother called out from the kitchen stove. "Come back tomorrow and we can play." Mom turned to me. "He lives next door."

Then my mother continued telling me about a conversation she had with her brother Guy. Over the years, Guy and my mother had attended the funerals of all their other siblings. They were the only two of the ten still living. On the way home from the last of these funerals a few weeks earlier, Guy told her, "I don't want to be the last one to die."

Mom replied, "I'd be happy to relieve you of that burden!"

In their mid-eighties people began to treat my parents as elderly. Their pride diminished. It was not how they saw themselves. This label was about what they could not do. They disliked this designation, recoiling at the term the way I had when people called me a bleeder.

Their personal disaster came when my mother's brittle spine began to crack. She lay in bed immobilized by the small crevices in her backbone. It seemed sudden, like a shift in the tectonic plates severing the earth, upending paved streets, collapsing buildings, and snapping bridges, but the deterioration had actually happened gradually. Subtle shifts during the past years had widened the fissure between vigorous and vulnerable.

A series of reductions in health, each with its own restrictions, had contributed to their decline. The first few diagnoses seemed to have little consequence. The year my father learned he had diabetes, Mom threw out her familiar recipes and frying pan. She started adding large portions of low carbohydrate vegetables to their lunches and dinners. By managing his diet, she successfully controlled his blood sugar level without medication for thirty years.

Unlike me, my father seemed to enjoy compliance. I watched in astonishment each time we ate in a restaurant together. Dad would glance at the menu and then turn to Mom saying, "What can I eat here?" He never took the time to learn his own dietary needs. Why should he? He relished my mother caring for him as much as I valued my independence.

My mother paid little attention to her own health. It was her habit to mask her own problems, diverting attention away and onto caring for others.

When her eyesight began to deteriorate, she put off making an appointment with the doctor. "I can see well enough," she told my father. "I've got an appointment for a routine eye exam in a few months." After the ophthalmologist finished his exam, he recommended macular surgery.

As I sat by her bedside after the attendant brought her down from the operating room, her deathly cold body and gray skin tone shocked me. I fed her warm broth. I whispered, "You'll be all right." I hoped that was true. The surgery had not been successful, the doctor reported. The retina had a buckle. Too much time had gone by and the doctor could not repair the damage.

Disappointed by the result, she still had some vision. She focused on what she could do. Most of her friends noticed little difference in her behavior. If they noticed the dusty shelves, no one said. The house smelled clean and fresh, her cooking was as tasty as ever, and her flirtatious smile as engaging.

My father had served in the US Navy during WWII. He had worked on the diesel engine of a ship. He blamed his hearing loss on the constant banging of the engine during those years. Dad relied on mother's ears to identify bird songs. She began to depend upon my father's eyesight. He read her wildflower books aloud to her.

Mom noticed a tremor in her hands after her seventieth birthday. She ignored this symptom until a friend urged her to see a doctor. The Parkinson's disease medications had side effects but she took them. She also started exercising her fingers several times each day as the doctor recommended. She would touch each finger to her thumb on the right hand, then the left. Her flexibility increased. She was still able to walk with the Wednesday Walkers, still energetic and proud. She was capable of identifying wildflowers as accurately as one of the retired college botany professors.

All those abilities were in the past. Now people described them as elderly and frail. That July in 1998 when I found my mother lying in bed, she had changed both in body and spirit. Unable to get to her own kitchen or bathroom, there was little she could do except listen to her Talking Books. She did not have the same enthusiasm for longevity that she had had all her life. Shocked and saddened to see my parents so worn out, so in need of assistance, I tried to piece together the how and why.

For several years her doctor had treated her for osteoporosis. By the time she was eighty, however, spinal fractures cut her off from doing the things that gave her life meaning. She could no longer garden. Her walking was limited. A few of her friends in the Wednesday Walkers group visited her or called, but she was no longer able to join them on their outdoor adventures. She lost the passion she had had for life.

Startled by resignation in her voice and the look of panic in my father's eyes, I had an obligation to take care of them. I plunged in without knowing what to do first. With only one purpose, damage control, I drove the two hours to their home each weekend.

# A House for Linda

Mom was making dinner and the three-room apartment warmed from the stove. There was no central heat in the apartment. The smell of meatloaf in the oven filled the air. Mother mashed the potatoes and put the peas on the four-burner gas stove to cook. Intrigued by her quick, confident actions, I wanted to be just like her. It was a few months after Dr. Dameshek diagnosed my bleeding disorder in 1950.

Mom set the plates, napkins, and silverware on the table. She ducked into the bedroom to put on red lipstick before my father got home from work. Thrifty even with her lipstick, Mom applied a small amount on her lower lip and then smoothed her two lips together, spreading the color onto her upper lip.

The best part of my day was when my father got home. Running to greet him, I sang out, "Daddy's here!"

"No running, Linda!" I heard my mother yell from the kitchen. I could hear her moving my high chair back into the kitchen. There was not enough room for the chair while she was cooking.

Dad set down his black tin lunch bucket with a clank and put his wide-brimmed felt hat on my head, gave me a hug, and then kissed Mom. He inhaled deeply and sniffed. "Smells good, I'm hungry."

After we sat down to supper, my mother said, "We have to buy a house. Linda is walking now. Her friends come to play in our apartment. That's fine, but she needs to play outdoors on the grass not on concrete."

We lived on the second floor of a gray stucco building. The apartment house took up the entire city block with no space left for grass or trees. It had an exterior staircase where the children played. Mom did not allow me to play on the metal grates of those stairs since the day Dr. Dameshek said I had hemophilia.

My father had lived his entire life in rented housing. He had never considered home ownership. Dad put down his fork and stared at his hands. He looked like he was shrinking. He glanced at me. He lowered his voice to almost a whisper. "I'm worried that we don't know yet what Linda's medical bills will be in the future. I'm not sure we can afford a mortgage. It took my father most of his life to pay off the medical expenses for my mother and my sisters."

Mom reached out and put her hand on Dad's. She patted it gently. "I know it's been tight since I had to quit my job while I got pregnant," she said. "I grew up poor on the farm, but we never went hungry. If we had a house with a yard, I could grow vegetables and save money on food. I could can them for winter."

Dad shrugged. He looked doubtful.

When my mother made up her mind, she rarely changed it. "We can do this," Mom said. "We must do this…for Linda. Besides," she added, "if we had a house, you'd have a place to use those tools that your father owned. That big wooden toolbox is just taking up space in your sister's home until you have a place to put it. Why, you could make us furniture for the house and round all the edges, so that Linda would not bruise herself on the corners of tables or bookcases."

Dad brightened. "I guess that would help," he said.

"Soon Linda will need a room of her own, and we will have to move anyway," Mom persisted. "You're eligible for a GI loan, and we will find a way to pay the bills," my mother said, standing up from the kitchen table.

"Some vets are using their loans to go to college," he said, sounding sad. "But you're right, we need to buy a house for Linda more." Dad looked at me. He winked and nodded.

"I'll find out what you have to do to apply for a veteran's loan tomorrow," Mom said as she began spreading out the newspaper opened to the real estate pages in front of my father. "What about this one?" she said. "Or this one?"

One weekend we looked at a Cape Cod house that had been constructed only three years earlier. Barren of trees or shrubbery, crabgrass crisscrossed the yard. "Look," Mom said, "there's a fenced-in backyard."

Inside, the house had two bedrooms, a kitchen, bathroom, and living room with a basement and an attic. My mother's footsteps echoed in each empty room. Dad and I poked into closets and cabinets. He carried me down the steps to the basement.

Mom said, "It's not far from the elementary school or the bus stop, and the fence will give Linda a free space where she can play and won't wander off. Let's make an offer to buy it."

Dad hesitated one last time, then agreed. His veteran's loan had been approved and he would use it to buy a house even if it meant that he would not go to college as he had dreamed. With pride he wrote a letter to his nephew Bill. The letter began, "I just bought a house for Linda."

# *Battleground*

Early in the spring of 1951, I heard my mother scream from the living room, "Oh, no!" As fast as she could, Mom was vacuuming up insects that swarmed across the carpet like an army. Some fluttered their wings, but they could not fly well. The bugs crawling across the carpet were sucked into the vacuum.

Fascinated by the insects and my mother's rage, I stood on the easy chair to get a better view. Mom was pushing the vacuum cleaner back and forth with quick jerks. "What are they, Mom?" I yelled.

"I don't know," she yelled back, "but I'm going to find out."

When she could see no more bugs on the rug, I heard her on the telephone. "Yes," she said, "I captured one in a glass jar." Then after a pause she stared at the jar. "The body is like a tube with no waist. They have four wings all the same size." Another pause and then she said, "Termites? We can't afford to pay for an exterminator, how can I get rid of them myself?" It sounded as if she was arguing with the person on the phone. "I don't care how dangerous it is," she said, "tell me what I need to do and I will do it."

Dad worked in a factory that made envelopes. He stacked heavy reams of paper onto a cutting surface and sliced the paper into the required sizes and shapes, while standing on his feet, lifting, and carrying all day. He left the house long before I was awake and returned home by four o'clock in the afternoon. He took the bus to and from work, since we didn't have a car yet. Arriving home, he would often sit and read the newspaper until dinnertime.

That day, Mom greeted him at the door saying, "We've got termites. I need you to drill some holes in the foundation, so I can pour in the insecticide."

My father sighed. "I'll do it this Saturday."

"No," she said, "I want you to do it now. One of the neighbors drove me to the hardware store so I could buy DDT. I dug the holes outdoors but the Extension Service told me that it's best to also pour some DDT through holes in the concrete basement."

With a heavy sigh Dad got out his toolbox and drilled a hole in the spots my mother had already marked.

"Keep Linda busy while I pour the DDT in the holes. It's poison and I don't want her anywhere near it," Mom said as she put on her gardening gloves and went outside to the faucet to mix the powder with water from the hose. I looked out the window and watched her pouring it into the holes. After that day we never saw another termite.

Mom slew the winged dragons before they destroyed our house. She fought back and she won. I watched in awe.

My mother dealt with my hemophilia the way she had exterminated the termites. Preventing damage was the first step, and anything she could treat at home, she did. She used rest, elevation, and ice as her weapons. She took me to a dentist for regular checkups when I still had all of my baby teeth. She purchased sturdy laced shoes that gave good support. No flip-flops or sandals for me in the summertime.

When I was four years old, I sat cross-legged in front of the television each morning watching the *Howdy Doody* television show. I cheered when I heard that Clarabell the Clown would be in our city at one of the local parks. Clarabell didn't speak, still fans like me knew what she was thinking when she honked the horn on her belt, or squirted seltzer on someone. I envied Clarabell's ability to show her frustration, sadness, and anger without words. Words got me in trouble. Worse than words, fists or kicks left bruises on my body. But honking a horn or spraying someone with water seemed harmless.

"Can we go, Mom?" I begged. "My friend Connie is going. Her mother is driving—we can go with them." At first she said, "Maybe," in that slow drawn-out way that usually meant no. I didn't give up. Mom avoided taking me to places where crowds of people might step on my toes or bump into me. I repeated my plaintive request until Mom finally agreed.

At the park, Connie and I got out of the car and began walking toward the crowd of people when we heard Clarabell honking her horn. Connie took off in a run. "It's her!"

Running behind Connie's strawberry blond curls bouncing in the breeze, I squealed in joy. I could hear Clarabell's "honk, honk" from the center of a gathering crowd. All I wanted was to see her striped puffy suit, her single tuft of hair on top of her head, the big outlined white rectangles painted around her eyes and lips. I forgot the lessons my mother taught me.

Behind me I heard Mom yell, "No running!" It was too late. I slipped on the gravel and landed on one knee. I didn't get to see Clarabell that day. Instead my mother cleaned the scraped knee and pulled out the first aid kit she carried in her bag. After she covered the injury with antiseptic and a gauze pad, she put me in the backseat of the car with my leg up while Connie went off to see Clarabell.

"Can't I go too? My knee doesn't really hurt," I begged.

"No, your knee will only bleed faster if you walk on that leg."

It took ten days before the scrape stopped oozing. My four-year-old body wanted to be in motion, not lying with my leg propped up and wrapped with several layers of gauze and tape.

The things my mother saw as reckless were what all the other children my age were able to do without consequence. When I let down my guard or made a miscalculation, the price was both prolonged bed rest and self-blame. I had disappointed my mother. Each time I promised myself to do better the next time. It was a struggle, and sooner or later I would forget.

Mom knew that preventing injuries could save my life. She began early to train me to stay alert to my surroundings. She was convinced I could prevent injuries if only I learned to suppress my impulse to act quickly without thinking ahead.

If I got injured, my mother's first question was, "What did you do?" The accusation was pointed. Mom would put me to bed with a bandage or an ice pack and then leave my room. Then I would hear her banging the floor mop across the linoleum in the kitchen, carrying the laundry to the basement, and rattling the pans on the stove as she prepared dinner. She worked furiously. She viewed my injuries as her failures. Soon I began to internalize that sense of blame and guilt. She no longer had to accuse me of not being careful enough. I would do that on my own.

# *Ghosts*

After I discovered my parents in distress and in need of assistance, I drove to Western Massachusetts each week. By mid-August Mom was showing improvement. She could stand and walk with less pain. I took a day off work to help her get to a bone scan appointment. Since the appointment was in the morning, I traveled to my parents' house the night before.

"These scans are so hard for me," she had told me pursing her lips tightly together. "The doctor ordered it, so I have to go."

My mother had turned my old bedroom into a guest room. Gone was the twin bed I had slept on before leaving home. In its place was the bed my parents had used for sixty years, and I tried not to imagine having been conceived on that thin mattress.

When I visited my parents on a weekend, it was the only place for me to sleep. I shifted from one side to the other in bed, tossing the sheets into a tangle. The room seemed inhabited by ghosts from the past.

Childhood memories buried long ago resurfaced. In the predawn darkness, I saw the sewing machine cabinet. The machine tilted down and under the lid, hiding it from view. In the past Mom used that machine to make most of my clothes and all of her dresses. I had used it too. Now the battered cabinet served only as a place to pile the medical records and numerous bottles of pills. There were two medications for mother's Parkinson's disease. The next row was her osteoporosis medication and a bottle of Dad's diabetes pills.

Above the cabinet hung a calendar. Several doctors' appointments filled the spaces in the coming months. Mom and Dad had scheduled visits to their primary care doctor, dentist, and ophthalmologist. My mother's shaky hand had written in appointments to the neurologist and arthritis specialist. I had made a copy of all the dates and times, so I could go with her on the checkups. During the sleepless night, I had laid out a plan in my mind for managing the difficulty of getting Mom to the next day's appointment.

At two o'clock, I heard a shuffle in my parents' bedroom. I went to check on Mom and discovered her trying to get on the commode by herself. "I didn't want to wake you," she whispered. As I had guessed, Dad had not heard me get up. I helped my mother back to bed and returned to my room.

When the clock showed six that morning, I went to the kitchen to prepare breakfast for Mom. Dad was already in the kitchen, eating toast and peanut butter. I brought Mom some hot oatmeal for breakfast in bed.

"You didn't have to do that, dear," she said looking at the tray I was carrying. She had been getting to the kitchen the past week for her meals.

Pulling out some clean clothes from her closet, I said, "I thought you might save your energy for getting dressed."

When she had finished eating, I brought her morning medications. "The doctor wants you to drink a full glass of water."

She shook her head no, as she swallowed the pills with a gulp. "I'll only have to go to the bathroom more often."

"Drink the water, Mom," I said in a firm tone of voice that I noticed sounded like the way my mother used to speak to me when I was a child.

I carried a basin of warm water, a face cloth and towel, and a bar of soap to her next. "You do your front and I'll do your back,"

I pulled off her nightgown and guided her to the commode. I dipped a facecloth in the basin of warm water and rubbed it with the bar of soap, then wrung it out and passed it to her. I watched as she scrubbed herself, remembering how she had loved taking a bath each night. Even though she could no longer get into the bathtub, I knew how refreshing it felt to have a sponge bath after being in bed a long time.

When she finished washing, I covered her with a towel and emptied the basin. I refilled it with fresh, warm water. I ran the damp cloth gently over her hunched back. Each knobby vertebra protruding through her thin skin made me wince. I heard her exhale a sigh. "It doesn't hurt," she said. "It feels so good."

Once she was dry, I began getting her dressed. "No hurry," I said, pulling on her socks and clean panties. I thought about how she had dressed me not only when I was a toddler, but also later if I had a bruised hand or swollen elbow.

Twenty minutes later she was wearing a warm jersey and elastic waist pants. "We have plenty of time," I said. "Why don't you lie down for a little rest?" She looked exhausted.

Going into the kitchen again, I poured myself a bowl of cereal and made a cup of coffee. Standing at the window over the kitchen sink, I ate my breakfast alone. After I washed the dirty dishes, I went to the living room to find Dad sitting in his brown recliner. His pile of books on the round end table overflowing, like the two bookcases at either side of his chair. He bent over the morning newspaper, not hearing me when I entered. I feared that if I sat down, I might doze off. Raising my voice and lowering my pitch, I said, "Good morning,"

Dad looked up and smiled. "What do you need me to do?"

"When we're ready to leave," I said with the same authoritative bossiness my mother would have used, "here are the keys to my car. I want you to open the front passenger side door for Mom before I come out with her." He nodded and looked relieved to have an assignment.

Step by painful step, my mother made it to the back door. She refused to hold my arm saying, "I might leave a bruise." She would not have had the strength to grip me tightly enough to cause a bruise, but I did not argue. When we got to the four steps down to the driveway, Dad had the car door open. He came to assist her down the stairs and into the car seat.

I drove up to the door of the radiology center and sent my father in to get a wheelchair for Mom. She uttered a feeble protest. "I can walk," she said.

"I know," I lied, "but why not make it easier and ride?"

When the technician called out my mother's name in the waiting room, I pushed Mom in the wheelchair toward the inner door. "I'm going in with her," I said.

The technician stepped aside saying, "That isn't necessary."

"I'm going in with her," I repeated.

The technician hurried to get my mother in position. Tears came up in her eyes when she saw the metal table the technician instructed her to lie on. Mom grimaced when she laid back on the cold rigid surface. I saw my mother's jaw lock in silent resignation. The technician did the scan without seeming to notice Mom was in pain. When I helped my mother off the table and assisted her back into the wheelchair, I wanted to cry. The torture of the scan had undone the progress she had made in the past few weeks of bed rest.

When I got Mom back home and into her own bed, she looked exhausted. I brought her a cup of tea and a Tylenol. "Do you want any lunch?" I asked.

"No dear, I'll just rest awhile," she said.

I kissed her and covered her in her quilt and sat with her until she drifted off to sleep. I tiptoed to the kitchen, enraged at the doctor who had ordered the bone density test. I telephoned his office, asking to speak to his nurse. By the time the nurse picked up the call, I had control of my righteous indignation.

"I can't see how these tests are doing my mother any good. It's agony for her. Unless the doctor can give me a compelling reason to continue, tell him not to order one again for her," I said without raising my voice.

"I'll tell the doctor," she said. The nurse sounded surprised, but she knew enough not to argue.

My mother believed doctors to be infallible. I knew they were human. A doctor who did not know how to improve the health of a patient rarely admitted it. Their default was often to order tests without considering whether the tests would do more harm than good.

Mom would not contradict a doctor's recommendation. I had spent almost fifty years learning how the medical system functioned and malfunctioned. It was time for me to use that knowledge to advocate for my parents' benefit.

# Magic, Jell-O, and Peanuts

Blood ran down my upper lip even after the pediatrician had stuffed packing into my nostril. Mom called the doctor who said, "I'm afraid she will need an infusion of fibrinogen to stop this nosebleed. Take her to the hospital, and I will telephone them with the order."

Our neighbor Kay drove us to the emergency room of the Springfield Hospital. Most children had not been in a hospital since their birth. In a few short years, hospital visits were already routine for me. This visit was different though. The on-call doctor gave me an antihistamine, believing that it would make me sleep and dry up my nasal passages at the same time.

When he came back to check on me several minutes later, he was surprised that I was still awake. My nose was dribbling blood. I tried to contain the oozing blood with a wad of tissue. I lay the saturated tissues on the table beside the bed and grabbed a handful of fresh ones.

"Okay," the doctor said, "let's get this infusion going." After several needle sticks on my arms and hands, he realized that this was not going to be easy. He asked the nurse for a surgical kit and injected a local anesthetic in my wrist.

"Watch me carefully," he said, snapping his fingers. Then like magic the nurse was gone. I heard a chime from the other side of the curtain, and poof the doctor disappeared too. They must have created a distraction. I lay there amazed by the trick, not worrying what would happen next.

In a few minutes, I looked up to see the nurse and doctor in front of my bed again. He cut a small slit on my wrist and inserted a tube so the bottle of fibrinogen could flow into my body. When the bottle was empty, he bandaged the cut on my wrist and pulled out the packing from my nose. I grinned, no more bleeding.

Most doctors wanted to be able to help. They were sad when it seemed there was nothing they could do to make me better. Medical science had benefited me and also failed me. In desperation for a cure, my parents and my pediatrician had grasped at theories. It seemed to me that there was not much difference between their theories and magic.

The day my pediatrician noticed that the fibrinogen concentrate looked like clear gelatin, he mused to my mother, "Fibrinogen is a protein and so is gelatin." He wrote on my hospital chart to give me Jell-O.

For two days the only thing on my food tray was Jell-O. When the doctor came back, I complained I wanted something else to eat. He replied that he did not mean to only give me Jell-O. He had intended that I get as much Jell-O as I wanted.

He said to my mother, "Why don't you give her lots of Jell-O if she has a bruise?"

After that Mom would mix the Jell-O in boiling water and cool it with ice cubes until it was a drinkable temperature before she gave me a cupful. Some days while I lay in bed with an ice pack on an injury, I drank several cups of the thick, sweet Jell-O.

My parents wanted to try anything that might help my blood to clot. In February 1960, the *New York Times* published a story that claimed eating peanuts could increase the blood's ability to clot for a person with hemophilia. My father purchased a fifty-pound bag of roasted, unshelled peanuts. When he dragged the bag to my bedroom and put it in my closet, he said, "What do you have to lose?" It took me months to eat all the peanuts in the bag.

Neither the Jell-O nor the peanuts helped my blood to clot. The only benefit was in making us believe we were taking some positive action. However, I never looked at a gelatin salad or a jar of peanuts the same way again.

# *Child's Play*

When summer arrived that first year in our new house, my mother set to work on preparing her garden. She turned the first clump of weeds over with her spade and let out a sigh.

"Sand," she said. "We'll need better soil than this if we are to grow vegetables." Then she continued to dig large clumps of weeds, flipping them over like pancakes on a griddle. She dug holes and raked the decaying autumn leaves for compost. From that day on, she carried all the vegetable peels and other organic waste from the kitchen and buried it in the sand. I played in the dirt as Mom worked.

Each summer while my mother worked in the garden, she taught any child who entered the yard the names of all the plants and how to pull the weeds. As I grew older, my friends and I picked off the nonproducing squash blossoms or carried buckets of water to the pole beans. From my point of view the yard was a playground. In between helping with the gardening, we played tag or ran through the water sprinkler, squealing in delight.

Most days I was able to participate in the activities. There were times, though, when I was not. Through the open window of my bedroom I could hear some children helping my mother water the vegetable garden. They filled water buckets from the outdoor faucet and laughed if the water spilled on their toes instead of on the plants. Mom was weeding and listening to one of my friends chatter.

I longed to be free like the children I could hear outside my window, running and laughing. Instead I was confined to bed until a bruise on my knee stopped swelling. No doubt, I was in pain. Worse than that, my friends forgot me.

Once pain ended, however, it was immediately forgotten, but what lingered were the memories of disappointment. No one seemed to understand that. The doctor told my mother that learning to ride a bike was unsafe for me. I watched my friends with jealousy as they careened up and down the street with their new two-wheel bikes. I resented the decision of the swim class instructor who refused to accept me because I might fall on the cement. Swimming would have been a safe and beneficial exercise for me—one I could do as well as any other child.

Annoyed with the people who did not understand, I concealed my anger when doctors, nurses, and technicians asked, "How long have you had this condition?" I answered politely and wondered if they had read my chart, which gave my diagnosis as "congenital afibrinogenemia." Perhaps they just did not know the meaning of *congenital*. That was a word I had learned by the time I was three.

I could forgive the inane questions of my playmates, but not the comments or advice of adults. A church schoolteacher dismissed my mother's explanation of my bleeding disorder with, "I bruise easily too. Give her vitamin K and she won't have that problem." Under her breath, I heard my mother's indignant tone as she muttered, "If only it was that easy."

People who had fibrinogen offered their own opinions to me as well as my mother. When they did, I imagined myself fading away. Like the Cheshire cat from *Alice in Wonderland*, I disappeared, leaving my smile hanging without a body.

My parents had each grown up in large families with brothers and sisters. Whether they desired more children of their own, or whether my mother wanted me where she could structure my play and keep watch on my behavior, I don't know. Either way there were few days when I was the only child in my house. Our house was a sanctuary for many a child in the neighborhood. Inside their homes hid violence, abuse, and degradation. Inside my house was praise, respect, and dignity.

Unlike so many parents, mine told the children to call them by their first names. Instead of being Mrs. Wright, every child called my mother Daisy. The children called my father by his first name too, Horace. Their names were as unusual as the atmosphere in our home.

The children who were most often present were the ones who received little attention or only negative attention from their own parents. Greg lived with his mother and grandparents at the end of our street. Very few children would play with him. Most parents banned him from their homes. He smiled if he made someone cry, and he could turn violent without any reason. He cut a slit in my favorite doll's throat saying with a satisfied grin, "I took out your doll's tonsils," then added with a smirk, "My father's a doctor."

I shrugged and walked away. After he left to go home, I cried for my injured doll. Better not to let him see I cared, I thought.

My mother told me that when Greg was born, his father had already filed for divorce. Greg's mother had moved back to her parents' home near us and got a job teaching school in another neighborhood. Greg lived in a home where his father's name was only spoken in contempt. He had never met his father. His grandparents and his mother didn't have the energy Greg required. My mother didn't turn any child away from our door, and although Greg cut my doll, he never lashed out at me.

My friend Marlene often came to my house to play. She and her two sisters smelled of mustard or whatever they had eaten for lunch. Her parents didn't have dinner with them. They drank cocktails instead of eating food. When Marlene's father would come to pick up his children, the little girl threw her arms around my father in a hug and wouldn't let go.

"You want her? You can keep her," the child's father growled. My father carried the little girl back to her house where her mother was already too tipsy to have walked the half block to our house.

"Can you imagine not wanting a child?" I heard Dad saying to Mom. "So sad."

As time went by, children realized they needed no invitation. There would be a knock on our kitchen door, then another, and another. Before there were childcare centers, parents often sent their children out to play on their own.

On most rainy or snowy days my mother would be in the kitchen surrounded by children. She knew which tasks small hands could manage successfully and which should be left for more experienced fingers. We kneaded dough, forming it gently into a ball. An hour later we would lift off the tea towel and be amazed at how the dough had filled up all the space in the bowl.

When we made cookies, my mother gave each child instruction: "Barbara, you may sift flour today. Helen, will you measure the sugar?" The children took their places around our small wooden table or at the kitchen counter. "Maryanne, we need a teaspoon of cinnamon. Can you bring the cinnamon to the bowl? Everyone may take a turn at stirring."

Mom would spread the sticky goo on the waxed paper. Then each child took a turn with the wooden rolling pin squeezing the mixture flat. We chose our favorite cookie-cutter shapes of people, bears, stars, and hearts to cut the cookies. Then we placed the cookies in rows on the metal sheet and decorated each with cinnamon hearts and currants before baking.

Mom taught more than cooking. She taught children the satisfaction of success. Each child left with a bag of cookies they had helped to make. Some of those bags would be empty by the time they got home.

My father's imagination and sense of wonder surpassed my own. Dad painted half of the basement pink for my playroom. At the bottom of the basement stairs he drew a Disney version of Pinocchio with Jiminy Cricket standing on his nose and scolding about the importance of honesty. Pinocchio stood as large as the children who walked down the stairs. Mickey Mouse tipped his hat over the daybed where my friends and I sat to read our library books.

My father left objects of interest on top of the piano or the card table. A slice of a maple tree trunk from my uncle Byron's sugar orchard revealed the rings of age and the scars from taps each spring. He transformed the room into a mismatched museum. He made paper geodesic designs, hanging them from the rafters of the basement one year. He liked to plunk on the upright piano that had once belonged to his mother. In the playroom he told me about his sister who played background music in a silent movie theater. "She only played on the black keys," Dad said as he picked away at "Chop Sticks."

When the museum of science put out a call for volunteers to dig out dinosaur tracks discovered when the ground was cleared to build an interstate highway, Dad seemed like a child who had been asked to test the latest toy. Each volunteer was given their pick of the imperfect ones the museum did not want to keep.

After digging in the Connecticut Valley clay all day, he returned home with three of these tracks. He laid the indented pieces of shale so that they pointed to our trash bucket. He loved to show children the tracks and ask if they thought the dinosaur had been foraging in our waste bin. Children would stare at the tracks with their mouths agape, look at the lid of the garbage bucket, then look at my father. Dad would wink, and then the children and my father would begin to giggle.

Once I tiptoed down the stairs and found him by himself. Having no child to read to, he had propped up one of my dolls beside him, tilting its head slightly so it seemed to be looking at the pictures in the book he was reading.

When it became too cold to be outdoors, my father spent most of his free time in the basement. His table saw buzzed, blowing sawdust in every room of the small house. My father made a maple picnic table and benches. The table was long enough for ten people to sit around comfortably. On one end of the table was a used aquarium. In the spring, Mom showed us how to make a terrarium that could serve as a critter habitat. Dad attached a piece of screen to a wooden frame so the latest hotel guest would not escape until my friends and I had observed its habits. I carried food and water for garden snakes, praying mantis, spiders, and toads.

My friends and I made drawings and crafts in the basement playroom my father had created for me. There, glue was drizzled and paint dropped without adult anger. Mom supervised activities for us. One day she announced, "Today we're making curtains for the basement windows. Let's go outside and pick up some of the autumn leaves from the ground and bring them back here. Then I'll show you how to spatter paint." She spread out paint, brushes, and sheets of plastic cut from an old shower curtain. When we placed our leaves on the plastic, Mom gave us a used toothbrush that we shared and a tongue depressor.

"Dip the toothbrush in paint and drag the tongue depressor over the brush to spray the paint. Be careful and pull toward you or you will spatter yourself with the paint."

We giggled as the drops of mixed colors covered the plastic wherever there were no leaves.

Every activity Mom supervised was one I could do safely. My mother used distraction to keep me from becoming bored. If I was occupied, I had less chance of injury. As a result, I spent far fewer days in confinement while an injury healed than I did in happy abandon.

# Chosen Sister

Driving to Springfield every weekend in August of 1998, I arrived on Saturday morning to cook, clean, and organize my parents' medications. There was always more to do when it was time for me to leave my parents on Sunday evening. In between my visits, my parents depended on Kay.

In 1951, when my parents had purchased the house, Kay was the first neighbor to knock on the door. She lived at the end of our street. As I was growing up, it was a rare day if Kay did not stop in at least once for a steaming cup of coffee with my mother. In those years, Kay would drive my mother and me to the hospital if my father was at work. She would bring my mom in to visit me, then return when my mother was ready to go back home.

Now that Mom was confined to bed, Kay came every evening to help get her ready for sleep. At eighty herself, Kay's auburn hair was not gray yet. She had laugh lines at the corners of her eyes, and she smiled often. She no longer knocked on the door, knowing that my father would not hear the sound and my mother could not get out of bed to let her in. Kay opened the back door with the key Mom had given her and waved at my father as she passed the door to the living room. Dad had the television volume up as high as it could go so he could hear the nightly news.

After Kay got my mother settled for sleep, she returned to the living room and sat for a while watching television with Dad.

Mom said Kay also went with her to doctors' appointments. "She comes along with us, but Dad drives."

When I asked Kay if this wasn't more than she could handle, she said, "Oh no, you're like my family now that my sons have married and moved away." Then she added, "Your father is an excellent driver."

I cringed, remembering that although he had once been a safe driver, I knew other drivers tailgated him when he drove below the speed limit. He was no longer quick to react to sudden changes. I shuddered at the thought that he might one day hit a neighborhood child. Kay was undoubtedly the better driver, but she knew that my father's self-esteem would be damaged if she offered to drive.

Since my parents were not walking with their naturalist friends every Wednesday, few went out of their way to visit or call. My father's hearing loss had left my mother in a wall of silence. Kay was the only person who knocked on their door regularly now. Instead of acting like Kay was a friend, Mom treated Kay as if she was an annoying younger sister. She criticized how Kay did things. "She's slow as molasses," Mom told me.

My mother had never been gracious at accepting help from anyone. Her longtime friend was now one of her caregivers. Mom preferred to be the giver, rather than the receiver. Watching my mother simmer in resentment, I realized that she needed more than just medical care.

Dad was easy, I thought, as long as he had a book to read and his imagination, he did not need any friends or further distractions.

However, mother alone in her bedroom was sinking into loneliness. I needed to find diversions. Immediately I thought of another friend of my mother's, Renée.

I asked Mom, "How long has it been since you have seen Renée?"

"It's been a long time. She's busy with her grandchildren these days."

"Think I'll give her a call," I said.

# *Zest for Life*

My mother and Renée were both Girl Scout leaders for different troops. Together they planned leadership training events, and I often heard them giggling as they bounced ideas around and made themselves costumes for the skits they did together.

Renée and her husband were artists, and their home was a jumble of chaos that contrasted sharply with our hazard-free home. Their house was under construction each time Mom and I went to visit. The stairs to the second floor bedrooms were unfinished plywood. Walls were often framed months before the wallboard was set in place. When they had enough time and money, Renée's husband would plaster. I could sense my mother's tension as she watched me maneuver around the clutter of lumber and art supplies.

Although Renée and Mom had similar interests, they had different approaches to the world. If Renée saw a pretty flower, she would put it in a vase of water on her kitchen table and sketch it in her drawing pad. Mom would go to her gardening encyclopedia and identify the plant. "I like to know the names of my friends," my mother said.

Renée responded, "People need beauty to feed the soul, like the body needs food. I don't care if I know their names or not."

They both sewed. Mom made almost all of her own clothing and mine. While my mother would carefully measure and pin, then baste before going to the sewing machine, Renée would cut, pin, and run the fabric through the machine, finishing in half the time as Mom. Renée's actions were as spontaneous as my mother's were deliberate.

Renée and Mom didn't have much money for their households. In search of bargains, Renée shopped salvage stores. Items damaged after a warehouse fire or in transport were cheap. She also frequented the musty fabric mills where huge bolts of cloth were wrapped around cardboard tubes and tossed in unsorted piles. Mom focused on the obstacles that I could trip on or sharp edges of shelves that might injure me while Renée saw only the glorious colors and textures.

"Watch that bolt sticking out of the row, Linda," I heard my mother say.

Renée dodged and weaved through the jumbled bolts of remnants until her sparkling dark eyes glimpsed a jewel. Despite her petite size, Renée would pull out a heavy bolt from deep under several other fabric remnants. "Wouldn't these colors make lovely sofa pillow covers?"

I worshiped Renée for her ability to plunge into life without thinking ahead. I breathed in her energy for life.

In addition to Renée's four children, their house was as full as ours with other children and adults who came to find adventure or diversion. There was always something going on in her house or someone visiting. It reminded me of home.

Renée had cheered me up when I was in the hospital many times.

"Your mother told me not to visit you when you needed bed rest," Renée told me once. "She said you get too excited with me around." It was true. Renée boosted my spirits and often made me forget my sorrows. She could do that now for my mother, I imagined.

Renée responded to my call with enthusiasm. She promised to visit while I was home the next time. I wasn't sure that I had called Renée because I knew my mother would like to see her or because I needed her exhilaration for life.

Renée arrived at my parents' home carrying a sugar-free apple pie. In her early seventies, her hair dyed red did not distract from her wrinkled face. Still her zest for life showed in her sparkling dark eyes.

"Mother is in the bedroom. Go say hello and I'll fix us some tea," I said.

When Renée came back to the kitchen, she leaned heavily on the counter beside me. "I wasn't prepared to see her looking so different," Renée said.

We both stared out the window, wiping tears off our cheeks, trying to hold back from sobbing. Together we looked out the window over the kitchen sink. Outside the kitchen the garden looked deserted, weeds reclaiming the ground. Birds had abandoned the wooden house my father had built for a chickadee nest. We were unable to find words for several minutes.

"I remember your ninth birthday so well," Renée said finally. "I was helping your mother make your birthday cake. Daffodil cake she called it. I was beating the egg whites for the angel food while your mother was mixing the yellow sponge cake. I noticed her eyes were tearing up and I asked her what she was thinking."

Your mother said, "One of Linda's doctors told me that she won't live past the age of ten. Today she's going to be nine years old."

I was shocked and struck by the courage my mother had to banish her fear and never show defeat. When I was in the hospital, Mom would arrive wearing her pink-checkered dress. She didn't look sad. She never mentioned that she was worried I would die. It had not occurred to me that my parents were among those who assumed I would not survive childhood. They appeared so confident. They didn't speak in front of me about their doubts.

Keeping my thoughts to myself, I sniffled, took a deep breath and set the teakettle on the stove to boil. I needed to be as strong for my parents as they had been for me.

Shaking off the gloom from our conversation, I said, "I hope you can drop by again to seem Mom."

"Of course I will," Renée said. "Let me know if there is anything else I can do."

# The Naughty Bench

At five years of age, I skipped along beside my mother on my first day of kindergarten. I chattered as we walked the four blocks to the neighborhood elementary school. Even the weight of my brown and white saddle shoes could not slow me down. As we entered the schoolyard, I watched the other five-year-olds. Some were clinging to their mothers' skirts; some were sniffling; some were wailing as they begged their mothers not to leave. Not me. Finally on my own, I sensed excitement.

I crossed the threshold into a schoolroom where the rules were as rigid as the wooden blocks stacked in the corner. My fellow classmates and I lined up in neat rows and marched into the school when the bell rang. We were not allowed to leave until the bell rang again. We learned how to raise a hand before speaking. We had to ask permission to go to the bathroom and then we could not leave the room alone. The independence I had imagined when I waved good-bye to Mom did not exist.

Even so, I knew I was luckier than several of my friends. In the mid-1950s there were no laws requiring the inclusion of children with a disability in a public school. Lenore had cerebral palsy and Down's syndrome. Rose had to go to a special boarding school for blind children. These friends of mine were unknown to the children who sat beside me in public school. It was as if Rose and Lenore did not exist.

Before the school year began, my mother completed the enrollment application for kindergarten. The principal rejected it, explaining to my mother, "I cannot be responsible for her safety." Anticipating this response, Dr. Dameshek had sent a letter to my mother. The letter read, "There is no medical reason why Linda cannot attend a public school."

The letter from my doctor did not reassure the principal. Nonetheless, she admitted me on the condition that I would not go to recess.

"I guess you'll have to play games in our backyard," Mom said to me.

During recess each day, I sat on the bench outside the principal's office door with the naughty children. When the other children went outside to play and even when they were indoors during recess, I sat on the wooden bench. The forced inactivity bottled up my frustration like compressed steam. Did the principal really believe that learning to bounce balls or to square dance would be hazardous to my health?

Some days, I sat alone on that wooden bench. I would stare at the door, longing to join my friends at play. On other days, I found myself sharing the bench with another child. Those of us who sat on the bench understood why the principal was punishing us. Broken, disabled, or disruptive in the classroom, we were all too much trouble. The naughty children and I had a lot in common: we were all angry at something. The difference between us was that if one of the other naughty children punched out their anger, they would not have to go to the hospital to stop the swelling in their own hand. I would.

Weary of being called, "You poor dear," I enhanced the myth that the bruises on my legs and arms came from fighting in the schoolyard. Although my mother had tried to train me to suppress my temper, I still was quick to defend a friend. I had hit Greg, the meanest boy in our school, when he pulled my friend Audrey's ponytail. I was the only child in the neighborhood who stood up to him. To my surprise, Greg cried when I hit him. Sitting on that bench solidified my reputation as a bad child. Many classmates no longer thought of me as a fragile girl.

I liked to think my school records also suggested a hint of truancy. Each time I handed a report card to my parents for their signature, it noted the days absent. Each year the total days absent exceeded the number of days in attendance.

Instead of skipping school deliberately, Mom kept me at home for reasons no other child could understand. If I woke up in the morning swallowing blood from a wiggling baby tooth, I would be out of school until the adult tooth filled the gap and the bleeding ceased. If I had a large bruise, I would spend several days in bed elevating the injured arm or leg. One day I would be practicing the multiplication tables. The next four days I would be out of school lying in bed with an ice pack on my elbow. I experienced school as if it were a stop-action film.

My mother contacted my teacher and asked if one of my friends could bring the day's worksheets home to me. Mom taught me what I could not figure out myself. With lots of time to practice while in bed, math came easily to me. Our house had more library books than the school classroom. Inspired by my father's reading aloud to me, I had learned to read before going to school.

The more days I missed school, the more fearful I became about returning. I worried about what the other children had learned that I had missed. What does everyone else know that I don't? Will there be a test today that I will fail? I didn't want to stay home another day, so I would go off to school in spite of my fear.

At the time, I did not perceive that I often returned to the classroom knowing more than those who had perfect attendance. My school report cards had above-average grades, but each began with, "Despite her poor health..." To me, the words discredited the grades that followed. It confirmed that I only received good grades because the teacher was sorry for me. School taught me less about arithmetic than self-doubt.

# Fantasy, Facts, and Family Secrets

My father read aloud to me each night before my bedtime. His favorite stories were from Andrew Lang's *The Green Fairy Book*. Images of magic swans, enchanted snakes, and golden mermaids swam and danced in my childhood dreams.

When he read *Alice in Wonderland*, I thought he had fallen down the rabbit hole himself. My father's voice made the Dormouse and the Red Queen come alive. I didn't need to look at the illustrations to see old Father William standing on his head. At the time it all seemed like nonsense to me. Already I was a serious child, but my father was determined to enhance my imagination.

During the warm summer afternoons I often walked to the end of our block and met my father as he walked from the bus stop home after work. He would listen to me chatter about my day. Dad seemed disappointed because I had not created an imaginary friend. At his urging, I fabricated a make-believe playmate and named it Pity. I can only guess why I chose that unusual name, and my father never questioned my choice.

"How's Pity today?" my father would ask in an ordinary tone of voice as we walked home together.

"Oh, he's fine. Off on one of his adventures," I'd reply. I didn't believe in any imaginary friend. I would try to change the subject, but Dad would persist.

"Where has he gone today and how did he get there?"

"Dad!" I groaned with exasperation. Then seeing the eagerness in my father's eyes I said, "He went to Toronto to see Uncle Bill. You know he flies—like Superman."

My stories were based on places I had been or people I knew. I preferred the truth. Fantasy was undependable, like the lies they told in hospitals. In my experience the nurses and doctors in a hospital had their own stories. They worked as if patients were just another broken item on an assembly-line conveyor belt. They dispensed pills, changed bandages, drew blood samples, and emptied bedpans, but rarely showed their emotions. I learned to do the same. They would say anything just to keep the line moving. Children who complained, fought back, or screamed out in pain were shushed.

I knew that if I displayed fear, the doctor would say, "It doesn't really hurt." If I got angry, they brought in a nurse to hold my hands down. If I cried, they told me, "It will be over soon." If those lies didn't work, they blamed me. "You need to be braver," or "You're making this even harder than it needs to be." They appeared to believe they could fix or cure anything if only the patient were cooperative. They would order one more test, try one more medication, and never admit defeat. I could see the truth, and I wanted to yell out like the child in my storybook who said, "The Emperor has no clothes!"

One story my dad never read to me was "The Princess and the Pea." The first time I heard the story, Carol Burnett pranced around on the screen of our black-and-white television in *Once Upon a Mattress*. I sat cross-legged on the carpet in front of the television shaking my head. No, no, no. A real princess would not claim she felt a pea on a bedstead buried under twenty feather mattresses. A pea was too soft.

What they did not say, but what I was sure they meant, was that a real princess would bruise easily. She would have hemophilia. That ridiculous princess lost a good night's sleep and gained a prince. How silly.

By the age of ten, I was an expert in bleeding disorders. Doctors believed that the only women who had hemophilia had both a father with hemophilia and a mother who was a carrier for hemophilia. That wasn't true. Many women who were carriers had the same bleeding problems as their fathers or sons. Often I found myself teaching doctors or nurses that girls could have hemophilia too.

My type of hemophilia was rare. My blood was missing the first factor in the clotting chain. Fibrinogen formed a sort of platform for a clot to build. People with the most common forms of hemophilia were missing other factors in their blood that would build upon that fibrinogen base. The chain reaction was complex, but if any one of the links was missing, the ability to form a clot and sustain it until healing could take place wouldn't occur.

My encyclopedia described hemophilia as a royal disease, but in truth there were many children born with a bleeding disorder. Before the twentieth century, only royalty had the resources to keep such a child alive. A prince had the luxury of being able to stay in bed when injured. Servants would bring the child food and take care of his basic needs. Children with hemophilia in other families died early. They weren't given special care, and no one wrote about their lives.

I don't remember when my mother told me my family secret. She lowered her voice even though there was no one else around to hear. "Your father and I are related by blood. We thought it would be okay. Almost everyone in my hometown was related in some way," she said "The doctor told us we are both carriers."

I already knew about the secret, but I did not know that was why I had no fibrinogen. My cousin Bill called my father uncle and my mother second cousin. He did not notice when my parents looked uncomfortable. He did not seem to understand that his joke triggered my parents' sense of guilt for my bleeding disorder.

I had my mother's eyes and my father's wavy hair. My fingers were short, and my mother said they looked like her sister Ivy's. Dad had read a book about genetics. He learned I had one chance in four of having afibrinogenemia. Ashamed that he had somehow helped to cause my bleeding disorder, he had not shared the information with me. If I had not hit the lottery of one in four, the afibrinogenemia in our family would have remained a secret.

"It's better if you don't tell anyone your dad and I are related," my mother said. I knew why. The comedians on television made jokes about children born to people who were related. They called children like me stupid. People did not care as much for the truth if they had already formed an opinion. If people thought you were inferior, they would treat you as if you were unworthy.

# Neighborhood Orphanage

The Robertson children were in our house more often than in their own. They lived in the house behind ours. The eldest was a girl, Sharon, just two years older than I. Mrs. Robertson was several years younger than my mother. I heard her explaining that Sharon was her child from her first marriage. She made a deep throaty laugh as she explained why she had left her first husband. I listened intently. In the early 1950s divorce was rare, especially if the couple had a child.

The next child Sharon's mother gave birth to was a boy named Logan. He was an attractive child with large, brown eyes and sandy-colored hair. He looked like his father.

By the time Logan was old enough to go to school, neighbors began gossiping about Sharon's mother. I didn't know what they meant when they said she was a loose woman. The city bus driver visited her on his lunch break, leaving with a broad smile and liquor on his breath an hour later. When Sharon's second brother was born, he showed no resemblance to Sharon's stepfather. The child had an olive complexion and coarse dark brown hair.

When Mrs. Robertson was pregnant the fourth time, her husband in a drunken rage shoved her down the stairs. The baby was born prematurely weighing two pounds at birth. They named the infant Ruth. After spending the first few months of her fragile life in an incubator, she emerged to meet the world totally and permanently blinded by the oxygen.

One morning, a few weeks after Ruth came home from the maternity hospital, there was a knock on our back door. The staccato knock was hard and sounded frantic. When my mother opened the door, Mrs. Robertson handed her the baby. "I've got to take Sharon to the doctor. Will you take care of Ruth while I am gone?"

"Of course," my mother said, cradling the infant in her arms. Blind and passive to the world around her, she appeared like a fledgling bird. She clung to any human who held her.

Mom closed the back door. "She looks a little like her daddy," Mom mused as she uncurled the translucent fingers. It was distressing to see her tiny fists pressed deeply into the sockets of her sightless eyes. "I'm Daisy," Mom said, even though Ruth was too young to understand. Mom cuddled Ruth and cooed soothing sounds, fed her the warmed bottled milk, and changed the soiled diaper. Ruth didn't make a sound as my mother laid her on the bed.

Mom turned to me. "Time for you to go."

That afternoon when I came home from school, Ruth was still at our house.

"I didn't expect Mrs. Robertson to be gone this long," Mom said.

"Can I hold her?" I asked. I had never held a baby, only my dolls.

"Sure, but you have to sit in a chair. Go sit in the living room on the sofa." Mom gently transferred the infant to my open arms and helped me to support the baby's head. "Don't pat her too hard. Stroke her cheeks and feel how soft they are—like peach fuzz, isn't it? You can sing her a lullaby if you want."

I nodded.

"Now I can get a few things done," Mom said.

A few minutes later, there was another knock on the back door. This one was so quiet that if Mom hadn't been in the kitchen at the time, she might not have heard it. When she opened the door, Logan was standing there sniffling and looking frightened. "Are you here to pick up your sister?" Mom asked. The seven-year-old shook his head.

"Something's very wrong in my house," Logan said snuffling back his sobs. "There's stuff everywhere." Then he added, "There is a piece of paper on the kitchen table, but I can't read what it says."

The second-grade boy could not read the angry note, yet he knew what the message must say. His mother had left him.

"Wait here with us until your father gets home," Mom instructed him.

Within a few minutes, my father arrived home from work. He took a look around and wearily dropped his lunch bucket on the kitchen counter. Instead of the evening newspaper, he picked up one of the children's books scattered in the living room, sat in his favorite chair, and selected a story to read aloud. Logan sat on the floor next to my dad. Even Ruth seemed to relax into the sonorous tones of my father's voice.

An hour later it was Mr. Robertson who knocked on the back door. He had come home to find the house torn apart. Upside-down chairs and books littered the living room; broken china covered the kitchen floor. The note from his wife ended with, "Ruth is at Daisy's house."

Mrs. Robertson had left two of her children behind—Logan and Ruth. She had taken the two children that did not look like her husband. She had sold what she could: china, silverware, and antiques. What she could not sell, she destroyed. Broken glass and slashed cushions showed the aftermath of her fury.

The next day Mr. Robertson filed a court order and the police posted a missing person's alert. She had made it to California with her new male companion and two of her children. The police arrested Sharon's mother and transported her back to Massachusetts. Sharon and her younger brother came back to Mr. Robertson.

I overheard Mr. Robertson telling Mom the judge said, "No sane woman would abandon two of her own children. He ordered her to ninety days of evaluation in the state mental hospital." Then the judge granted Mr. Robertson sole custody of all four children. After Sharon's mother served her time, she left town alone.

Mr. Robertson brought Ruth to our house each morning before he went to work. For years these four children were under my mother's care whenever they were not in school. Each child was left with scars visible only in their behavior.

When Ruth acquired language skills, she would ask, "Why did my mother leave me?" She asked this question to every new person she met, bringing tears she could not see to many eyes.

Logan preferred to climb the fence, sticking his bare toes into the diamond squares of wire and slinging first one then the other leg over the top and landing with a thud on the grass. He displayed the trauma of losing his mother with controlled rage. As he helped my mother or father pick off the Japanese beetles from the flower garden, he smiled as he crushed each insect. Logan seemed to get the most glee out of gently removing a tomato worm and then slicing it in half with the shovel. When neither of my parents could see him, he would catch a grasshopper, snap off its head, watch the green blood stain his fingers, and then pop the grasshopper into his mouth and lick the juice from his fingers.

"Eeeeeey, yuck!" my friends would scream.

If Sharon and I were left alone to play together, Sharon would tempt me into some behavior that my mother would punish. "I'm going to pull the pages out of your book and burn it," she said one day.

"No, you won't!" I yelled, thwacking her with my doll.

As the doll connected with Sharon's arm, Mom walked in. "No fighting! Linda, go to your room and stay there until I say it is all right to come out." I left without argument.

I turned back to glare at Sharon and saw the smug smile on her face. Soon I caught on to Sharon's tricks and learned to hold my temper, but Sharon had learned too. She simply lied. She would let out a shriek of mock pain and call out, "Ouch! Linda hit me!"

Sharon would then get my mother's full attention while I would be confined to my bedroom. If I told my mother the truth, she would reply, "Sharon doesn't have a mother now. You do."

Listening from my bedroom I could hear my mother and Sharon. It seemed to me that my mother had more fun when I was not there. I certainly was having less.

In my isolation I convinced myself that I brought my parents more sorrow than joy. The fear that I was a burden on my parents crept into my thoughts.

As children, Logan and his sisters didn't tell anyone that their father came home from his job each night and drank. Like throwing gasoline on a flame, the alcohol he drank spread his fury in all directions. When Sharon was an adult and living on her own, she told me that her father had frequently threatened to kill them all in their beds. More than once she had sneaked out of the house and slept in the bushes of their front yard listening for gunfire from inside the house.

These children didn't have hemophilia, but that didn't mean their lives were easy. They envied me as much as I envied them.

# *Home Care*

When Logan had knocked on our back door for the first time, he was seven. That was the day his mother had left in a rampage. After that he would infrequently come inside our house. He would only knock on our door when he needed first aid. Once my mother had cleaned his scraped elbow and applied a bandage, he didn't hang around.

In 1970 Logan finished his freshman year at the state college and came home. Mom opened the kitchen door to see Logan standing on the steps with a bloodied face and a laundry bag full of dirty clothing slung over his shoulder. He explained that his dad was drunk again. Logan had come home for the summer. His father had announced that he would not pay for any more school. It was time, his father screamed, for his son to go off to the war that was in Vietnam. No more would he have a son who shirked his duty and hid behind books to evade the draft.

"Take the dirty clothes downstairs to the washing machine," Mom said. "Dinner will be ready in an hour."

By the time I arrived home from college a few weeks later, I could hear John Lennon's music filling the space that previously had only held empty suitcases and dusty photographs. My parents had offered Logan their unfinished attic as a sanctuary.

Logan said very little to anyone. Some evenings, after we had dinner together, he would linger long enough for a game of cards after the kitchen table had been cleared of dishes. Most nights he would go directly to his private space with the unpainted plywood floor and bare rafters stuffed with insulation.

In a few weeks, Logan had a job as an orderly in the city hospital. He applied for nursing school and was accepted. Whether he was truly a pacifist or whether he did it to spite his father, he received an exemption from the draft. His war was a private one. His spirit seemed full of inward battles fought in solitude.

Each morning, before he dressed for work, he arose earlier than any of us and left the house to run. He ran in the heat and the cold, in the rain, and even in the snow. He ran, it appeared, not just from his abusive father, not just from the war he opposed, but to save his own life. His goal was to run a marathon, not to win the race but to finish. The first few times, it took him so long, the race officially ended two hours before he reached the finish line. It didn't seem to bother him.

During the next two years, while he lived with my parents, I drove him in my dad's old green Chevy to and from the site of several marathons. The physical demands of long distance running were foreign to me. I could not fathom why someone would volunteer for such an arduous and punishing experience. I had spent years becoming attuned to the early warning signs in a twinge of a muscle. For me, pain was a warning signal that something was wrong. The smallest of body aches could indicate the need for medical intervention.

I did understand the importance of a cheering section and a friend to reach out with some fresh water. So, at several points along the marathon route, I would stand until I saw him come into view. Then I would begin calling out his name, shouting encouragement until I saw his dazed eyes acknowledge me.

When he had saved enough money, Logan moved out of my parents' home and eventually married a woman who was also a nurse. My parents saw Logan rarely after he married. He sent them postcards each time he and his wife went to Disneyland. He had bought a house a few miles away, but he didn't like to come back to the neighborhood where he had spent his childhood. His father still lived in the house just behind my parents.

Mom told me that Logan was working for a home care agency now. I hadn't seen him in more than twenty years. I found his unlisted phone number in my mother's address book and gave him a call. Surprised to hear from me, he listened to me as I explained my parents' distress and how the trips to their house were depleting my energy.

When I stopped long enough to take a breath, he said, "I'll arrange for your parents to have an aide stay with them overnight. Your parents live in my catchment area anyway."

"That would be so wonderful," I exclaimed, grateful for his help. "I'll be here myself next weekend. Could you drop by the house?"

"Sure," he said. "I'll be there."

Taking a deep breath for the first time all day, I thanked him. I had not had time to relax since returning from the vacation in Maine. Now that seemed as if it had been a year ago, not just a few months.

"Logan is coming to visit," I yelled in the hope that my father could hear and understand what I had said. I found it exhausting to shout at Dad, not knowing whether when he smiled and nodded if he really understood what I meant.

Whenever I could, I spoke only to my mother. Now she could not raise her voice loudly enough for Dad to hear her either. If they sat in the same room together, I noticed them glancing up, as if to check that the other was still there, then giving a slight wave of a hand to the other in recognition.

When I got to my parents' house the following Saturday, Logan had already charted my parents' daily medications. There were some notes for me to read. He had visited them, as promised, and recorded their blood pressure and Dad's glucose levels.

Logan arrived in the afternoon and we sat at the kitchen table. Then he went to say hello to my father in the living room, and Mom in her bedroom.

Just before he left, he reassured me. "I'll come check on them every week."

Handing him a scrap of paper and a pencil, I said, "Let's exchange email addresses in case we need to get in touch during the week."

My parents would not think it was charity when Logan came to visit. I reached out to hug him, but he stepped back.

"I can't thank you enough," I said. He shrugged. I searched his eyes for any sign of emotion, but saw none. He had been withdrawn and closed-mouthed in his youth. I wondered if he was capable of displaying affection for my parents who had given him shelter. Had the wounds inflicted by his parents left scar tissue the way it had stiffened my ankles and knees?

# *Baby Dolls*

One of my childhood friends had a younger sister who was born with cerebral palsy and Down's syndrome. Her parents refused to institutionalize their youngest child, despite the advice of doctors. Even though her father had a good job, he had no health insurance. They went into debt paying for the medical care their youngest child needed. The family had filed for bankruptcy, and in the process the bank took their home in California. They moved back to Massachusetts to be near family and rented a little house next to the dry cleaners. I worried that my parents would be unable to pay for our house because I had overheard them talking about how much my medical bills cost.

One day when we were eight years old, she and I sat cross-legged on the living room rug. On that October afternoon, we could see the skeletons of trees outside the window. We were making new Halloween costumes for our dolls. We had spread around us several spools of thread, bits of rickrack and lace trim, small scissors and a round tin box of spare buttons. Scooping the buttons in my fingers, I let them drop a few at a time, clink, clink, clink, back into the box.

Absorbed in our sewing projects we did not talk much. When we looked up from our sewing, we saw the sun had set.

We could hear my mother rattling pots and pans in the kitchen. We picked up the scraps and stuffed our sewing projects into a cardboard box.

After my friend left, I went to the bathroom. When I stood up to flush the toilet, I noticed that the water in the bowl looked pink. The good day had turned scarier than a Halloween goblin. I knew what to do if I had a bruise. I had no experience with blood in the toilet.

I called Mom to come look. "You're pretty young to have started your period," she said. We had already talked about menstrual bleeding and I knew what she meant. Mom checked my underpants, but the panties were clean. "If your urine is still red in the morning, I'll call the doctor."

Kay drove my mother and me to the pediatrician the next day. He examined me and then said, "I'm going to call Dr. Dameshek, your hematologist in Boston." He asked my mother to come with him while he made the telephone call. He told me to wait in the examining room.

I sat alone on the table swinging my feet up, first the right leg, then the left. It reminded me of when the doctor checked my reflexes with the brown rubber hammer that looked like an Indian arrowhead on a stick. I wanted to know what they were saying about me in the doctor's office.

The nurse came in after several minutes. She took me to the office where the doctor and my mother sat. My pediatrician usually had a smile for me, but today there were wrinkles on his forehead.

"Dr. Dameshek wants you in the Floating Hospital in Boston," the pediatrician said. "He knows best how to treat whatever is wrong."

The drive to Boston would take several hours since the interstate highway had not been completed. "If it was the Springfield Hospital, I would have the time to take you there," Kay apologized.

When we got home, my mother called her friend Renée. Renée had family in Boston. I had heard Renée say she liked an excuse to go to Boston if we ever needed a ride. Mom hurried to pack a bag for me and one for her. Then she left my father a note. She couldn't call him while he was at work. Dad would be alone for as long as I was in the hospital.

I was the only one glad to be going to the Floating Hospital. I had been in that hospital before. Unaware of the strain it placed on my parents, I cheered, "Yippee!" when Renée's car came in the driveway.


In the Springfield Hospital, not many children were brave like I was. The walls echoed with children's cries of "Nurse!" Often the nurse did not come in time and the children wet their beds. The smell of soiled bed sheets hung in the hallway outside of their rooms. Parents could visit only during a few hours each day. Children cried day and night. They were lonely and afraid. They were more frightened when they heard other children crying and no one came to help. Like that very first time in the emergency room, I just wanted to get out and go home.

I didn't dread going to the Floating Hospital for Children in Boston. I had never been afraid there. In the hematology ward, where I would be admitted, many of the children had leukemia. I heard nurses whispering that these children would die soon. Still I did not hear any child crying for help. The hospital subtracted money off the cost of the medical care if one parent would stay overnight beside their child. My mother, like many other parents, took their own child's temperature, brought bedpans, and read stories. Mom invited other children to come to my room so we could play card games on my bed. Nurses had time to give extra attention to the children whose parents were unable to stay with them.

Dr. Dameshek was a famous doctor. He talked directly to me and I listened to his every word. He explained the big words, like *coagulation*, so I could understand. He believed that infusions were only for emergencies. He wrote instructions in my chart that I had to stay in bed. He didn't want me to get up even to go to the bathroom. Each morning the nurse bottled a small sample of my urine and taped it to the foot of my bed next to the sample from the day before. Each day the sample looked less pink.

"That means you are getting better," Dr. Dameshek told me. "You won't need an infusion if you keep getting better."

A student doctor carried a vial of my blood in the pocket of his white coat. Each morning he would stand at my door, pull out the tube, shake it, and then shake his head. He looked amazed. I asked him why, and he replied, "I don't know why you are still alive." He told me he was waiting for the blood to clot, but it never did. Silly I thought, and yet I couldn't forget the confused look on his face.

Dr. Dameshek led Grand Rounds every morning. He walked fast into my room, and I could feel a breeze as the other doctors' white coats flapped behind him. The students formed a circle around my bed. The medical students came from all over the world. I listened to what Dr. Dameshek told them about me and to the students' questions. Sometimes the students asked me questions too. I pretended to be a witness in a trial, like on television. I was giving them testimony so they could get the facts.

One of the student doctors was a woman. She asked if I had had my monthly period yet. "No," I replied.

"Well, you should have a hysterectomy before you do."

I asked her what she meant. She explained, "We could surgically remove your uterus, so you won't bleed to death from a period. You can't have any children anyway."

My mother had talked with me about monthly periods. She showed me a book and I knew what a uterus was, but she never said it could kill me. Dr. Dameshek frowned at the student doctor. He looked angry with her.

"You'll be fine," he said to me. I wanted to believe him, but I worried that the woman doctor knew more than he did about my future.

"When I grow up, can I have a baby?" I asked him.

"You could adopt one," Dr. Dameshek said.

I realized the answer was no. Later I would learn that without any fibrinogen a placenta does not attach to the inner wall of the uterus.

I waited until the doctors had left the room and my mother had gone to the hospital cafeteria for lunch before I cried.

In ten days the urine sample finally showed no sign of blood. Dr. Dameshek said I could go home. In my own bedroom at last, I picked up my favorite doll and threw it against the wall. "No babies for me," I yelled at the doll lying on the floor.

# *Becoming a Woman*

A few days before I celebrated my twelfth birthday, I began my first menstruation. It was a rainy, chilly Saturday, and I was glad it wasn't a school day. Mom had already shown me where the new elastic sanitary napkin belt was in the bathroom, right next to her package of pads. I put on the belt and attached the pad to the plastic clasps on each end. An ache just below my belly made my fingers shake a bit, and it took a while for me to get the contraption on in the correct position between my legs.

"Cramps?" Mom asked, as if I knew what that meant. It certainly was not like any pain I had experienced before. Then she said, "I guess you are old enough to have coffee. Would you like to try a cup?"

The hot liquid looked so appealing. I cradled the cup in my hands and sniffed the familiar scent. I tasted it. "It's bitter," I said. "You like this stuff?"

"Put some sugar in and a little milk, at least until you get used to the taste," Mom said, passing me the sugar bowl and a spoon.

"Mom," I wailed, "is this normal?"

When she nodded her head yes, I couldn't believe her. Never in all the explanations had anyone described the intensity of what she called cramps. In my Girl Scout troop we watched a film showing a pear-shaped uterus preparing a soft cushion lining. The reassuring voice in the film described a period as the discarding of that lining each month. The information had not equipped me for the gut-clenching ache I felt that day and the thick bloody discharge that poured out of my body. My mother had been careful not to frighten me.

"You mean all women have this experience every month?" I remembered the student doctor who had said I could not survive a period. Four years had passed since then. I realized for the first time why the doctor had been afraid of the consequences of menstrual bleeding for me.

"I'll plug in the heating pad. That will help the cramps. You can also use it on your back," Mom advised. "I wish I could give you an aspirin, but you know what the doctor said."

Years earlier a doctor had told me never to take an aspirin. He had helped to discover that it worked to prevent clots from forming. That was good for some people, but dangerous for me.

I turned to my mother. "I can't believe I have to go through this every month for the rest of my life." Only then did my mother confide in me that she had heavy periods, as had her sister Ivy. Everyone accepted it as part of becoming a woman. In disbelief I listened to my mother share her ways of coping.

"A heating pad will help the pain, putting your feet up will lessen the flow of blood," she said. Through her voice I could hear an underlying anxiety.

The first two days I managed to cope with the flow by changing the thick sanitary napkins every few hours, but by the third day, I soaked through the pads in a few minutes. They stank as I folded them up and tried to hide them from view in the bathroom trash bucket.

On the telephone I heard my mother calling the doctor. When she hung up, I asked her what he had said. He suggested that you lie down and keep your feet raised above your heart.

He told me you're still in the normal range and often the first menstrual period is the heaviest. He wants me to call him back if you soak through more than one sanitary pad an hour.

For three days I lay on the living room floor with a pile of newspapers underneath my rear and my feet propped up on the sofa. It was hard to read in that position, holding the books up and in front of my face. I couldn't see the television, but my mother turned it on so I could listen to my favorite game shows and programs during the day. It helped to laugh at reruns of *I Love Lucy* or listen to *Truth or Consequences*.

Uncharacteristically I had no wish to get up more often than to eat and go to the bathroom. When I did, the blood flow increased. On the heaviest days I soaked through the extra thick pad and onto the magazines and newspapers Mom put under me to protect the carpet from bloodstains.

After three days of lying on the floor, the flow slowly tapered off and so did the cramps. It was eight days before the stains of blood ceased completely.

"Why don't you stay home from school a few more days," Mom suggested. "You look so pale."

"No," I said, "I've lost enough time already."

Two weeks after my first menstrual period ceased, Renée called my mother and said, "I'm taking the kids to the fishing derby at the park. Want to come with us?"

None of us caught any fish that chilly gray day in mid-April, and when we got back to our house, Renée's children and I decided to play a game of tag outdoors while our mothers sipped tea inside. The soil was soft, now that the frost had left the ground. We were running, as an excuse to celebrate the day off from school. None of us cared about the rules of a game.

I froze not because of the game of tag, but because of a stab of pain in my belly. It was sudden, sharp. It doubled me over in a rigid pose, clutching my center. I was afraid to inhale and unable to speak. I held onto myself tightly and managed to get inside the house.

Renée said, "Come on, kids, we're going home." Then she turned to Mom and said, "I'll call you later."

Once I was inside, the pain continued. It curled my body with its pull. I walked hunched over, my hand gripping my lower torso. Even when I lay on the bed, I could not straighten my back without increasing the pain in my belly.

My mother called the pediatrician. "He's out of town," Mom reported when she came back to my bedroom. "I spoke to the doctor who is covering for him. He said you'll be better in a day or two."

I had heard her on the telephone say, "She isn't running a fever. She hasn't been sick to her stomach. I'm sure this is more than the flu."

As the afternoon turned to evening, then to night, the pain grew. Restless I got out of bed several times, compelled to walk, to change position, trying to escape the pain. I moved, doubled over, from bedroom to living room, to bed again. I watched television, but could not concentrate. I couldn't divert my attention from the pain. The pain punches took my breath away. I paced, then lay in bed. Hours passed, forty-eight maybe seventy-two.

I could hear Mom talking on the telephone. "She's growing paler. No, she doesn't have a fever, no vomiting, only pain." I could hear the agitation in her voice.

Straining to hear what my mother was going to do next, I called out, "Mom!" when I heard her hang up the telephone.

"I'll be there in a minute," she yelled. "I'm calling Renée."

When Mom came into my bedroom, she explained, "Renée suggested I call Hazel. Her husband's a doctor."

"What can she do?" I asked.

"We'll see." Then Mom went back to the kitchen telephone and I could hear her talking again.

In prolonged pain and mounting alarm, I waited to hear what my mother would try next. Finally she came to my room again.

"Hazel says she'll ask her husband to come over after they finish dinner tonight. If he thinks it's necessary, he will admit you to the hospital." Then she said, "I'm going to fix dinner for us now and then I'll get clean sheets on your bed. Can't have a doctor in here seeing wrinkled sheets." Off she went.

I had brushed away my father's offer to sit with me. He looked too sad, too helpless. When my mother came to change my bed sheets, she had me roll from side to side so I didn't have to leave the bed. It was difficult enough for me to roll to the left side of the bed while she made the right side, then roll over again onto the clean side while she folded and tucked in the sheets.

When she was done, I said, "No supper for me." I hadn't been able to eat all day. She kissed my forehead and left. There was silence in the kitchen while my parents ate. The first sound I heard was Mom putting the plates and silverware in the sink and running water to wash the dishes. I imagined my father drying the items Mom placed to drip in the drainer. Still no conversation I could hear.

Our front doorbell rang an hour later. Mom came into my room with the doctor. He smiled at me and I tried to smile over my fear.

He took my blood pressure, looked at the palms of my hands, and then gently pressed down on my stomach. When he let go, I screamed involuntarily at the sharp pain I had not anticipated. He asked to speak to Mom in the living room. He wanted to know about my bleeding disorder. I could have told him, but he didn't ask me. I heard him on our telephone talking to someone.

Mom came back to my room in a few minutes. "He's ordered an ambulance to take you to the Floating Hospital. He talked to the doctor who is on call for Dr. Dameshek. A doctor will be waiting for you there."

I took a deep breath for the first time in days and immediately regretted it since it hurt more afterward.

In a few minutes I could hear the wail of the ambulance arriving at the front of our house. Standing over my bed, the ambulance driver reminded me of one of the giants in a children's fairy tale. He left the stretcher in our living room. It would not fit through the hallway door. He bent over me, one arm under my knees, one behind my shoulders, and picked me up. The room around me swirled. In our living room he placed me on the stretcher.

I heard the doctor's voice say, "She won't make it to Boston. I can't find a pulse. Take her to Springfield Hospital."

As if it was far away, I could hear the siren above me as the ambulance sped toward the hospital. Each time the ambulance bumped over a pothole, I screamed. The last thing I remember before I lost consciousness was my mother blocking the ambulance driver from picking me up and carrying me to the emergency entrance. She appeared to be half his height and weight. "You are not going to lift her like that again! We're at the hospital. Get help if you can't get the stretcher out by yourself," Mom ordered.

Thankful for my mother's courage, I drifted into unconsciousness.

I awoke in the recovery room of the hospital unaware of place or time. When I opened my eyes, my father's face came into view. He looked more frightened than I had ever seen him. My mother leaned closer to hear what I whispered. "Am I going to die? Dad never takes a day off from work."

"It's all over, honey. You had surgery," she said stroking my hair. "You'll be fine."

I dozed on and off, and each time I awoke, I asked the same question, not believing what I heard for the answer.

The surgeon came to visit me the next day. He had spoken to my parents the night before. During the exploratory surgery, he found the source of the internal bleeding. I had ovulated and the cyst had ruptured.

He said to me, "When other women have an ovarian cyst rupture, they lose a drop or two of blood. Then the bleeding stops. In your case it didn't stop since your blood does not clot. I sponged away the excess blood and then sutured the incision. I've ordered the clotting factor to be infused until you heal from the surgery. You're going to be here for a while."

I was older than most of the other patients in the children's ward of the Springfield Hospital. As soon as I was able to get out of bed, I began to explore. Brian and I were the oldest patients and also the ones who had to stay for an extended amount of time. In those days there were no televisions in the hospital rooms, no telephones.

When I met Brian in the hallway, I was pushing my IV pole. The skin on his face and body puckered into crazy-quilt patterns. His eyelids didn't close fully and his lips were swollen. He saw me stare at him. He looked about my age, too old to be a child, too young to be a teen.

"Tossed a spray can into a fire. Won't do that again," he said with a snicker.

Brian knew people found his ghoulish appearance tragic and he liked to watch them squirm with their discomfort. He used sympathy like a get-out-of-jail-free card in a game of Monopoly. "I'm gonna grab that empty wheelchair and race down the hall. Bet I can get that nurse to spill her tray of pills!"

I guessed that in his school he had sat on the naughty bench many times. When he was not creating havoc for the nurses, he liked to play a staring game with other patients and their visitors to see who would blink first. He almost always won, unless he played with me. I admired his belligerent attitude.

When Renée came to visit me in the hospital, I introduced her to Brian. I saw tears pop up in her eyes when she looked at Brian's hideous scars. When he had left my room, Renée gasped, "Why didn't you warn me, Linda?"

The truth was that I saw no reason to be sad for Brian. Some of us had scars on the outside and some, like me, had them where they didn't show.

The day I was released from the hospital, the doctor recommended that I get a home teacher for a month while I continued to get my strength back.

Two weeks before the end of the school year, I returned to my sixth-grade classroom. The teacher was attempting to keep the class amused. She seemed to have no interest in teaching the class. Each child was making a paper maché puppet head in preparation for the grand celebration on the last day of elementary school. I picked one of the inflated balloons and began covering it with glue-soaked newsprint. I stared at the stiff-faced puppets with the painted smiles and wondered if that was how I looked too.

We would all be going to a new school the following September. I didn't think I was ready to face the challenges of a new school where I would need to follow a schedule and walk from class to class. Because I had missed so many days of school, the principal recommended I be put in the eighth track. The students who were in tracks one, two, or three had already been labeled as college material. Tracks four through eight were expected to learn a trade or find a job after completing high school. Those in tracks nine and ten were not expected to finish high school.

Glancing around the room, I envied my classmates' naiveté. My education had come from hospitals and doctors.

Mom reassured me that I knew more than I thought I did. "Starting slowly in a class that isn't too challenging is a good idea," she said.

"But I want to go to college," I wailed. I wasn't even sure what that meant. I knew it had been my father's dream and his biggest regret. Now it was my dream.

"You will," she said with conviction. "You will."

# *My Turn*

I took several days off work whenever one of my parents had a medical appointment. The primary care doctor advised me to have my father's hearing tested and get both of them to the ophthalmologist for eye exams. My mother's neurologist explained her Parkinson's medications. I quizzed the arthritis specialist about the medication Mom was taking to strengthen her thinning bones.

In October trees fluttered gold, crimson, and burnt umber. The wind picked up the leaves tossing them in piles that buried the grass, cluttering the sidewalks, and drifting against fences. Each week there were more naked branches. Goblins and ghoulish carved jack-o'-lanterns sat beside doorways. I groped like a living corpse at times myself, dragging my tired body from home to work to parents and back to work again. As a minister of a Unitarian Universalist Church, Robin preached on Sunday. I traveled alone many weekends, collapsing into Robin's arms when I arrived back home late on Sunday evenings.

Weighted down by the trips back and forth and the stress of being able to provide only minimal care and attention for my parents, I returned to work each Monday without any time for rejuvenation.

My father had given up his dream of getting a college education to buy a house for me. In my childhood I heard my parents whisper about the things they could not afford because my medical bills had to be paid. Hospitalizations were only partially covered by my father's health insurance. There was no reimbursement for a visit to a doctor. Dad had longed to start his own business, but he had given up when it would mean no affordable health insurance. There was never enough money because of my medical expenses. My parents did not speak about it, but it was obvious to me that my mother's ability to economize was a necessity.

I realized that they took care of me even when there were half-moon shadows of fatigue under their eyes. They never spoke about their anxiety.

They protected me, inspired me, and believed in me. They were the ones who had taught me how to be safe. They encouraged my dreams even when others doubted my abilities. I knew I had had the rare gift of a happy childhood. The sacrifices they made for me were because they loved me. I would do whatever it cost to care for them. It was my turn.

My mother was able now to get out of bed and walk to the bathroom, kitchen, or living room. These gains seemed fragile. She still had advancing bone loss. Her Parkinson's disease was responding less well to the medications.

Logan described to Mom what the rest of us already knew. He said, "If you fall, you will break a bone. If you break a bone, you will have to go to a nursing home. You'd be miserable in a nursing home. You must use your walker." She was listening, but I knew she did not believe this warning.

She was still leaving her walker in the bedroom when she walked to the kitchen or living room. "I don't really need it in the house," she told me after Logan left.

Dad still walked around the neighborhood park twice a day. The park had been the city's reservoir, and there was a paved road, no longer accessible to cars, circling the small lake. Motorcycles zigzagged through the barricades. In the shadows under the trees, people were arrested for selling drugs. My father didn't believe he would come to any harm in the park where they had walked for years. I tried to turn off the images in my head of him being mugged, left unconscious, lying in the park until someone might happen by and discover him. It also made me nervous when I sat beside him as he drove his car to the grocery store. He annoyed the people driving behind him with his slow pace and indecision.

Since earning a master's degree in 1974, I had worked as a librarian until 1980 when I took a job as a consultant for the state library agency. That job had included improving libraries in institutions, such as prisons, jails, mental health hospitals, and schools for children born with learning impairments. In 1984 I returned to working in a public library—this time as a director.

I told Robin, "I used to love my work. Now I'm scrambling to get the basics done. I'm not doing a good job anywhere. I want to expand the ESL program. The children's room is not big enough, and the architect's drawings are buried deep in a pile on my desk. I think more about my parents than about my work. I'm not taking good enough care of them, but these trips to see them every weekend are exhausting."

"It would be easier if we moved them in with us," Robin suggested.

"How could we possibly manage that?" I looked around the house we owned. It was half of a duplex. The town was full of houses like ours. They had been built for mill workers near the beginning of the twentieth century and were intentionally designed so that no two houses were exactly the same.

The mill constructed looms for weaving fabric. When polyester began to replace cotton and wool, however, the mill shut down its production. The mill workers no longer had free housing from their employer, but the mill sold each half of the duplex individually, as if they were condominiums. It was a less expensive way to purchase a house, and many of the previous mill workers now owned the home they had lived in for years.

In our half of the two-family house, the previous owners had added a bathroom on the first floor. It had an undersized sink, a toilet, and a shower. The space would not be large enough for my mother to get into with her walker. The bedrooms and another bathroom were on the second floor. We used the third floor as storage. In the basement was our washer and clothes dryer, a small wood stove, and all our gardening tools.

My mother would be able to use only the first floor, but getting into the house would be a problem, since there was a long flight of steps up to the deck.

"It's silly to discuss these details now," I said as we listed off the obstacles. "They'll never agree to move in with us."

My father had told me that he was proud of his father because Grandfather didn't want to be a burden to any of his children in his old age. My mother tried to talk my father into moving into senior housing ten years ago when she thought they were still able to move on their own. Dad wouldn't even discuss it with her. It was memorable because my father usually agreed to whatever Mom thought was best.

Now she might not have the energy to move. She would know that I would have to manage all the details. I would be in control, not her. Surely that would not be easy for either of us.

"You will never forgive yourself if you don't take care of them now," Robin said, interrupting my thoughts. "You've always told me what a wonderful childhood you had and how extraordinary it was compared to the other children you had as friends."

"You're right," I said, "but even more than that, I don't want them to think they are a burden. I know what that's like." I hesitated. "The truth is, living with my parents again will be difficult."

I had established a distance between them and me. We spent holidays together. I called them on the telephone once a week. Until the past few years we had met at a halfway point in a restaurant or picnic grove. It was all I wanted and it seemed to be enough to satisfy my parents. They had their own lives and I had mine.

I could not keep up the lies of omission if we moved them in to live with us and neither could they. Since August I had learned that they played the "I'm fine" game on me. Once I no longer lived with them, I had frequently told them I was fine when it was not true. If they lived with us, they would know every injury I sustained. I would know their every weakness. Despite the apprehension that crept over me like an army of ants, they needed me now to take care of them.

"Okay," I said. "We have nothing to lose by asking them to move in with us." How little we knew about what we were undertaking.

# *Pearls of Wisdom*

We stood in an awkward row with our fists on our waists, as my friend Bobbie's mother taught the Girl Scout troop how to do the Highland Fling. "Put your weight on your right foot," she demonstrated. "Raise your right arm toward the ceiling. Now lift your left foot so that it touches your right knee. Keep your toes pointed toward the floor, like this."

She looked remarkably light on her feet for a plump middle-aged woman. Still on one foot she said, "Now switch and put your weight to your left foot and your right arm up. Put your right foot up crossed in front of your left knee."

Impressive, I thought. If she can do this, then we should all be able to do it too. It wasn't as easy as she made it look. At thirteen most of my girlfriends slouched as they tried to conceal their expanding breasts. Our height was increasing as our bodies were transforming into the shape of a woman. All of our joints were being stretched. Our center of gravity was shifting. We practiced several times before she turned on the bagpipe music and told us to keep dancing. When I landed more to the side of the right foot than flat on my sole, I felt my right foot buckle. I kept dancing.

In agony that evening, I was unable to sleep with the throbbing ankle pain. By morning I couldn't touch the foot with my fingers. When Mom came to my room to check on me, I screamed, "Don't breathe on it!"

"I'm calling the doctor," Mom said.

A hematologist had opened a new practice in the city where we lived. Dr. Dameshek had been enthusiastic. "You won't have to travel two hours to see me. I'll send him a copy of your records."

Mother came into my bedroom sputtering, "The new doctor said you didn't need an infusion. He wants you to take an aspirin." Dr. Dameshek had told me years ago never to take an aspirin. It would only make bleeding worse. "I'll get you an ice pack."

Mom had not dared to contradict the doctor, but as she left my room, I saw her roll her eyes.

In pain and restless, I wanted to escape the bed. I stared around my room. I decided I could hop on one foot and rest my knee on the wooden desk chair.

"What are you up to?" My mother's voice threatened. I could hear her making our lunch in the kitchen.

"I've got my foot up, Mom," I yelled back. "I'm just going to the bathroom." Like an inchworm, I made slow and determined progress. Holding my injured foot in the air, I lifted the chair up and placed it an arm's length in front of me. Then I hopped forward and rested the knee back on the chair and took a breath. I looked up to see the distance between my bedroom and the bathroom: lift leg up, lift chair, place chair forward as far as my arms could stretch, hop, place knee on chair, and repeat. Not as graceful as dancing, I thought, but still better than using the cold metal bedpan.

The throbbing was unrelenting night and day. When my father came home from work, he no longer pulled up a chair beside my bed and attempted to distract me from the pain. On the weekend, however, Dad, then in his midfifties, purchased a Hula-Hoop and spun it around his middle. When I giggled at my silly father, Dad said, "It's so good to hear you laugh."

The laughter was a welcome diversion, but the pain never stopped. It took two weeks before I could return to school.

By the time I was fifteen, I had twisted both of my ankles several times. Each sprain led to internal bleeding that ate away the cartilage between the bones. I stumbled easily, reinjuring the ankle again and again. Each time the agonizing pain confined me to bed. When I was well enough to return to school, carrying my textbooks left bruises on the inside of my arms. I walked with a limp. I took the stairs one by one while the other students raced up or down. Each time the bell rang, I cringed at the thought of getting to the next class before the second bell. After a few months in grade eight, I was exhausted. Even with nine hours of sleep each night, I was tired.

In addition to the weakened ankles, I missed school at least three days each month because the flow from my menstrual period was so heavy. I was weak from the loss of blood. When my mother requested a home tutor for me, I cried. Defeated, I could not protest her decision. "These are the worst years of your life," my mother reassured me. "It will get better."

The city school department assigned me a home teacher. She came to tutor me at home six hours each week. "I'm really only supposed to teach elementary school-age children," she told my mother, "but the school department doesn't have anyone else to send."

The following September, I began the ninth grade back in school.

"Don't worry about missing so much school," the school counselor told me. "With your medical problems, you will probably only get a job as a receptionist or perhaps a secretary. You don't have to prepare for college."

Mom slammed down the pot on the stovetop burner. She tossed in the cut-up potatoes and turned the burner on to high. Gritting her teeth, she said, "How did he get to be a counselor? Hasn't he looked at your grades?"

Over the past ten years my mother had worked to put money aside in a college fund for me. At home she strung cultured pearls for four jewelry stores in the city. Each customer could pick out the size and number of pearls they wanted. The customer chose how many strands they wanted and selected a clasp. Weekly she took the bus to the city, stopping at each store, dropping off the completed work and picking up the new jobs in brown paper packets labeled with instructions.

I had often sat and watched as my mother picked up each bead with the flexible wire needle and slipped it onto the nylon cord, securing it in place with a knot before stringing the next pearl. It was work she could do at home. Every check she received, she put into a savings account for my college education.

By the start of the tenth grade my mother said, "You can't keep doing this. You need to get proper rest. You need to stop carrying those heavy books and climbing so many stairs." She continued, "I've talked to the principal and he will arrange tutors for you at home, but it will take an extra year for you to complete the required college preparatory classes."

My heart sank at the idea of not being in a classroom with my friends for four years. Four years seemed like an eternity. Even so, I knew she was right.

# The Taste of Bitterness

The friends who had come to our house to play were busy now with after-school activities, parties, or clubs. Some already had boyfriends. Only a few of the friends I had made in school remembered me now that I was not in the classroom with them every day. The longer I was out of school, the less often friends would call or visit me. I began to experience being an only child in a way that I had not before.

Dad sat glumly in his recliner until dinnertime, and then sat silently at the table. Evenings sitting in the living room were my loneliest times of the day. Dad stared at the television. The gulf between us contrasted sharply to the way we had enjoyed each other's company when I was a child. I missed my father's smiles, our chatty conversations. I believed he had rejected me. It didn't occur to me that my increasing medical issues were a drain on him both physically and emotionally.

My childhood friend Bobbie bounced through our back door whenever she wanted an audience for her jokes. Bobbie was active in a church youth choir. She was intent on saving my soul and converting me. I found it annoying, but she was sincere in her belief that I would go to hell. I thought that if there was a hell, she was the more likely candidate. Even so, she provided me with an entertaining distraction.

Bobbie's youth choir met once a week to practice and afterward they went out to a local diner. Bobbie often told me stories of their behavior after they left practice each Wednesday evening. One evening the choir devised a plan inspired by Bobbie who had purchased a can of octopus from the grocery store. "It was as if the can was challenging me," she told me. Bobbie took the can of octopus home, opened it, and drained the liquid. She was pleased to see the slimy black octopus was almost whole.

At choir practice she outlined her plan to the group. At the diner that night they filled themselves with French fries before the soprano said, "I'm still hungry." She ordered a bowl of tomato soup. The waitress set the steaming bowl on the counter. After the waitress left the table, Bobbie surreptitiously slid the octopus into the soup. No one else in the restaurant seemed to notice either. The soprano gave the soup a gentle stir with the spoon, waited a few minutes, and then scooped up the octopus, dripping red soup. She screamed her highest note in feigned horror and ran from the restaurant.

When the waitress came running to the table, Bobbie displayed the octopus high in the air so that all in the room could see its tentacles dangling over the spoon, apparently bleeding. Bobbie asked innocently, "What is that in the soup?" The choir members got up suddenly from the table pretending to be alarmed. They left without paying the bill. The remaining customers seated in the diner suddenly found they had little appetite and left without finishing their meals.

At the time I found this story hilarious. Anger and frustration were the things that Bobbie and I had in common. Bobbie got to express her indignation. I didn't.

One afternoon in early summer, Bobbie carried a chocolate cake up the steps and knocked on our door. The cake was warm and covered in thick frosting. She had walked the four blocks from her house to mine. She set the cake on our kitchen counter and cut two large pieces, one for each of us.

Bobbie loved cooking almost as much as she loved eating and practical jokes.

"Want a piece, Daisy?" she called to my mother, knowing that my mother was trying to lose weight.

"No, thanks," came the quick reply. Mom turned her back and left us in the kitchen.

In my bedroom, Bobbie and I each ate a large piece of the delicious cake with its gooey fudge frosting. "So when does your dad come home from work?" Bobbie asked.

"About three thirty, why?"

"Oh," she said slyly, "I thought I would offer him some cake too." Then she winked. I knew Bobbie was planning some devilish joke.

When she heard the back door open, Bobbie darted back to the kitchen to greet him. "Horace, go sit down. Put your feet up in the living room, and I'll bring you some cake," she told him in a sympathetic tone.

"Thanks, Bobbie. I am tired," Dad said, eager to do as she suggested. Bobbie cut a slice of the cake and made some instant coffee, dumping in a heaping teaspoon of salt, instead of sugar, before pouring the hot water into the cup. She was at the counter and I had no idea what she had done. With a wide smile, she set the cake and the coffee on the table beside Dad's easy chair.

There was a muffled, "Thanks," from behind the newspaper. Bobbie returned to my bedroom and waited for the yelp she knew would come. My father rarely showed anger, he didn't swear or lose his temper, but that afternoon was a memorable exception. Probably the giggles he heard coming from my bedroom did not help. Within minutes however, Dad had transformed his fury into disappointment and gone back to looking unappreciated. My father believed that he had no right to complain. He had long ago decided anger would only harm relationships. It wasn't the explosive thrill Bobbie had expected.

I thought her prank on my father was funny too. I got a vicarious thrill from my father tasting the bitter salt. Resentful that he had recently pulled away from me, when I heard him in the bathroom spitting out the salted coffee, I tasted revenge. From that time on, each time Bobbie saw my father she would offer him a cup of coffee and watch him wince.

I didn't appreciate the ways he still cared for me. He would have left that morning for work at five o'clock and stood on his feet all day. Trapped in a job that did not challenge his mind or his creativity, he worked only to pay the mortgage and buy the things his family needed. He came home exhausted to find a daughter suffering and a wife who was frightened by the doctor's prognosis.

Too young to realize that my father's withdrawal was a sign of depression, I was angry with him.

# *Pair Ants*

The last time my parents had moved was 1951. They melded into that house over the years in ways I could not fully understand.

"I can't imagine that they will move in with us," I told Robin one more time as we drove toward Springfield on a chilly November morning.

"Maybe they'd agree if they thought they were doing something to make your life easier. They both would do anything to keep you safe."

When we entered their house, I hugged Dad and gave Mom a kiss. Because she had shrunk by more than a foot in the last few years, I had to stoop to reach her cheek. While Robin filled a bowl of water for our dog, Penny, I flipped through Logan's meticulous records. There was a note attached that read, "Check with your father's doctor. Blood sugar levels going up. May need medication." I groaned at the thought of another visit to the doctor. I did not know how I was going to find the time.

When Robin returned, we all sat in the living room. My mother sat in her rocking chair. Dad sat in his recliner. Beside him he kept a stack of books precariously arranged on a slender end table. I could see from the top of his pile that he was currently reading *Harry Potter and the Philosopher's Stone*, the Museum of Natural History magazine, and some of his favorite poetry collections.

"We have something we'd like to discuss with you," I began. Dad straightened up in his recliner. Penny was the only one not paying attention now. She circled around several times and then snuggled next to Robin's legs.

I took a deep breath. "I'm sure you know that it has been hard for me to travel here and back so frequently." My mother's jaw tightened. Dad sat back in his chair. "So I want to know if you would consider moving in with us."

My mother paused. "What do you think of this?" she said glancing in Robin's direction.

"Actually, it was my idea," Robin said.

There were a few moments of silence. I waited for the disagreement to begin and the arguments. Instead Mom said, "Well, if it would make it easier for you, dear, of course we will move." She looked at Dad who bobbed his head up and down.

"Wonderful," I said as enthusiastically as I could, ashamed of my mixed emotions.

"I'm going to walk Penny before we have lunch. Want to come along?" Robin asked my father.

Dad nodded, putting on his hat and picking up his walking stick.

My feet moved automatically to the kitchen. Mom shuffled behind. I put the soup in a saucepan and turned on the burner. My fingers reached for the bowls and silverware. The discussion had not gone as I thought it would. It was too quick, too easy. I doubted we had thought this through adequately. We were like flotsam washed ashore, being pulled out to sea on a tide of obligation.

As I stirred the soup, I consoled myself that my parents had made the right decisions for me when I was young. I could shoulder the responsibility for their health care now. They needed to live in a home, not an institution. They needed me to help protect them during the last years of their lives. More than that, they needed ways to enjoy life. They needed the dignity and respect they had offered generously to me and to others. No one understood their wants and needs as well as I.

As much as my mother needed to be with people, my father needed solitude and tranquility. My father could disappear into another world when he read a book and become fully present when he walked in a forest. He had trained himself not to display anger or disapproval. Once he told me, "After my mother and my two sisters died, I decided people are too precious to let angry words divide us."

I understood Dad's quirky sense of humor. For me it was a skipping stone across the water of despair. He liked to tell stories that were like trickster tales. It was people that gave him a good-natured chuckle.

Recently he had told me, "Your mother thought I was losing my memory and she wanted to ask the doctor about it." Then he paused. I could see a glimmer in his eyes.

"Did you?" I asked on cue.

"Yes. The doctor said he was going to show me three objects and at the end of my appointment he'd ask me what they were. He showed me a pen, a letter opener, and a stapler and then put each into the top drawer of his desk." Dad paused again for my straight line.

"What happened at the end of the appointment?" I prompted.

"He forgot to ask me about the three objects. I think the doctor has a memory problem," he chuckled.

By the time the soup was hot, Robin and Dad were back. Mom was opening the box of crackers.

After lunch Robin and I prepared to leave. "I'm going to make another doctor's appointment with your primary care doctor," I said as I kissed them good-bye. "See you soon."

When I stopped the car at the Mass Turnpike tollbooth, I said to Robin, "I'd like to move them before January. If it takes longer than that, we might all be trapped with a blizzard."

"Let's start that list of things we need to do right now," she said pulling out a pencil and some scrap paper from her bag. "We'll need to get a contractor. The man who expanded our porch into a sunroom two years ago did a good job. I also liked the contractor who did some work at church recently. I'll call them both and ask for estimates."

As we continued with list-making, I was reminded of a poem written by a friend when she was in college entitled "Pair Ants." The independence we treasured was going to be encroached upon by the needs of my "pair ants"—the pun completely intended—because what lay ahead for Robin and me wasn't going to be a picnic at all.

# *Identity Crisis*

The first time I met another person with a bleeding disorder, I was a teenager. I had been staring at the door of my hospital room, attempting to keep my face expressionless, while an intern prepared to stick one of my veins with a needle. A nurse had already made three puncture wounds on my arms before she paged the resident doctor. The doctor had missed twice, making a total of five sites oozing blood from my arms and hands. I was polka-dotted with gauze bandages.

Years earlier, I had asked my parents to leave the room when I was having an IV line started. I told them that it made me nervous to have them present. It did. The sadness in their eyes made it harder for me to pretend. It only made it worse, not only for me but also for the person trying to get access to a vein if I said, "Ouch." It was better to look as if it did not hurt, as if I felt nothing.

That day, I tried to look nonchalant during the first three stabs with the needle. Not to shed tears or complain was a performance that I had mastered over the years. Sometimes I even convinced myself that the sticks were no big deal. However, after five failed attempts, I feared I might not be able to maintain my indifference.

Before he was about to try again, the intern muttered, "Your tiny veins shift position at the last minute."

I stared blankly at the door. I wanted to tell the doctor that it wasn't my fault and make a sarcastic remark about how he needed more training. That wouldn't help. At that moment a boy walked by the doorway singing "Waltzing Matilda" and swinging his IV pole from his left hand to his right. The boy stopped walking and stood at my door. He had thick blond hair and a mischievous twinkle in his eyes. He had overheard the doctor's remark.

To my astonishment, the boy called out, "Stick her once for me, Doc!" I laughed, relaxing the tension in my body. I appreciated the absurd statement. The intern registered the insult. There was now a witness, and blaming the victim ceased. Relief washed over me. On the next attempt, the doctor punctured a vein.

The teenager turned toward his IV pole and said, "Come along, Matilda, let's dance."

As the nurse connected the blood products to the IV tube, the boy returned to my room. He said his name was Don and he had classic hemophilia. He was two years younger than I.

That night we talked until the nurses announced lights out. After we were discharged from the hospital, Don and I spent hours each day on the telephone. We each had home tutors. During those phone conversations we laughed together over things other teenagers would not think were funny. We talked about things that we shared with no one else, things we thought no one else could understand. We spoke frankly about the changes we were experiencing in our adolescent bodies. For us, the altering of hormones led to medical crises. Growing pains required medical intervention. Don described the pain of a bleed into his scrotum. I shared the sensation of being kicked in the gut whenever an ovarian cyst ruptured. Our intimate discussions eased the loneliness and anxiety we had about our own sexuality.

"No son of mine is going to be a sissy," Don's father had announced. Then he gave his son hockey skates as a Christmas present. By the time I met Don, his knees were swollen and restricted from repeated episodes of bleeding into the joints.

To minimize childhood injuries, my parents had given me a badminton set. "It's safer," my mother said. "A tennis ball could leave a bruise if it hit you."

Don and I talked about the doctors we knew. We each had the same hematologist, Dr. Davis. His desktop was tidy with plenty of open space. His bookcase was half empty, each row of books neatly held upright by ornamental bookends. There was space at the end of each shelf for a vase or framed photograph. How different it looked from Dr. Dameshek's cluttered office, where his collection of books and medical journals filled each shelf, file folders covered his desktop, and piles of reports were stacked on the floor.

When Don and I compared our experiences, we learned that the hematologist flirted with both of our mothers.

"Mom," the hematologist would say with deepest concern, "how are you doing?"

Don's mother adored the attention the doctor gave her. She poured out her sorrow and anxiety. As she talked to the doctor about her unfaithful husband and her labor-intensive son, Don sat in the chair listening.

When we compared our experiences, we were curious why he did not order blood tests. "Does he do a rectal exam each time you see him?" I asked Don.

"Yes, it's weird, don't you think?" he said.

My mother didn't like Dr. Davis any more than I did. Often my mother deflected his questions about her by asking him for an evaluation of my health.

"I don't think Linda's bleeding disorder is severe," he said, waving his hand as if brushing away a gnat. He seemed to have forgotten the medical records he received from Dr. Dameshek.

Don confirmed what I already had suspected. Dr. Davis was dangerous. He didn't believe a girl could have a bleeding disorder. I had come to dread his examinations. The way he had ignored my ankle injuries was leaving me more and more disabled.

"I want to go back to Dr. Dameshek. I don't care that he is in Boston and we live in Springfield," I told Mom.

"He seems to be well respected, but I don't like him either," my mother confided in me. "I'm afraid you might need him if you go into the Springfield Hospital for an infusion. Doctors don't like patients who question them. You should have a doctor you can trust though."

I hoped Dr. Dameshek, the hematologist who had diagnosed me with afibrinogenemia, would take me back as a patient. Mom scheduled the first available appointment for me, March 17, St. Patrick's Day.

"I want to go by myself," I told my mother. "I'm almost sixteen and I've been traveling on the city bus since I was ten—and I've saved my babysitting money, so I can pay for the bus fare."

My mother agreed, although she admitted that she would not have the courage to leave a doctor. She encouraged my independent streak, knowing that my safety depended on my ability to make my own decisions.

When the day came, I chose a window seat on the bus because I wouldn't be getting off until the last stop. I spread my green stadium jacket over the back of my seat. If I sat on the wooden toggle buttons, they would bruise my back. The bus glided at a steady speed along the interstate highway, moving away from Western Massachusetts toward Boston.

Absorbed with my thoughts, I shifted my weight and leaned toward the window. The cars in the left lane whizzed past the bus, kicking up bits of sand and salt left on the highway to melt the snow and ice of winter. My emotions were as cloudy as the glass spattered with grime.

Like the legend of St. Patrick, I had my own snakes to banish. St. Patrick's Day was a holiday in Boston. Most businesses, schools, and public buildings would be closed for the celebration. People would be watching the parade, eating corned beef with cabbage, and drinking green beer. Crowds were dangerous for me. My body seemed like a magnet attracting anyone who was clumsy or awkward. More than once an elbow poke or another person's foot pressed upon mine had bruised me. When I stepped off the bus and onto the sidewalk in Boston, I was on high alert. I constantly scanned my surroundings for potential hazards.

I first went to the lab to have my blood drawn and tested. It was a familiar routine. The lab technician seemed to be only half listening to my nervous chatter as she scrubbed my arm with an alcohol wipe.

Without glancing up to look at my face, the phlebotomist mused aloud, "So you have met a young man with classic hemophilia. They don't usually live to be older than twenty."

I realized that this meant my friend Don could die in the next six years. Did it mean that I would die in the next four? Leaving the lab, I walked through the familiar hospital hallways in shock. The white tile surrounding my pathway gave me the sensation of being in an igloo. I took a seat in Dr. Dameshek's waiting room and picked up a magazine. I stared without seeing the print or photographs.

When the nurse called my name, I entered Dr. Dameshek's office. He jumped up from behind his desk and exclaimed, "Let me take a good look at you!" He grabbed my hand and smiled saying, "It is so wonderful to see you again." I stood tall when he said with enthusiasm, "You look so well."

I had missed his optimism and could not remember an encounter with him when he did not raise my spirits. To my shock he said, "I know that there will be a cure for your bleeding disorder soon." His smile was radiant and sincere.

As if I was in a car crash, the idea that I should die in a few years had thrown my emotions backward. Only a few minutes later the doctor's words flung me forward. Instead of being comforted, I was dazed by whiplash. I had trouble remembering the purpose of my visit. My reactions could not keep up.

Unaware of the impact of his words, Dr. Dameshek leaned across his desk, saying, "I can't take you back as a patient. They are making me retire now that I am seventy. I'm going to leave Boston and go to New York City." Then he added, "I'm sorry things didn't work out for you with the Springfield doctor. I'm happy to refer you to an excellent hematologist here in Boston."

On the bus ride back home, the windowpane separated the chilly outside air from the warm air inside the coach. I could not distinguish my tears, reflected in the window, from the water droplets formed by the condensation. My eyes were as unfocused as my worries. The passing cars in the fast lane were a blur.

The possibility of a cure did not bring me joy. I'd never taken gym class and I didn't want to start. My life experiences had trained me how to avoid and treat injuries. I had no experience in picking out the best-looking prom dress. There was only one thing in my life that I could count on as constant, my bleeding disorder. Now, that might change.

The weight of the lab technician's remarks settled in my chest. What if they don't find a cure for hemophilia and my friend dies in a few years? What if they don't find a cure soon enough for me and I die too? There was no need to plan for college or a career the way other adolescents did if I wasn't going to live that long. Which is worse—living or dying?

As the bus pulled into the Springfield terminal, I saw my parents standing on the platform waiting for me. I waved and smiled. They would never know what I was thinking.

"I did it," I said to Mom when I hugged her. "I have the name of a new hematologist in my purse. I won't have to see Dr. Davis again."

# *Braced*

In a recurring nightmare I dreamed I stood in the driveway watching a vulture loom over my head. Its red head tilting at the end of a crooked neck. It was holding me in a one-eyed stare. I tried to decide if I could make it safely to the car before it swooped down and carried me away. I told no one about my night terrors. Awake, I could hear the echoes of people who doubted I would live past my adolescence. I wavered between my plans to apply to colleges and being afraid I would die before I graduated from high school.

When I took the college entrance exam test, I didn't recognize anyone in the room. My friends had all taken the test a year before. My peers had been in classrooms while I was at home studying alone with tutors. I doubted that I received the same education as the other young people in the room. My fingers gripped the number two pencil as I filled in the dots beside each answer. When I finished, I handed my test to the proctor and left, dejected. The test scores arrived in the mail a few weeks later. They were higher than average. I could apply to colleges with confidence, but would I be able to walk, carry my books, or keep up with the physical demands of life on campus?

If I had been unable to climb the high school stairs, how could I expect to manage the physical demands of a college campus? I decided to make an appointment with the orthopedist who had replaced one of Don's damaged knees.

The orthopedist had sandy blond hair, lake blue eyes, and a confident smile. He glanced at my x-rays before asking the standard medical history questions. When I explained I had a bleeding disorder, he responded, "Do your menstrual periods stop?"

I blushed. "I'm told they are within the normal range."

"Then you don't have a serious bleeding problem. I'll operate on your ankle, fusing the bones, and you won't hurt anymore; otherwise, you'll be in a wheelchair soon."

I thought I'd rather be in a wheelchair than bleed to death in surgery. After sixteen years, I knew my blood did not clot unless I was treated. No way was I letting him take a knife to me if he didn't understand. It could be disastrous. He looked as handsome as one of the doctors on television, but that didn't mean he understood how to control a joint bleed.

"I don't want surgery," I said.

With a hint of scorn, he said, "Don't be so nervous."

I sat up in my chair and tried to look older than sixteen. I wasn't going to let him see there was any room for doubt. Unlike my mother I wasn't afraid of what a doctor might think of me. "I'm not nervous," I said firmly. "I don't want the surgery."

He looked amazed as if no patient had ever declined his recommendation. "Okay," he said. "Then if you don't want me to operate, I'll get you fitted with braces so at least you won't twist your ankle again. I'll have them do the right leg first since that is the ankle that has the most damage," the orthopedist said. "I warn you, though, without surgery you will be in a wheelchair soon."

In a few weeks I picked up the brace. The brace looked like an instrument of torture. I sounded like Frankenstein when I walked—clunk, squeak, clunk. If I had not already been out of place with other sixteen-year-olds, the orthopedic gray shoes with two aluminum rods attached solidified my misery. Connecting the rods was a leather strap designed to wrap around my leg just below my knee. The brace prevented me from twisting my ankle.

I had only worn the brace one day when a deep blue welt appeared behind my knee where the strap pinched my skin. The bruise spread wider each day, and when the strap was loosened, the eggplant color covered my calf. I took the brace back to be adjusted, and the orthotist shortened the upright bars and lowered the strap. Still I got a bruise. By the time he cut the brace down again, the brace offered little stability to my ankle. The threat of a wheelchair seemed more real. Pain shot from my ankle to my knee with each step I took.

"If I have to go to college in a wheelchair, I will," I told Mom.

In the library I found a directory of accessible campuses. I searched for schools in New England, finding only a listing for a women's college in Connecticut and Boston University. The women's college returned my application fee with an enclosed letter. Because of my disability, they advised me to consider a college where I could live at home. Sourly I thought even though they had made their campus accessible, the college had not changed their assumptions about people with a disability. Their smooth sidewalks and first-floor classrooms would go unused by those who needed them the most.

Boston University sent me an early acceptance letter in an envelope bulging with forms and instructions. A note asking me to schedule a meeting with the housing office dropped out of the envelope too.

On the day of my appointment with the Boston University housing office, I wore my leg brace. My childhood friend Marlene offered to go with me on the drive to Boston and back. Like my other peers, she had graduated from high school a year ahead of me. Marlene had not gone on to college, but had found a job.

"I'll take the day off from work and we can explore the city. Maybe have lunch. I'll treat," she said enthusiastically.

When I went into the student housing office, my friend wandered around the campus. The admissions counselor offered me a chair. "It seems," she said, "that you have requested a dorm room in an accessible building." She did not meet my eyes, staring instead at the leg brace. She released a heavy sigh and said, "Well, we do have some accessible dorms, but I doubt anyone will want to be your roommate."

Hiding tears of humiliation, I shrugged. I lowered my voice the way my mother did when she was angry and said, "I have already been accepted to Boston University and I will be attending."

As I left the housing office, shame turned into rage. In defiance I lifted up my clunky shoes off the pavement and skipped down the sidewalk to meet Marlene.

When I got home, I threw the orthopedic shoes and brace in the back of my closet. I refused to wear them again.

# Shedding Skin

When I was a child, I once watched a toad shed its skin. Bubbles of perspiration rose to the surface of its lumpy back. "Like a woman in menopause, change begins with the sweats," Mom said. She stood behind me watching over my shoulder. The toad rubbed and tugged at the outer skin revealing the inner layer, tender and glistening. Much to my astonishment, the toad wrapped the outer layer up and over, back to front, until it stuffed each piece of old skin into its mouth. Then it swallowed. The toad looked exhausted.

I remembered that toad when we began preparing our home for my parents to move in with us. In a burst of activity that came in the autumn of 1998, Robin and I peeled away our possessions. We had acquired more things than my parents. If we were going to make the merger of two households work, we must get rid of treasured items we had collected over the past twenty-five years of living together.

The china cabinet Robin's mother had given her went to an auction along with the sideboard we had custom built to fit in our dining room. We gave my bone china cups and saucers to a local antiques dealer. My aunt Ola had sent me one cup each year on my birthday. With each piece I wrapped and packed in a box,

I also folded in a memory. When we netted only small amounts of cash, we began giving things away in a crazed frenzy. I stuffed my emotions and swallowed my tears remembering the toad I had watched so many years ago. The marathon of purging lasted until the week before construction was scheduled to begin.

"You can have two of three things," the contractor cautioned us, "but only two. The three things are cheap, fast, and good. Which two do you want?"

"We need the entire first floor remodeled in five weeks," I told him. "We want fast and faster."

We learned that fast not only required speed from the contractor, but from us as well. Robin made checklists of jobs we needed to do together, so we could schedule them. We didn't linger over choices. We charged into stores, wasting no time picking plumbing fixtures, lighting, cabinets, and flooring.

Construction was set to begin the day after Thanksgiving.. The week before the holiday, we moved everything portable out of the kitchen, dining room, first-floor bathroom, and living room. We shifted our refrigerator, microwave, living room couch, dining room table, and various canned goods into the only room on the first floor that remained intact, the sunroom. A table lamp sat precariously on top of a canister of sugar. We tucked spices into gaps on bookshelves. Who could remember where we put the coffeepot or the mugs?

We couldn't get to our back door because the carpenter had torn down the steps to create a ramp. The front door opened through the obstacle course that had been our sunroom. We had no place to cook, or sit, or eat. Friends invited us to Thanksgiving dinner. Grateful to be able to sit at a real dining room table, we attempted to make cheerful conversation.

The next day, the demolition team ripped apart our dining room, knocked out the wall between the first-floor bathroom and the kitchen, and removed the oak built-in bookcases in the living room. I averted my eyes from the second-story window so I could not see the contents of the dumpster in our driveway. When we came home each day from work, we saw another destroyed wall or another row of shelving gone.

"Don't walk on the flooring in the kitchen until I say it's okay," the contractor said. We peeked through the thick sheets of plastic covering access to the kitchen. Dust had settled into the heating ducts and blew allergens out into all the rooms in the house. Instead of making an appointment with my own doctor, I lived with the wheezing and cough that kept me awake most nights.

Each day I had off from work, I drove to my parents' house. I pulled items down from the highest shelves so that my parents could examine them and decide what to keep and what to discard. In my job at the library we called it de-acquisitioning; in our homes I called it desolation.

With a stoic, no-tears-shed attitude, my parents decided to give away almost all their furniture and the contents of the kitchen cabinets. Mom had not baked for years. She used the small convection oven and the stovetop to cook. On the metal racks inside the unused oven, Mom stored her few battered pots and pans. Nothing—not appliances, flatware, plates, or mixing bowls—was less than twenty years old. Most items had been acquired not long after they had married sixty years ago. Some people would have spent thousands of dollars to remodel their kitchen and replace appliances. Not my mother.

Mom's old friend Renée dropped by to help. "Whatever you leave behind, my grandchildren might use," Renée said. "I can have a yard sale if there are things my grandchildren don't want," Renée added.

My mother smiled. Reduce, reuse, recycle had become her spiritual practice, not just a way of saving money.

I began carrying down things from the attic. Renée let out a squeal when she discovered the holiday decorations I had designed and made during the years when I was unable to join my friends who were going to high school dances and football games. Each set was used once before I packed them up and put them in the attic for storage. The following year I would make another color scheme. There was the Christmas of the red silk and gold felt, the year of sugarplum purple with white sparkles, and the royal blue metallic silver combination. "May I have these?" Renée asked.

"Sure," I said. I was too numb to be attached to them.

"The patio tiles Horace made with the leaf prints—you can't leave those behind!" Renée exclaimed.

My father had built a garage for the car and framed a patio on the side. When the garage was painted, Dad purchased a bag of cement and mixed it with water. He laid a flattened leaf in the bottom of a six-inch wood box he had made in his workshop. Then he poured in the wet concrete. When it hardened, he extracted his leaf fossils and set each block in place on the sandy ground of the patio. There were the impressions of sassafras, maple, birch, oak, ginkgo, sycamore, and several species of ferns. Dad could name each one and tell where he had found that particular leaf.

"We can't move them and neither can you," I said with a pang of regret.

Dad was staring out the living room window watching the brown oak leaves flutter to the ground. "Dad, can you sort out your books and decide which ones you want to keep?" I asked. He nodded.

By my next visit, Dad had neatly stacked a small pile of books on the floor beside his chair: a poetry book his mother had owned, *Watership Down*, several wildlife identification manuals, and the log he had kept while serving in the navy during WWII.

Most of his books remained on the two bookcases. He had reread his favorites many times over the years.

Dad pointed at the pile on the floor and said, "This is all I need to keep."

"Are you sure? Don't you want this book?" I said pulling *The Iliad and Odyssey of Homer* off the shelf. He lowered his head and shook it to signal no.

"Mom, don't you want to keep your knitting needles?" I asked.

"My hands shake too much to knit anymore. You can have them if you want them," she replied. "Give the yarn and buttons away, unless you can use them."

I could not imagine my mother without her knitting basket. I suppressed the desire I had to break down and sob. Mom, however, seemed almost invigorated by the downsizing of possessions.

When I asked him, Dad admitted he could not navigate streets in a city new to him. Without protest he agreed to sell the sixteen-year-old car he had purchased when he retired. He had driven that car to classes offered at the senior center and to visit friends and explore woodland preserves. Overlooking his loss of independence, I thought we would all be safer with him no longer behind the wheel.

Unlike my mother who seemed excited to be moving, Dad's silence was no longer amiable. He was detached from the conversations around him. "What about your tool box?" I asked him.

"It was my father's," Dad mumbled as if that meant it had no value. I knew how he had admired his father, and in the past he had spoken reverently about that toolbox.

I hadn't seen my father look this sad since I was a teenager. Yet I was too eager to check off one more thing from my to-do list to pay attention. My mother had taught me to be unsentimental, and I needed to use that strength now. I shut out the sense of mourning my father had at leaving this house. He was leaving the one thing he was most proud of, the house that he had purchased. He hadn't expected that he would ever own a home. He had lived in rented apartments and rooming houses for the first thirty-eight years of his life. This house had sheltered the family he loved and had sustained his pride and dignity. It was more than a home; it was part of his identity.

# At Sea in Uncharted Water

It's just a double date," my friend Bobbie said when she telephoned me from her dormitory at the nursing school. "Hank is an old friend of Larry's. It's time you had a little fun," she pleaded.

She was right. I had an underlying depression during my high school years being home schooled. I had missed the parties and dances that my friends were enjoying. The teen magazine I read called it the "Elizabeth Barrett Browning Condition," and love was the only cure according to the article. What could go wrong on a double date? Then again, with Bobbie, anything could happen. She loved a practical joke.

Bobbie didn't have to ask me twice. "Okay," I said.

"Good," Bobbie said. "Larry and I will want to sit in the backseat together, so Hank will pick you up. Hank's in the navy and home on leave. He can drive us to the restaurant."

I had a suspicion that perhaps she was asking me to go as a chaperone. Larry, the boy she planned to marry after her graduation, had gone to work in a machine shop after high school. Bobbie had told me that Larry wanted to have sex before they were married and she had been tempted. She believed she would burn in hell if she gave in.

Hank rang the doorbell. He wore his navy uniform. He rolled his hat in his hands and glanced shyly at my parents standing behind me. My father shook Hank's hand formally and asked him to come in. I stared at the door. Dad restrained himself from asking probing questions or otherwise embarrassing me. My mother was remarkably quiet, but I could see her eyes evaluating Hank's appearance, trying to find clues to this stranger's character.

Hank breathed an audible sigh of relief when Dad closed our front door behind us. He opened the front passenger door for me, closing it gently as I settled into the seat. Hank smiled at me before he started the car's engine. A wave of pleasure rippled through my body. "Are you going to sit way over there by the window?"

"I always wear a seatbelt," I responded.

We picked up my friend Bobbie at Larry's house. It wasn't long before I could hear groans from the backseat. Hank rolled his eyes each time he looked in the rearview mirror. I don't remember the conversation at dinner, but Hank took me home after he had dropped off Bobbie and Larry. When he parked in front of my house, he gave me a kiss before he got out of the car and opened the door for me. I could not remember when I had been that happy.

The next morning I had finished eating breakfast when the phone rang. It was Hank. "I have to go back to the barracks day after tomorrow. Will you go out with me again before I leave?"

"Sure," I said. It wasn't love but it was romance.

When he came to pick me up, he announced, "I spent this afternoon putting a third seatbelt in the front seat of my car, so you can sit right beside me." Hank took me to his house to meet his mom and dad and see his prized miniature railroad. The trains were in the basement. I remember standing on the top step, then landing at the bottom of the stairs. I must have bumped each stair with my ass on the way down.

Frightened, Hank ran to the bottom of the stairs and helped me to stand. My backside hurt, my nylons had a run, and I felt a flush of embarrassment on my face. Hank's sister gave me a new pair of stockings to wear, and I decided, what the hell, you only get one first date in your life. If I pay a price tomorrow, at least I'll have a good time tonight.

We went out to dinner as planned at the Polynesian restaurant. Over dinner I blurted out that I had a bleeding disorder. He listened and asked me several questions. My anxiety drifted away as we talked. "Are you sure you don't want to go to a hospital?" he asked.

I thanked him and shook my head no. "Thanks, I'll be fine, really."

"Well if you need medical attention, I have a two-way radio in my car," he said. "You're safe with me."

I had never imagined that I would find someone so considerate.

At the end of the evening when he parked his car in front of my house and kissed me, he said, "Will you marry me?"

"You can't be serious, we just met," I replied swallowing a laugh.

"I'm a serious guy and I want to be married. Will you marry me?"

"I think we should get to know each other first, don't you?"

"I'll be back late in January. By then I'll have finished training and I'll be going out to sea."

"Okay," I said, "but I've got to go into the hospital in Boston to have my wisdom teeth taken out."

"I'll drive you to the hospital," he said.

Elated by the idea of having a boyfriend take me to the hospital instead of my mother, I said, "That would be great."

It took several weeks for the bruises on my buttocks to fade away. I hardly noticed the discomfort. Letters from Hank arrived daily from Richmond, Virginia. On the back of each envelope, he drew a cartoon. He portrayed himself as an eager-to-please dog, full of puppy love, like the Peanuts character Snoopy. He drew me as the cynical and uncompromising Lucy. I responded to each letter immediately, aware that what we each needed was someone to care and listen.

In late January, I kissed my mother good-bye and got into Hank's car for the drive to the Boston Hospital. Dad was at work that day. My mom had only had her driver's license for two years. I could see in her stiff smile that she was partly relieved not to have to take me to Boston by herself and unsure about entrusting Hank with my safety. Gleefully I waved good-bye to Mom as Hank backed his car out of our driveway.

Hank kissed me before he left me at the hospital. I changed into my pajamas and robe, then I wrote on the notepad beside my bed in large black letters, "Do not blue dot this patient." I had been in the hospital frequently enough to learn a blue dot was code for do not resuscitate. I knew that I would not have a blue dot on my chart. I was too young, too healthy. I simply wanted the medical staff to know that I was savvy enough to have figured out their dirty little secrets. I wandered around the ward.

I was seventeen years old, and for the first time I was going into the hospital for a planned procedure, not an emergency. A doctor I had not met before came to my room to ask if I would test a new coagulant. The new medication had only been used as a last resort on soldiers who had deep tissue burns from napalm blasts in Vietnam. I was old enough to sign the consent form myself and I did so with pride. After all, the first time a doctor asked me to volunteer for research, I tested the oral polio vaccine in the 1950s. There had been many subsequent requests from researchers and I had always agreed. It satisfied a need in me to be useful.

A nurse started the IV line in my right arm before the doctor arrived. A technician made a tiny cut in my left arm. She explained that it was one millimeter long and one millimeter deep. Every thirty seconds she used absorbent paper to draw off the blood. Normally the bleeding stopped in a few seconds. I watched as the blood bubbled up one drop at a time. Ten minutes later the blood was still seeping from the small cut.

The doctor hung the bottle of the new coagulant on the metal pole and connected the tubing to the bottle. He stopped the saline drip and started the medication. I turned my head to look at my left arm and the little drops of blood had stopped surfacing. Amazed, I looked back at the face of the doctor and noticed that his lips were moving but I could not hear what he was saying. A second later everything went black and my last thought was, I'm dying.

When I opened my eyes, I was startled to see a small crowd of people by the bedside. Astonished, I glanced at all the faces staring at me. There was a crash cart that had not been there before. I heard one of the doctors say, "The adrenaline worked, thank goodness!"

Rising up from my chest, like bubbles in a can of soda pop, came a giggle, then more giggles until I broke out into a full belly laugh. The audience of doctors and nurses looked concerned. I had evaded death one more time. The experiment had failed, and I was overjoyed to be alive.

After my laughter subsided, the medical staff scurried to check my vital signs and test my reflexes. They cleaned up the clutter and debris from the event. The echoes of trauma still reverberated in my room. A few hours later the nurse came and said I could get up and go to the bathroom. When I stood up, my legs collapsed and I fell to the floor before I could take a single step. It was twenty-four hours before they allowed me to try standing again.

The doctor postponed the planned dental extraction for a few days. Prior to the surgery I was given my standard dose of fibrinogen concentrate. The doctor released me from the hospital when my gums had healed. Dad drove to Boston on the weekend to pick me up and drive me back home.

Hank had gone out to sea. A few days after he left, I received a letter from him in the mail. He wrote me that the navy chaplain advised him to have a vasectomy if we should marry. He wanted to marry and he wanted children. His older brother had a wife and they had a child. He would be happy to adopt. I rolled the images of wife and mother around in my imagination.

I was grateful to him for his understanding, but in truth I did not love him. My brush with death in the hospital experiment had given me a chance to reflect on how I wanted to use my life. I had dreamed of going to college and becoming independent. As long as I could remember, I'd been working toward this goal. I had not dreamed of marriage. I no longer wanted to raise children of my own. That was Hank's dream. We both had a right to see our dreams become reality. I turned down Hank's proposal and set my sail toward Boston University.

Disappointed, Hank, responded, "Would you continue to write me letters while I am at sea?"

"Of course," I said.

# *Be You*

The high school guidance counselor who said I didn't need to go to college because of my bleeding disorder saw my disabilities, not my abilities. He underestimated my determination. The orthopedic surgeon who said I would be in a wheelchair if I didn't have surgery miscalculated my ability to heal. The Boston University housing officer said I would have trouble finding a person who wanted to be my roommate. She saw me as a pariah. Someone who was pitiful. Her prediction proved to be wrong too. None of them knew me.

Those naysayers left cracks of doubt in my wall of stubbornness. In late August of 1968, my parents drove me to Boston University. I would have liked to send that guidance counselor, doctor, and housing officer postcards with the message, "You were wrong about me."

Sentenced to four years of rest and recuperation during my high school years, I had served my time under my mother's vigilant supervision, and that had given my damaged ankle joints time to strengthen. A second orthopedic surgeon advised me to wear shoes that had a one-inch heel. "It will take the weight off your ankle," he said, "and relieve the pain."

I took his advice. I purchased short, unlined boots with laces I could tighten. The boots supported my ankles better than the inappropriate braces had ever done. I walked without pain for the first time in years.

Instead of limping, I swaggered into the dormitory as if I owned it. I could now walk with ease, but stairs were still a challenge. I needed an elevator. The dorm was one of the newest ones on campus and the only accessible dorm within easy walking distance to the lecture halls and classrooms. The three towers housed fifteen-hundred students. One tower was exclusively for men; the other two towers were for women.

Joining the swarm of students, I rode the escalator up to the lobby as I gazed through the plate glass windows overlooking the granite exterior of the College of Liberal Arts. Clattering and squealing, the MBTA trolleys popped up from beneath the ground and onto the tracks in front of the dorm. My heartbeat quickened with energy at the city noises.

My dorm assignment was on the sixth floor of the first tower. Dad carried my sturdy luggage. Mom held a bag of sheets and towels. I clutched a shopping bag with my desk supplies and the one-cup coffeemaker my friend Bobbie had given me. Men were not allowed in the women's sections of the dorm without permission. My father had to sign in before getting on the elevator. As instructed, he announced his presence by shouting, "Man on the floor," when he stepped out of the elevator. The smell of marijuana drifted in the air. My parents exchanged wary glances. I strode ahead.

As we turned the corner to my room, we saw a young woman no taller than five feet, blond and wearing nothing but black lace underwear. She seemed to be smoking a cigar and was cooing obscenities into the hall telephone in a seductive tone. My father's eyebrows rose, but he said nothing. The woman gave us an unconcerned glance. Apparently she didn't care that there was now a man on the floor.

The dorm rooms had two small beds that doubled as a sofa during the day when they were pushed to the wall, two desks, and two closets. The walls were white cinder blocks and the window looked out to another tower. To me the institutional decor looked luxurious. New beginnings could be made here.

My roommate wasn't there when I arrived and unpacked. When my clothes were hanging in the closet and my bed was made, I walked my reluctant parents back to their car and kissed them good-bye.

"I'll be fine," I grinned. "I'll write you lots of letters and call you if I need anything." Their facial expressions were muddy with a mix of pride and worry, as they got into the car and drove away. I let go a sigh of relief. Reminded of that day years earlier on the first day of kindergarten, I practically danced back to my dorm room excited by the possibilities.

I made friends with the young woman who had been talking on the hall telephone when I arrived. She turned out to be as raucous and bawdy as I had hoped. She and her roommate evaluated every man they saw on his potential sexual prowess. I savored each titillating tale, attempting to keep my naiveté to myself.

Most of my classes freshman year were in large amphitheater spaces where five hundred or more students listened to the professor lecture three times a week. We submitted our written assignments and tests to a graduate student. I found the assigned reading easy. If I skipped a class or two because of a heavy menstrual period, it didn't seem to matter. No one would notice one person missing in the large lecture hall.

My hematologist was within walking distance from my dormitory. For the first time in my life I could count on knowledgeable doctors to provide medical help within fifteen minutes. If I felt a twang from an ovarian cyst rupturing, I could be treated with clotting factor quickly and back in the dorm in a matter of hours.

At BU I had a fresh start at defining who I was. I could be just another college student. I could be a girl with hopes and dreams. I could be me.

There was only one rule my mother believed was unbreakable—no lies between us. A secret was a form of a lie in her dictionary. We were more than mother and daughter; we were allies combating the same enemy, and we needed to work as a team. Unlike most of my peers, as a teenager I did not battle with my mother over the shortness of my miniskirts or the music I played on the radio. Those things did not concern her. Her only goal was my survival. I didn't lie about where I was going or what I was doing. Secrets were not easy to keep, living in the same house with an observant mother. My mother for her part gave me wide latitude for making choices of my own.

Once I was living away from home, Dad wrote me each Sunday evening, often enclosing a clipping of the Pogo cartoon from the morning newspaper. He wrote about the television shows that amused him and the changeable weather. His letters to me were as positive as my replies.

Mom, who previously trusted me, became suspicious. She had far more trust in me when she could see me. At first I was startled by the weekly inquisition that never seemed to satisfy her. I became resentful dreading the weekly telephone calls. When Mom asked direct questions, squeezing out truth like juice from a bitter lemon, I did not lie. It was never enough for her though. She began to accuse me of withholding the truth. I dreaded her intrusive telephone calls. Perhaps I needed to change my tactics, I reasoned. So I began doing what she dreaded most.

Mom did not need to know that my boyfriend had decided to test the maximum speed his car would go on a dead-end street, slamming on the brakes and coming to a stop a few feet in front of a brick wall. That was a memory I would prefer to forget myself. She also did not need to know that the night several of us went to a bowling alley I put on the rented shoes and started a bleed in my right ankle that required an emergency visit to a hospital.

As a child I frequently went for a walk with my father after he came home from work. It was a special time for me as we sang or told stories. And before we went home, we often enjoyed an ice cream cone from the corner store. According to Dad, when I was four years old, I stopped licking my ice cream long enough to advise him, "You know, Mother doesn't need to know everything." I knew my father liked sweet things as much as I and my mother wouldn't approve since, "It might spoil your appetite for dinner." Dad apparently thought this secret amusing.

Over the years there were more secrets I would keep from my parents. It quickly became a habit. It protected them from worrying, I thought, and it certainly protected me from hearing the lectures and accusations.

# *Teach Your Children Well*

At Boston University, the School of Education was a tower overlooking the Charles River. In my freshman year, I enrolled in the required introductory class for elementary education. The instructor told us to make tags to symbolize ourselves for the next class. I was the only one to make a tag that was not a happy face or a flower. My collage of orange and brown paper was impressionistic and reminiscent of yin and yang. The professor scowled at the tag I wore confidently on my blouse.

"We're going to do a trust-building exercise now, everyone. Find a partner and then fall back until the other person catches you."

I raised my hand. "I'm not going to do that, I bruise easily."

"Well, if you can't do that, then you shouldn't be a teacher."

My hope that I had left the naysayers behind me evaporated. I clenched my jaw. Really? I thought it absurd that this exercise was required to be a good teacher. The professor looked surprised the way a bully does when his victim does not surrender.

The elementary education classes didn't challenge me. My grades were consistently As. Frustrated by the tedium of lectures by professors who hadn't seen a grade school classroom in years, I chose most of my electives from the College of Liberal Arts. In my junior year I opted for an independent study, tutoring math to children in South Boston. Perhaps I could find out for myself if I was able to teach.

I took the trolley from my dormitory once a week stepping out in front of the local soul food restaurant. I inhaled the aromas of bacon on the grill and collard greens simmering in a pot. I walked the few blocks past the red-brick row houses. The neighborhood was changing as affordable rental units were transformed into trendy single-family homes. Aunts, uncles, and cousins were squeezed out of their single occupancy rooms and into apartments already overcrowded. Others slept on the sidewalks and in alleyways. Few people on the street met my eyes or smiled. I walked the few blocks to the school undeterred.

Unlike my elementary school, this one was badly in need of repair, the books out-of-date, and the teachers frustrated. Most of these children didn't have parents who could help them with their homework.

On my first day, the fourth-grade teacher sent me one of her students. Darrel plopped down in his chair and tilted it backward. "I hate math," he said. "I ain't no good at it."

I emptied my bag of colorful educational blocks called Cuisenaire rods on the desk. Darrel raised an eyebrow and then sat up for a better look. His eyes widened. In a few weeks he had practiced addition and subtraction, multiplication and division using the blocks.

One day I configured forty-nine rods and turned to Daryl. "Can you tell what the square root is?" It was a new question and a term he didn't know. After a few minutes, he said confidently, "Seven."

"Wow," I said, "you're pretty good at math."

He grinned and nodded. I knew how it had changed my life to have a few people believe in me when others had not.

Antiwar demonstrations on the campus escalated after May 1970 when students were shot and killed while protesting at Kent State University. By the autumn of 1970 the atmosphere led to bomb threats in the larger Boston University dormitories, during the day and night. Whenever the alarm sounded, we were ordered to use the stairs not the elevator. Many students stayed, but each time the alarm sounded, my heart would pound. What if there really is a bomb this time? I'd limp down the five flights to the emergency exit door and leave the building until the all clear was announced.

At first it was an excuse to meet outside with friends. We would go out together for bagels at two o'clock in the morning. One night when the alarm sounded before ten o'clock in the evening, I took the MBTA to my old roommate's apartment and asked if I could sleep on her floor. I cuddled up with her spare blankets and was just about to drift off to sleep when I noticed the cockroaches crawling across the floor, marching over my torso. I never went back to her apartment after dark again.

Partway into the semester I decided that I could no longer stand being awakened night after night to the bomb alerts. My ankles had begun to ache again from the trips down the stairs. Sleep deprivation was making it difficult to concentrate on my studies. I decided to petition for a room in a smaller dormitory.

Supper in the dormitory cafeteria included what my friends and I called mystery meat, whipped instant potatoes, and overcooked vegetables. I would put a blob of this or that on my plate as I strolled through the long line at the steam table. The consolation was that later each evening the kitchen would open up a soft serve ice cream stand in the dormitory lobby. For a quarter, I could buy a cone filled with four inches of creamy swirls.

One evening as I was standing in the lobby licking my cone, I saw Robin. The year before she had lived on the same floor of the dorm as I. We were casual friends and had double-dated once when her boyfriend came to visit. He was enrolled in an ROTC program at a college in Vermont. After that date we laughed over how our two boyfriends had nothing to say, while we couldn't seem to stop talking to each other. I was glad to see her again.

She seemed pleased to see me again too. "How are you?" she asked, as she brushed aside her long brown hair from her face.

"I'm fine except that I need to move out of this dorm. I just can't stand the bomb threats every night."

"I want to move too," she said. "Perhaps we should find a room together."

"Sounds good," I said.

We were assigned a room that would be vacant in January. Before the holiday break, my parents and Robin's parents helped to pack up our belongings and move us to our new dormitory.

The next autumn when I began my senior year, I took a single room so that I would not have to wake Robin when I needed to get up early each morning. My father purchased a used car for me when I learned my student teaching assignment was in a Boston suburb. During rush hour traffic it took me an hour to get to school in a car. It would have taken two hours by public transportation.

It was one of the most affluent towns outside the city. This school was free of barriers in more ways than one.

The school complex had been constructed only a few years before. The single-story classrooms and school library formed a quadrangle along the edges of a grassy lawn. Each classroom had new furnishings, the latest textbooks, and a large window from which children and teachers could view the surrounding trees and picnic tables. The contrast from the school where I had tutored math the previous spring was jarring.

The curriculum I taught had to be followed without diversion. I forced myself day after day to show up and do what I was told, but my heart was not in it. Children practiced their reading with me each day. Flipping the pages easily, they looked bored. They could read well already.

In my first month at the school I was standing on the playground monitoring the first graders when from the other side of the yard an older child came running directly at me. I had never seen him before. He stopped when he got to me and landed a punch on my right arm with a boxing jab. The power of his thrust was astonishing. In seconds, he disappeared into the crowd of children standing across the quadrangle. No one had seen what he had done. I was stunned. Even the angriest children I had grown up with would not have lashed out and hit an adult for no reason.

No one would understand the impact it had for me. Had he spotted me as an imposter? Had he recognized that I had never been allowed to go to recess when I was in elementary school? Did he intuitively know that I found the rules and regulations of the classroom abhorrent? Within seconds my arm began to swell and burn. I could not abandon my six-year-old charges to find an ice pack.

After that, when I was not teaching, I wrapped myself in a cocoon of silence. I had been unable to protect myself from a violent attack by a child. I had no ability to sufficiently treat my injury. I felt trapped and powerless. I began to wonder if I really did have the physical stamina to be a teacher.

For weeks, I spoke only when necessary. When I was in the dormitory, I hid myself in my single room and avoided human contact as much as possible. Robin came to my room early each morning to remind me to go to the cafeteria for breakfast and pick up the brown bag lunch prepared for student teachers. She would return to my room at dinnertime, knocking on my door. We shared meals together, but I found it impossible to tell her about my day.

Midway through student teaching, the Boston University interns were switched to different grades and new supervising teachers. The first-grade teacher had been only a few years older than I. The sixth grade had multiple teachers. The homeroom teacher had wispy gray hair and alert eyes. More than her appearance, her interests in art, classical music, intellectual conversation, and gourmet food did not seem entirely compatible with her profession. Her life outside of work was much more colorful and appealing to her than her day job. The children warmed to her, as did I.

The middle school offered instruction in music and art. It was a shock to my system after having spent the previous year in the inner city of Boston tutoring children who had long ago given up on getting anything worthwhile from the public school. I taught the class math since the math teacher was often absent or late to arrive.

In student teaching I didn't believe I made much of a difference to any child, with the exception of Andrea. Andrea would occasionally leave her desk and take a perch on the radiator. If she didn't understand, she wouldn't sit passively as the other students; she asked for clarification. Her eyes were wide with a hunger to learn. The other students didn't seem to mind; in fact, they probably benefited from Andrea's boldness. I didn't mind either. Her attentiveness made me a better teacher. I was energized by her curiosity.

"I've recommended that we hire you next semester as an aide to teach math to the class again," the homeroom teacher told me. "It seems, well, the assistant teacher is in drug rehab. He won't be coming back."

I accepted the offer, glad for the opportunity.

One afternoon, my supervisor from the university came to the school to observe. I saw the professor slip quietly into one of the desks in the back of the room. I was too busy teaching to pay much attention to him.

When the semester ended, the supervisor met with each of the student teachers to give them their grade. As I sat in front of his desk, he began to shake his head sadly.

"I'm giving you a C," he said. "What were you thinking, letting that student get up from her desk during class to sit on the radiator?"

I gulped. Was this really his priority? Somehow I found the courage to answer honestly. "I was thinking that she was learning and I didn't care where she chose to sit."

"You know, you will never get a job teaching if I give you a C," he said.

I didn't know. I knew teaching jobs were hard to get but at that moment I didn't care. This conversation had confirmed to me that although I loved to help children learn, I disliked most of the rules, the intrinsic inequity, and the one-size-fits-all curriculums. On the whole I agreed that I was an average teacher.

I stood up to leave saying, "Thank you."

"That's it?" the professor said. "I expected you to argue with me, like the others have. The students I gave a B to argued for an A. Some of them badgered me and some begged me."

I was startled. None of those things had occurred to me.

"I'm changing your grade to a B because you didn't do any of those things."

"Thank you," I said again, although the professor had given me yet another reason to dislike the education system. Then I walked quickly out of his office fearing that if I lingered my grade would become an A.

Back in the dorm, I got drunk for the first and last time in my life. I staggered down the dorm hallway. When Robin found me trying to unlock my room, I turned to her and babbled, "I hate teachsing and I doonut care."

When graduation day came, I picked up the cap and scarlet gown but purposely did not attend the ceremony. Graduation ceremonies were held in the stadium, and I had neither the ability to maneuver the steps or the desire to attend. I had a degree and no idea what to do next. All I knew was that I had made the wrong choice when I had decided to become a teacher.

# Change in Direction

After I graduated from college, I moved back to my parents' home in Springfield. I had spent four years getting a degree in elementary education to discover that I intensely disliked schools and classrooms. With my transcript and degree I applied for a teaching position in the Springfield school system because I needed a job. As I unpacked my belongings, organized my closet, set up my stereo, and shelved my books, I sniffed the dust of defeat.

Merlin, the guinea pig, squealed in his cage expressing his longing for carrot peelings. We both craved independence. The last thing I wanted was to be back under my parents' care. Certainly I had made some mistakes in judgment, but I had returned home stronger and healthier than I had been four years earlier.

Only a week after moving back to my parents' home, I received a call from the assistant director of the City Library. "There is an opening for a children's librarian at one of the branch libraries. Do you want it?"

I had forgotten that while home during the midterm break I took Rose, the child who had lost her vision when she was born prematurely to our neighbor, to the library. Rose was twelve. My parents were still taking care of her when she was home from the Perkins School for the Blind, and my father often read to her.

Wanda, the children's librarian, had helped me pick out books to read aloud to Rose. Wanda took me aside and said, "So what are you doing when you graduate from college?"

"I'm not sure," I said. Even I could hear the resignation in my voice.

"You should be a librarian. You'd love it."

"I don't think so," I said.

As if she had not heard me, she said, "Go right upstairs now to the assistant director's office and complete a job application. I'll read to Rose while you are gone."

I had never considered being a librarian. What do I have to lose, I thought as the elevator door opened.

The job application asked how many sick days I thought I might use in a year, and I wrote the lowest number I could imagine. The assistant director looked at what I had written on the application form and then advised, "If you want to be considered, you will have to reduce the number of estimated sick days." I erased the number I had written and lowered my estimate, not believing I could fulfill their expectations. The assistant director smiled and said, "We will call you if something comes up."

Months had passed and I had forgotten that spontaneous application. Shocked, I heard the woman on the telephone say, "This is Miss Jeffers. We met a few months ago when you applied for a job in the library. There is a position open as a children's librarian in one of our branch libraries. I'm calling to offer you the job."

I didn't need to consider the offer before accepting.

"Come to my office on Monday morning and you can fill out the paperwork before you go to the branch library."

I hung up the phone and let out a whoop. "I'm going to be a librarian!"

My only concern was that there would be a few months before I had any medical insurance coverage. My bleeding disorder was what the insurance plans called a preexisting condition. If I could avoid an injury or spontaneous internal bleeding at ovulation, I would be a winner. It was a game of roulette and I had no choice but to spin the wheel.

The branch library had a staff of three: the branch director, a clerk, and a children's librarian. In addition, a high school student came after school each day and put the returned books back on the shelves. It was the smallest branch library in the city.

On my first day, I knew nothing about being a librarian. When I reached the granite steps, several children were already waiting for me to unlock the door and let them inside. Public schools had closed for the summer.

Among the children I saw a toddler still holding a bottle to her lips. She would occasionally remove the bottle and curse obscenities. The other children ignored her epithets. When I reached the top step, she stopped long enough to look up and smile. "Hey, the liberry lady!" she announced to everyone. Since she was not old enough to read, I wondered why she would be so impatient to get inside the library.

My key unlocked the door, and the older children moved to form a queue in front of my new desk. Some of the children were gregarious, some shy. The youngest children were two to four years old. Many came with their older siblings. Most children had parents who worked all day. These children were usually waiting for the library to open each morning. It was a safe shelter for them where adults were available to protect them and where they could meet other children. They would stay until it was time for dinner. They often carried their lunches in paper bags. They went outdoors to the front steps at noontime to munch on their peanut butter and grape jelly sandwiches.

They came several times each week to pick up a fresh pile of books to take home or ask what to feed the stray kittens that lived behind the housing complex. They came to trade postage stamps from the envelopes that arrived from relatives in other parts of the world or listen to me read stories.

No one required them to sit still in desks and raise their hands before asking questions. No question was considered stupid in the library. Bit by bit, I realized that these children had taken control of their own education. The library would change their lives.

Summer Reading Club was beginning, and I discovered that most of my day was spent listening to the seemingly endless row of children who stood patiently in line to tell me about the books they had read.

There were children of Irish, Italian, Portuguese, and African descent. Some children were first-generation immigrants who were learning English. Each wave of immigrants had moved up in pecking order status, when the latest newcomers arrived. The library was the one place they gathered together voluntarily.

Seven-year-old Victor lived with his uncle. When I first saw him, he had a broken arm and his large brown eyes stared into mine like a puppy in a pound. He told me that his birth mother had died and his father had gone back to Portugal to find a new wife. Victor spoke English well.

It did not take me too long, however, to realize that when Victor came up to me to report on a book, his summary bore no relationship to what the book was actually about. Victor, I discovered, had not yet learned to read English. I enjoyed his clever stories he derived from the illustrations in the book. Together we would work on learning a few words from each book he brought to share with me until the end of the summer when he could read his own books. His face beamed each time he unlocked the story written between a book's covers.

Monica at eight years old was in charge of her little sister Charlene. When they entered the library, I could hear four-year-old Charlene chattering away like a little bird. Then I would hear Monica's voice in a mothering tone saying calmly, "Now you have to be quiet in the library, remember?" Charlene would nod her chocolate brown face solemnly. I could see that Monica was relieved to have a few hours when her little sister's voice was subdued. Still every few minutes, I could hear Charlene saying, "Monica, what's this?" or "Monica, can we take this book home?" or "Monica, will you read to me?" Monica would let out an exasperated sigh and then patiently answer each request.

Bonnie didn't have to tell me that her parents had come from Ireland, it was written on her face. Streetwise and sturdy, she didn't trust anyone. When she came into the library she softened. "I brought you a present," she said, sliding a piece of dime-store jewelry across my desk.

Only a few weeks after starting my new job I knew that I had found myself. When the Springfield school system called, I declined their offer for a teaching position without a second thought.

The summer of 1972 passed quickly at the library. I held a grand celebration for the end of Summer Reading Club with entertainment by a magician and prizes for everyone. The children returned to school more able to read than when they had left. They were eager for the first day of school in September.

Autumn leaves fell leaving the bony branches of trees exposed. By the end of October, Monica, Victor, Bonnie, and the other children came into the library subdued. They no longer came in full of energy and babbling conversation. Tempers flared easily. They looked somber as they pulled out worksheets from their bags. The questions they asked were for homework assignments, not the ones they had on their own. They left earlier each day to be home before the sun set.

As the daytime light shortened, my parents' home seemed cramped. I dreaded driving home after work. My parents had gotten into the habit of eating from tray tables in front of the television while watching the nightly news. I longed for some adult conversation.

One evening I grumbled, "Doesn't anyone talk during dinner anymore?" After that, my mother served dinner at the kitchen table. They had little to say to one another or to me. Once he had eaten, Dad went to the living room and turned on the television to watch *Jeopardy!*, giving the questions before the onscreen competitors. When my mother and I finished washing the dishes, Mom would sit in her rocking chair knitting.

I often left the house to wander through a shopping mall alone. "I'm going out. Is there anything you want?" I asked each time.

Dad would jokingly reply, "A color TV."

When the waiting period ended and I had my own health insurance, I decided to spend some of my paycheck. Until then I had deposited my pay into a savings account in case I needed medical care. My parents had refused to charge me rent or let me purchase groceries. One of the first things I purchased was a small color television. Dad tried to explain he had only been kidding. I knew that. The next weekend he began sawing wood to build a table for the new television. A color set was common in most homes, but my parents considered it a luxury they could not afford. Despite his protest he would exclaim at the way color improved every program he watched.

That winter I spent most of what I earned on items my parents had denied themselves. My mother was still using a wringer washing machine. With that machine, she filled the agitator with clean water, then drained the tub and refilled it with a clean water rinse. Each garment had to be hand fed through the rolling cylinders in order to squeeze out the water before it could be hung up to dry. If it was raining or snowing, she hung the lines in the basement. If it was a clear day, she carried the laundry basket to the clotheslines outside regardless of the temperature. When I told her I was having a washer and dryer delivered to the house, she said, "That's not necessary. I won't know how to use it."

"Trust me Mom, it's not that hard."

For Christmas 1972 my mother purchased a small tree planted in a pot and placed it on the bookcase. On Christmas Eve after they had gone to bed, I spread the presents I had purchased for them around my father's recliner and my mother's rocking chair. I knew these gifts would not be joyfully received. My parents would be more embarrassed than grateful. That is the way it had always been. Dad might use the items I gave him. My mother would put her gifts away saying, "I don't need this now."

Then I decided to open the bottle of Bénédictine liquor, which was a Christmas present from the library's custodian. Neither of my parents drank alcohol, and I had secretly stashed the bottle in my closet. The swig of liquid warmed my body and comforted me. I would make the bottle last for almost a year, taking one small sip each night after my parents had gone to their bedroom.

Many of my high school friends had moved away from the area. They had married or found jobs in other places. College friends had dispersed to different parts of the country. Most were in the process of starting jobs, beginning their adult life. We exchanged newsy letters at first. Gradually these became less frequent. Loneliness crept in with each drift of snow during the winter.

I wrote to Robin who had moved back in with her parents in New Haven after graduation. Attending Yale Divinity School, she was working on a master of arts in religion and working part-time in a warehouse assembly line. For the last two years at Boston University we had been almost inseparable. We had provided balance for each other. My happiest memories of those years were spent with Robin. We enjoyed simple amusements. Both of us had only a few dollars of spending money each week. We laughed at silly inside jokes and cried at the same movies. When we went out on double dates, we found each other more interesting than the young men who sought our attention. During my lowest times, it had been Robin who sat with me and listened with patience and empathy. She had helped me get to the hospital when I needed an infusion. She had refused to be an informant for my mother.

Her experience with moving back home was much like my own, lonely and constrained. We began driving from our parents' homes to a midpoint and meeting for dinner in a restaurant once a month. It was the only time I could be myself.

"Why don't we plan to go away on a vacation together this spring?" I suggested.

"I'd like to go to Cape Cod. That's where my parents used to go for vacation."

"There are some inexpensive cottages if we go before Memorial Day when the season starts. And if I need medical help, the Cape isn't far from Boston."

We began making plans. The week we went on vacation, it rained each day, but it did not dampen our fun. We used the cottage heater to dry out our jackets after we tried to golf in the drizzle or walk along the sandy shore. We collected shells and sand, put the sand in containers, and dug small holes rimmed with shells, then poured in melted wax and stuck a wick in the middle of the wax when it began to cool. For years, the sand candles held memories of our first vacation together.

When the summer arrived it was a welcome relief to see the children relaxed and playful again. They plunged into new books, new questions.

"Does lightning come down from the sky? Or does it come up from the ground?" Jeff asked one day after a storm.

Together he and I flipped through the reference books as a small gathering of children circled around to hear the answer. Merlin, my guinea pig, watched intently from his cage atop the card catalog. Most children were at eye level with Merlin when they looked up a book in the catalog. Merlin had become a confidant and friend for the children who often brought in a fistful of grass from the library lawn to feed him.

I had fallen into being a librarian by accident. I joked when asked why I had wanted to be a librarian. "I didn't. I was recruited," I would say. Now I realized how luck had given me the job I was best suited to do.

When autumn set in again, I applied for a better paying position in a larger branch library. The larger branch would give time off for employees to take classes in a graduate degree program. A graduate degree was essential if being a librarian was my career.

Another person was chosen for the job. Disappointed, I did not give up. I applied to the graduate degree program in the School of Library and Information Science at Simmons College anyway. Somehow I would find a job in the Boston area so I would not have to commute.

Included in the application form was a request for medical information from a doctor. I sent the form off to my hematologist in Boston. When he returned the form to me, he enclosed a note saying that the questions seemed irrelevant to him. He had signed the form writing "not applicable" to all of the questions. I would later learn that his instinct was correct.

"It is not our policy," the director of admissions told me later, "to accept students who are disabled. It gives librarians a bad image."

Thanks to my doctor's suspicions, I slipped by unnoticed. I received an acceptance letter in the mail a few weeks later. Again I was an imposter, pretending to be a typical student at Simmons College.

# Ready, Set...Go?

In mid-December 1998, the contractor announced that all he needed to do was to paint the walls. Modification of our house had only taken two months. The bathroom on the first floor could now accommodate a wheelchair. To make this possible the galley kitchen shrank to a pantry. The dining room was now an eat-in kitchen. The living room had space for my parents' beds.

Robin and I purchased a twin-sized bed for my father and rented an electrically controlled medical bed for Mom. We dusted the rooms, filled the kitchen cabinets, and prepared for the transition that would begin on New Year's Day.

One week before moving day, Robin and I went to spend Christmas Day with my mom and dad. We brought no gifts except for the groceries we carried to prepare dinner. The house was the only one on the street without colored lights outside or candlelight twinkling through the windows. I addressed holiday greeting cards to everyone in my mother's address book, passed the cards to my parents for their signatures, and slipped their new addresses effective January first into each envelope.

We gathered in the living room while we waited for the turkey to roast. Dad sat down in his recliner. He turned to face me and announced calmly but firmly, "You can take Mother with you. She needs your help, and I can't take care of her, but I've decided I'm staying here." My breath escaped my lungs and my knees gave way as I collapsed, landing on the sofa. Dad continued, "This is my home, the only one I have ever known and I'm not leaving."

For several seconds I could not find my voice. "Besides," Dad said, making his final argument, "I don't want to live in a house where everyone but me is female, even the cat and the dog!"

My heart rate spiked with anger. I had not seen this coming. My mind went blank. When I glanced at Robin, she jumped from her chair as if it was on fire, snatched the leash, and headed out the back door with Penny. As she passed by me, I saw tears in her eyes. Everything we had done was coming undone. She had willingly offered to sacrifice time, comfort, and treasured belongings in order to provide my parents with safety. She had volunteered to help care for my mother and father.

My mother froze in midswing on her rocking chair. She looked as shocked by Dad's announcement as I. It was if we had been caught in a stop-action film. I couldn't think. I lowered my eyes so my father would not see my rage. I tried to make sense out of what had happened.

Dad had frequently told me that if Mom died, he would not live long himself because he wouldn't want to live without her. Did he love his house more than his wife? Did he remember that we had already sold his car? What did he mean about not wanting to live in a household of women? He had lived in a household of women most of his life, adoring his own mother and sisters, then Mom and me. Did he think that we would all leave him to die alone?

The Lewis Carroll poem from *Alice in Wonderland* played in my thoughts:

"You are old, Father William," the young man said,

"And your hair has become very white;
And yet you incessantly stand on your head—
Do you think, at your age, it is right?"

As if it was an exhaled breath I said, "Dad, I can't do this without you."

All I could hear was the tick of the clock. We had planned to pack up the items my parents wanted to take with them but would not need in the next week, like their summer clothing. We had secretly sorted the items they would no longer need. I had already purchased new towels for them. The ones they had used for the past forty years were now so thin the light showed through the face cloths. The edges of the bath towels were frayed. They were to disappear on the day of the move. That was all we had left to do after two months of disruption and disorder.

Perhaps my face displayed my exhaustion and desperation because when I looked up again, my father shrugged and said, "All right…if I can help, then I'll move too."

# Part 2

# Together Again

At the end of January 1974, I felt a stabbing pain near the left side of my pelvic bone. I knew immediately this meant an ovarian cyst had ruptured and bled. I saw a new doctor in Springfield who ordered an infusion of a clotting factor called cryoprecipitate. I was told that fibrinogen concentrate was no longer being produced because it was a pooled product from thousands, perhaps millions of donors. Therefore it was vulnerable to viruses, which could be transmitted to the recipient of the product. Cryoprecipitate or fresh frozen plasma was now my only option for treatment of a bleeding episode.

"You're over twenty-one. I'll prescribe birth control pills for you, so this won't happen again," the doctor said after my bleeding had stopped.

The oral contraceptive not only brought me relief from the occasional internal bleeding at ovulation, it also reduced my monthly menstrual flow to a manageable level. The worry I had had about missing days at work each month vanished.

However, I began to feel vaguely ill a few weeks after the infusion. My skin had a yellow tone, and I was unusually tired. The doctor ordered a blood test and reported that I did not have hepatitis A or B, although I did have many of the symptoms of a hepatitis virus.

I called Robin. We had planned to meet for dinner. "I'm so sorry," I explained, "I don't think I'm well enough to drive to Hartford."

"That's okay. I'll drive to you."

"There's supposed to be snow. Are you sure you want to?"

Robin insisted and I easily gave in. I was deeply grateful. A surge of happiness rose in me as I thought of seeing her.

It had been a bitter cold winter with drifts of snow that came halfway up the bird feeder outside my bedroom window. Thick icicles hung from the eves, heavy with sharp points like spears.

When Robin arrived, she said, "It took me three hours to make an hour and a half drive. My old car slid and slipped in some of the drifting snow on the highway. But I was eager to see you."

Robin sat by my bedside. She said, "I'm getting my masters in religious education from Yale this spring. I've been accepted at a theological seminary in the Boston area. What I really want is to be a minister. I'll need a master's degree in divinity."

"I've been accepted at Simmons College," I responded. "Since I didn't get that promotion, I can tell I need to get a masters if I want to continue being a librarian."

Robin confided, "I don't have very much money for housing. I took out a loan to cover my tuition at seminary."

"I don't have a lot of cash myself. I withdrew my retirement account to pay the tuition. My friend Marlene might let us stay at her place until we find an apartment to rent."

Overjoyed at the thought of moving away from our parents permanently, we gave little consideration to moving without a place of our own or a way to pay for housing and food. What mattered most was that we would be together again.

In late August 1974 Robin and I moved out of our parents' homes for the last time. If someone had told us we would reverse that direction twenty-five years later, when it was our parents' turn to be dependent on us, we would not have believed them.

# In with the New

Early Thursday morning on New Year's Eve, Robin and I drove our cars for the last time to my parents' home. We needed both cars in order to transport the remaining furniture and my parents back to our house.

When I opened my parents' back door, I glanced around the emptied kitchen. The curtains my mother and I had sewn thirty-five years ago still hung at the windows. They were dusty and faded. We had eaten the last meal at the kitchen table where once laughter and conversation had mingled with garden vegetables.

The real estate agent would put the house on the market to sell. Logan dropped in to say his final farewell. When he finished, he looked stern. "Do me a favor, don't ever contact me again." My parents looked as if they had not heard him. Robin's eyes widened. It seemed so heartless to me. I wondered if he simply did not want to know the last chapter of my parents' lives.

"I won't," I said looking into his steely eyes.

Kay came to wish us well and say good-bye. I gave her a farewell hug. Keeping our emotions at bay, we all wore optimistic smiles. It was pretense. My parents went to bcd for the last time in their house. Robin and I stayed up late on New Year's Eve, not celebrating, but organizing the items we needed to squeeze into the two cars.

We wedged my mother's Boston rocker, a bedside table and television cabinet, a small collection of my father's favorite books, and a few plastic bags full of clothing into the back seats of the two cars. Internally I praised Mom for her disregard for possessions.

"Things are a waste of money. I don't care about them," she had said whenever I offered to purchase something new or improved for her convenience. It was her frugality and savings account that had made it possible for us to remodel our home.

As long as I was busy I could suppress the anxiety at ending phase one and beginning phase two of the rescue of my parents. There was no turning back.

"I want to get there as early as possible," I told Robin. "The weather forecast for tomorrow is freezing rain by afternoon." It had been hard enough to get my mother down the four steps from the back door and into my car when she had a doctor's appointment. The image of her maneuvering her fragile limbs step-by-step over icy pavement horrified me.

A cold drizzle of rain began early in the morning, not yet sleet or freezing rain but a degree or two in temperature would bring us sliding into danger. I balanced caution with urgency as Mom took her first step down the concrete stairs toward the waiting car in the driveway. Dad went out first and opened Robin's car door. Robin went in front, descending one step at a time backward facing my mother. I walked behind. If Mom teetered in either direction, we could steady her and prevent a fall.

My mother gingerly sat down in the front passenger seat of Robin's car. Her face was locked in determination. "I'm fine," she said, when I gently eased her into the car and snapped the seatbelt across her child-sized chest. She already looked exhausted.

We drove in a caravan, my car leading the way. There was something distinctly funereal about our procession. I had never thought about the day when they would need to move. Robin drove her car behind mine with my mother beside her in the front seat. As I backed out of the driveway, I glanced in the rearview mirror. We had left the only house my parents had ever owned and all of us knew we could not go back. The "For Sale" sign would go up the next day. I was glad I wouldn't see it. Sitting in the front seat beside me, Dad was silently staring out the window.

Now a new year had begun. Two hours after our departure, we arrived at the home we would share. Mother rolled her walker up the newly constructed ramp to our back door. Dixie, the cat, met us when we entered. Penny stood out of the way following a command to sit and stay. They both tilted their heads in curiosity at the two new humans moving in.

It took some persuading to get my father to sit down and read while Robin and I unpacked the car, but Mom went straight to her new bed and dozed with Dixie curled beside her. Soon I could hear my father gently snoring from the recliner in the sunroom.

A few minutes after we had unloaded my parents' belongings, the temperature dropped below freezing and the light rain that had been falling froze as it fell to the ground. The sidewalks and streets became treacherous. Relieved that we had all made it safely indoors, I lay down to rest for a few minutes.

My persistent cough from the construction dust kept me awake. I had been granted a month of personal leave from work to get my parents settled. There was so much yet to accomplish. I had no emotional energy left for grief.

None of us had had time for reflection. Each item on the to-do list had been checked off as quickly as possible. I stifled the underlying apprehension when I thought about how my parents would adjust to a new home. Our lives would merge the way they had not since I was a young adult.

# *Reversing Tide*

During my month of family leave I helped my parents become adjusted to their new environment and routines, chose new doctors for each of them, and assumed the responsibility of keeping them fed and cared for. My mother had relaxed the control she had gripped for most of her lifetime. She had been the one to decide what was best not only for herself, but for my father and me. I had not expected she would hand over the responsibilities of choosing doctors, making appointments, and administering medications without a struggle.

My parents' new primary care doctor had referred Mom to a neurologist and Dad to a cardiologist. After I had taken my parents to all of their new doctors for initial visits, I made an appointment for my father to have his hearing aids tested, persuading him that new hearing aids might be worth the expense.

When the month ended and I returned to work on February first, I wanted to get back to my position as director of a small-town library. I also wanted to get out of the house. I longed for time when Robin and I could have some privacy. Our only conversations now were in hushed late-night whispers when we were both exhausted and more than a little cranky.

Dad liked feeding Penny, opening the back door when the dog needed to go out and whistling her back inside again. He preferred to read, watch television, and take one-mile walks to the end of our street and back. He would not care that I was no longer around the house every day.

I knew my mother would miss my daily presence. "You should retire early," she told me as I left for work that first day of February. I could already see that my mother was feeling less pain. She needed less sleep during the day.

"I don't think so, Mom." She would like me to be a stay-at-home daughter, I thought.

Returning to my job meant that my weekends were the only time I had to give fully to my parents' care. After breakfast on Saturday I set up my mother's medications in her weekly pill counter and then went to the desk on the second floor. I sat at the computer paying my parents' bills and ordering refills of Mom's medications from the mail-order pharmacy.

Never able to fully agree on how to handle money, my parents had set up separate checking and savings accounts. Mom had opened multiple five-year certificates of deposit all staggered so that they came due in different years. She was proud they were accruing better interest than any savings account. She believed it was prudent to stagger the certificates, so if she needed cash at some point she would not have to pay a penalty. My parents knew nothing about stocks or bonds. Mom had been saving money all of her life, and she instructed me that the certificates should not be cashed in before the maturity date.

Years earlier my parents had put my name on their bank accounts. Now I was the only one capable of paying their bills and transferring money from one account to another. Managing their multiple accounts seemed ridiculous to me. I found it onerous to balance my own checking account. I longed for a lazy Saturday morning. I sat at my desk grumbling about so much work for so little money. Penny, the dog, looked confused by my heavy sighs of impatience.

When the telephone rang, I got up from the desk eager for a break. One of my cousins explained why she had called. "I'm worried about you now that you've moved your parents in."

"I'm fine," I said.

"You know, I ruined my health when I took care of my mother," she said.

I did not know. My cousin had been a nurse for years. She had skills I did not. Sixteen years older than I, she seemed quite healthy to me.

"Don't worry about me," I assured my cousin. "I have it all under control." I went on. "I contacted the Elder Care Services. A home care aide comes in once a week to give them each a shower and wash their laundry."

When I hung up the phone, I thought about the other ways I had constructed safety nets to protect myself from burnout. I didn't mention to my cousin that I had put several systems in place to cover the weekday hours from nine to five when I was at work. Two mornings a week, David, a retired Air Force veteran, came to take my father for a walk at the town park.

Walking out of doors had been one of my father's lifelong joys. Dad was safer with a walking companion. Both men seemed to thrive on their slow-paced hikes around the pond. David often brought his camera and shot pictures, as my father watched birds. They would return to the house together looking refreshed and cheerful. My mother took on the role of hostess, making tea and spreading out crackers for a snack.

My mother insisted that I hire someone to do housecleaning. I knew Millie from church was looking for a part-time job. She came to the house each week to vacuum the carpet and wash the kitchen floor. As she worked, she told my mother stories of her part-time job at Walmart and her trips to Arkansas to mine crystals. Mom thrived on their chatter and the companionship Millie gave her during the day while my father sat reading. There was at least one visitor each day from Monday to Friday.

In a matter of weeks after my parents moved in with us, my mother walked more easily. She liked being able to push a button and raise her head up or down until she found a comfortable position in bed.

Dad's blood sugar tests improved, since Robin and I were preparing the meals. His forgetfulness, which had irritated my mother before they moved, vanished. Now that he was free from worry about my mother, his memory seemed to be as sharp as it had ever been. He could remember what he and David had discussed on their morning walk that day and enjoyed telling Mom about the birds he had seen.

Astonishing to me, there was still plenty for Robin and me to do. My parents' new primary care doctor wanted to see them every three months. Mom's neurologist recommended regular checkups to monitor her Parkinson's disease. I still needed to find them a dentist. Mom's partial dentures now were too big for her mouth. As she chewed, the false teeth slipped up and down. They both had to have their toenails clipped by a podiatrist. They needed me to drive them to each appointment.

Earwax collected in my father's new hearing aids until he could hear better without them. Robin took responsibility for cleaning the hearing aids once a week. On Saturday mornings while Robin was picking out bits of earwax and checking the hearing aid batteries, I sat at the dining room table with Mom counting out her daily medications and filling the pill counter. She double-checked my work as if she did not trust me. One morning she accused me of getting the count wrong. I slammed the last bottle on the table.

"You watched me like a hawk open one bottle at a time, placing the correct number of pills into the time slots."

"You got it wrong," she insisted.

We continued to argue until I removed each pill putting it back in its bottle, counting as I went to prove that I had not made an error. Then I began again putting the pills into the plastic reminders for each day. My cheeks flushed with the heat of anger as my mother refused to apologize for doubling the time required to set up pills for the week. Now that my mother was stronger, she wanted her control back.

Mom was able to prepare her own breakfast and was puttering around the house seeking out chores. She folded the clean laundry after the home care aide brought the basket upstairs from the dryer. One day she announced with satisfaction, "I found your broom and swept the kitchen floor this morning." She had hated being in bed. She wanted to be useful again.

She expected to be thanked, but instead I said, "Mom! You're supposed to use your walker."

She huffed, "I don't need it in the house."

One evening I came home from work to find my mother sitting on the living room floor. I froze at the sight. Mom had inched her way off the couch to sit on the floor and comfort the dog. Penny was having one of her occasional seizures. The vet had prescribed phenobarbital, which had become less and less effective over time.

I watched the tender scene as Penny began to come back to consciousness while my mother cooed softly, "There, there." Mom's bony fingers gently stroked Penny. A few short months ago, my mother could not have gotten to the bathroom by herself. Now she was able to get down on the floor without injury. I helped her get up safely, restraining myself from telling Mom it might not have been a wise decision for her to get down on the floor.

Robin's Sundays were spent at church. Monday was her day off, but there was no more rest for her than there had been on any other day. While I worked, she took Dad to the grocery store to purchase the food we needed for the week. He enjoyed getting out of the house. It gave him a sense of purpose; however, Robin could have done the shopping in half the time without him trailing behind her.

We dashed home at noon each day to make their lunch and check on them. We found this took too much time away from our jobs, so I requested Meals on Wheels. Rather than a quick bowl of canned soup or leftovers from dinner the previous night, they enjoyed a complete meal, sized for elder appetites. It was a bonus that they also received another daily visitor.

When Robin and I had a few private moments alone, we spent much of that time venting about my parents.

"It's all my fault," Robin said one evening. "I was the one who suggested they move in with us."

"No, it's not. I hear the younger women at work talk about how much work it is to care for a new baby. They say if they had only known. But, of course, that would not have made a difference to them, and it would not have made a difference to me if I had known how hard this would be."

At the end of each day, when I had turned the dishwasher on, I pulled the bed covers around Mom and kissed her good-night. My father would be watching television, the volume up as high as he could turn it. When I entered the living room he would look up.

"Good-night, Dad."

Every night he replied, "Thank you for taking care of your mother."

I did not know how to respond, since it seemed to me that he had also benefited greatly. I'd smile, kiss him good-night, and tell him I loved him. He seemed to have no idea that he too needed care.

Dad walked up and down the neighborhood block each morning and again in the afternoon. Mom fussed at him about the dangers of icy sidewalks and below-freezing temperatures. He ignored her even after the day when he came home with an abrasion on his cheek.

"I fell on a snowbank when I went to cross the street," he explained. "A nice man stopped his car and helped me stand up. I'm fine."

"You fell into the street?" I gulped, trying to hide my panic. I wanted to scream. Instead I looked at my mother who had washed his scraped face and applied antiseptic and a bandage. She raised her eyes upward. She had already given him the lecture and it made no impression. There was no point to giving my father another scolding.

At work, the library budget request absorbed my attention for most of the day. I calculated the amount required to receive the additional funds from the state. The finance committee might reduce the budget request even further, but the library could not afford to lose the supplemental funds from the state grant award. I reduced the line items to a minimum. Library staff would take the brunt of complaints for fewer new books or reduced hours of service. Some people might lose their jobs. My shoulders ached at the thought of these possible outcomes. When I glanced at the time, I realized I had to finish my work later. I needed to get home, prepare dinner, and then come back for a board of trustees meeting at seven.

Before my parents had moved in, there would have been plenty of time, but now I would be slowed down as my parents shared the news from their day. They would feel compelled to tell me who had rung the doorbell and what was in the mail. They had lost any interest in my day.

As I started my car's engine, I was relieved to hear Robin's car in the adjacent church parking lot also start up. She had a meeting tonight too. Together we could get supper on the table and leave in time to be early for our respective meetings.

As I opened the back door to our house, I let out an involuntary gasp. Dad was standing at the kitchen counter in a blizzard of flour. He had white powder on his hair and his plaid shirt. There were fingerprints where he had wiped his hands on his navy blue pants. There was even a dusting on his shoes. The cherry dining table had a fine layer of powder covering the surface. It looked as if the flour canister had exploded. Mom was rolling a thick gooey blob across a piece of waxed paper. I could see a smudge of flour on her forehead. Dad lifted his hands in surrender when he noticed me. His right hand had been scooping out flour and dropping fistfuls as my mother tried to make the dough form a ball. Mom was accusing Dad of not understanding her instructions.

I stood speechless as I heard Robin come up behind me. When Mom noticed us at the doorway, she offered, "We thought we would surprise you by making biscuits for dinner."

Robin's mouth dropped open. I managed to stifle the horror swelling up in my throat. I thought, they are eighty-six, and they are acting like three-year-olds. Mom looked overwhelmed by a task she had done so readily for most of her life. Her lips were tight, her face flushed. It was against her nature to apologize. Robin and I had to clean up the mess before we could prepare dinner.

I had a momentary thought of turning around, getting back into my car, and going out to eat. Instead I heaved a sigh. "Why don't you two get cleaned up? We can finish here." The only way we could work quickly was with my parents out of the room. Besides, if they hovered, I might tell them what I was really thinking. I was furious at the extra time the cleanup would take, but they looked so forlorn.

My parents had been patient with my childhood foibles. Mom had showed me how to clean up the candle wax I dripped on the living room carpet and helped me to scrub the crayoned drawings off the painted wall in my bedroom. She must have been upset, but she remained calm. Other children had mothers who would punish their children for their mistakes.

The difference between raising a child and caring for an elder was that a child acquires skills day by day. My parents were losing their abilities. After eighty years of being capable people, pride did not allow them to see that this was no longer true. I was caught between my desire to improve their health and safety and my wish to help them maintain their independence as much as possible. My parents had moved in with us less than two months earlier. Perhaps my cousin had been right after all.

The next Saturday, I knocked on my neighbor's door. She had three children in elementary school. This is a crazy idea, I told myself as she opened her door.

"Can you go visit my parents a few afternoons a week?" I said, "You can bring your kids if they want to come along. My parents love children."

"Sure," she said without hesitation. "Do you want me to do anything special?"

"My mother likes to cook, but she needs supervision now. Just keep them from getting into trouble," I said. She looked confused. I imagine she thought it was an odd request. I left relieved and yet there was an encroaching sense of loss.

# Spring Forward, Fall Back

On my father's birthday in mid-March the gusts of wind promised spring. Robin stirred the biscuit dough and dropped spoonfuls onto the cookie sheet. She slid the aluminum pan into the oven. I cut the strawberries into bite-sized pieces and then put them back in the refrigerator beside the beaters to chill. Before whipping the heavy cream, I added a small amount of sugar. There was no sugar added to the berries or the biscuits. My mother had made this low carbohydrate dessert instead of birthday cake for the past forty years. It fit into Dad's diabetic diet. After dinner, my father smacked his lips in appreciation. In 1999, Dad was happier to watch the coming of spring than he was to turn eighty-seven years old.

"Winter's almost over," he grinned. "I saw a few snowdrops in the garden yesterday."

Each day had more sunlight. Morning fog rose from the ground as the earth began to thaw. The lavender Dutch crocus showed their faces. The yellow forsythia blossoms became a confusion of brilliant yellow along our stockade fence. Dad reported his observations each day to my mother.

My fiftieth birthday was in early April. It was an occasion I wanted to celebrate. Grateful that my parents were there, at dinner that evening I asked, "Can you believe it? I made it to fifty!"

I wanted them to share my joy, but my words met with no reaction from my parents. Had they forgotten all those difficult years they had spent trying to keep me from dying young? Had fear for my safety and well-being become such a habit that they could no longer appreciate success? I tried not to let my disappointment show on my face. Robin noticed and squeezed my hand. I chided myself for expecting my parents to see my birthday as a victory they helped me to achieve.

A few weeks later my left shoulder began to hurt. I had no time in my day to pay attention at first. When I could no longer sleep at night from the pain, I consulted my hematologist.

"Is there a microbleed in my shoulder?" I asked him.

After he examined me, he said, "You have what we call a frozen shoulder or adhesive capsulitis. If you didn't have a bleeding problem, you could have a steroid injection. I can't allow you to do that. Try physical therapy."

I added physical therapy appointments into my schedule by doing without lunch three days a week. I practiced the exercises at home before breakfast and at the end of each day. The pain only grew more intense. Meanwhile, my mother's back pain receded week by week. She moved easier from a chair to a standing position.

My mother's doctor had warned, "People with Parkinson's should not have wheels on their walker. Much too dangerous. Get some tennis balls and cut an X in the middle and then replace the rubber bottoms on the walker with them. The walker will glide easier over carpet indoors and grass outside."

Robin and I made checking the wear on the tennis balls part of our regular routine, replacing the thin, worn-out ones. When our garden flowers began to bloom, I did not notice that we were replacing the balls less often. In May, I came home early one afternoon. Driving past the front of our house, I spotted two figures arm in arm. Mom and Dad were admiring the pink and purple lilacs. What I did not see was Mom's walker. It seemed that while I was working, my parents were now in the habit of checking the garden daily.

"I don't need the walker because I hold onto your father," Mom explained before I had a chance to open my mouth.

I rolled my eyes. She feared that would be my reaction and had chosen not to tell me about their daily garden tour. My shoulder throbbed. I turned and went inside to get some distance before I said something I would regret.

When I regained my composure, I realized that it was unfair of me to deny her a simple pleasure in the name of safety, now that her back pain had decreased. She deserved a walk out of doors free of the encumbrance of her walker. Still I worried what would happen if she fell and I was not there to help.

By June we were able to eat at the picnic table in our yard. On most summer Saturdays as a child, my parents would gather up neighborhood children and head to a state park. Mom had learned to cook on the wrought-iron wood stove in the farmhouse where she had grown up. She amazed my friends when she prepared a full dinner with roasted potatoes, chicken, and vegetables on a barbecue grill.

Now Robin and I made the food, carried the plates, utensils, and drinks from the kitchen, and spread out the checkered tablecloth on the table under the black maple tree. By the time we had pulled up the plastic lawn chairs and guided my parents into them, the picnic had lost its appeal for me. Even though Robin had done most of the work, I was in agony with the shoulder pain.

As Robin tied Penny's leash to a stake, I glanced around at the untended yard. Over the past ten years, Robin had replaced much of the grass lawn with flowerbeds of star-gazer day lilies, peach German iris, coral honeysuckle, and lace-cap hydrangea. She had nurtured the garden. This year I doubted she would have the time to put the netting over the blueberry bushes. The birds would have a feast. I was glad that my mother's eyesight was not as sharp as it once was or she would be tempted to get down on her knees and pull out the weeds.

"Robin and I are thinking about going away for a vacation next month," I announced at the table.

"That's a wonderful idea," Mom said with a gleam in her eye. "Don't you worry about us. We're fine." Dad nodded in agreement.

"We'll only be gone a week," I said hesitating. "We're not going far. Just to Cape Cod. We can come back early if you need us. We'll take Penny."

"I'll take care of feeding the cat," my father winked. "No problem."

Before we left, I asked Millie to check in with them every day at dinnertime, in addition to her regular housecleaning schedule. She would clean the cat's litter box and make sure my parents were settled at the end of each day. I left her instructions on how to reach us in case of an emergency. I asked David to be vigilant about my father's safety.

Robin loaded all the supplies into and out of the car because of my shoulder pain. The cottage faced a tide pool. There was a kitchen where we prepared all of our meals . Going to a restaurant was impossible since it was too hot to leave Penny in the car alone, Dogs were not allowed on the beach, so we walked along the town's sidewalks trying to catch a cool breeze from the ocean. My shoulder pain did not magically disappear in that week. It kept me awake at night and drained my energy during the day. When the vacation was over, we were not relaxed. We wondered if the vacation had given us any respite.

In November we celebrated my parents' sixty-third wedding anniversary. After dinner, I asked my father to tell the story of their wedding day.

"I was so excited, that day," Dad began. "I went to the train station very early to wait for Daisy to arrive. I walked up and down beside the tracks eager for the train from Boston. My sister had arranged to have the minister come to her house to do the wedding. My father, my brother Ernest, and his wife, Eileen, were all waiting at my sister's house for us. I was glad Daisy and I were together at last."

I smiled at Robin. We had lived together for twenty-five years. Although the past year had been a drain of our energy, shrinking our time together, our relationship had strengthened. We leaned on each other for comfort and support. I loved her more deeply than I had ever before.

# *Why 2K*

By late in 1999 my shoulder was able to move more freely. The pain was less except at night when I lay down to go to sleep. I went for a checkup with the doctor. He shook his head at my blood pressure reading.

"That's too high," he said. "Maybe it's just temporary."

I made no comment. The increasing weight of responsibility for my parents' care weighed on my shoulders like an ox's harness. I pulled myself from task to task, day to day. I wanted to make their lives as easy and pleasant as possible. Until then, being a librarian had been a satisfying career. Now it only provided a salary. I did not have the luxury of enjoying my work as I had before. Caring for my parents was the priority now.

Even before we had moved my parents into our home, we had begun to hear the phrase Y2K. The rumblings of global catastrophe echoed the upheaval in our lives. It was as if there were earthquake tremors under my feet.

A friend left her planned career path to devote the entire year to preparing for the oncoming disaster. She stopped searching for a job and began volunteering for national and local organizations as a consultant. She lectured us each time we saw her about stockpiling food and medical supplies. Our friend's husband worked in a high-tech company, and he had encouraged his wife's activism.

The monthly meetings for department heads in Town Hall focused on keeping public services available after January 1, 2000. The horror stories my friend had been telling me were repeated at our meetings. When operating systems for computers were developed, the programmers had not been able to comprehend anything beyond the twentieth century. Worse yet, computer systems operated power grids and food distribution warehouses and mail deliveries. We were told that at midnight on New Year's Eve, the numbers would roll over to zero, and everything we needed to live safely and comfortably would cease to be produced or shipped. In that freezing January we would have no heat, no tap water, no groceries, no prescription medications. Funds in banks would be unavailable. There would be increasing crime and mayhem as those who were not prepared began stealing the supplies others had stored.

The details of what the next new year would bring infiltrated my thoughts during the day and quickened my heartbeat, keeping me awake at night. Convinced that it was easier to prevent injury than to treat a wound, my mother had taught me to look ahead. Her strategy had paid off—reducing my trips to hospitals. Would it be negligent of me to ignore these warnings about Y2K?

My parents weren't worried by the news on television. They had grown up before production of goods and services relied upon digital automation. I shared none of my anxiety with them. At the dinner table, I often prompted my parents to tell stories from when they were young. I treasured the stories of their lives before I was born.

One evening the topic of Y2K came up. Mom began, "When I was growing up on the farm, every so often the traveling evangelists set up a tent. Crowds of people squeezed in to hear when the world would end. When that day came, I saw people standing on the roofs of barns waiting for the rapture. It seemed silly to me. Did they think they could hitch a ride to heaven?"

"The thing that always amazed me," Dad chuckled, "was that the spiritual leaders claimed that it was their petitions to God that had prevented the world from ending. The believers went back to their sinful ways each time Judgment Day was postponed."

This time, instead of the religious fanatics predicting doomsday, it was the computer scientists. I kept my thoughts to myself.

My parents trusted me with their care. I was obligated to see they had shelter, food, and medical attention. I began ordering refills for my parents' prescription medications earlier than necessary, eventually building up a surplus that filled a storage shelf.

Robin purchased extra canned food and bottled water each time she did the food shopping with my father. We installed metal shelving in the basement so that we could fill it with emergency canned goods. We invested in a propane camp stove that we could use on the back deck of our house to cook.

We had lived in the house ten years and not lit a fire in the wood stove, so we hired a chimney sweep and started collecting kindling. Then we had a cord of wood delivered.

At work the town allocated funds for the library to purchase new computers. Without these, the town selectmen warned resources stored in the government computers, including those in the library network, would be unavailable. In a rampage of buying, businesses and organizations worldwide replaced their older computers with new ones.

On the morning of January 1, 2000, I turned on the light in the bathroom with the switch. I found Mom in the kitchen simmering her oatmeal. Dad was smearing his toast with peanut butter and drinking his coffee. I heard the furnace in the basement softly cranking up the hot air into the heating ducts. The internet still functioned, and stores were advertising they would be open as usual after the holiday. Y2K had been a false alarm—or perhaps a way to boost the economy.

Our storage shelves in the basement held plenty of pickled beets, creamed corn, and bottled water we would now force ourselves to use. My relief was overshadowed by the time and effort I had expended on preparing for an emergency.

# *Gut Reaction*

Two weeks into January, I went to work one Wednesday morning, a bit tired but that was usual these days. By noon, however, I stood up from a chair and felt a stab of pain in my abdomen. With me, sudden pain was usually a sign of internal bleeding. I could not afford to ignore it. Reluctantly I called my hematologist. I don't have time for this. I've got too many things I need to do today.

"Come right in and I'll schedule a CT scan for you," he said.

Lunch was unthinkable with the pain. Much as I wanted to ignore it, the pain was getting worse. "Okay, I'll be there as soon as I can."

I made a quick phone call to Robin, letting her know how my plans for today had suddenly changed. "I'll be fine," I said. "I can drive to Boston on my own. I love you."

After the CT scan results were in, the doctor ordered me admitted to the hospital. Soon there were two plastic bags hanging on the IV pole. The one with the clotting factor was running. I watched the steady drip, drip, drip. I shifted from side to side in bed trying to get comfortable. I watched the clock and worried. There weren't any distractions in the single-bed hospital room except for the television. I flipped through the channels on the remote control and then turned it off.

When the gastroenterologist came in to my room, she reported, "The scan showed you have diverticulitis and your large intestine has a perforation."

It did not sound like I would be going home in time to fix my parents' dinner or see that my mother took her evening medications. My body had failed me again. It wasn't reliable when I needed it to be strong. Old anger at my disorder spiked quickly.

I had drifted away from the news the doctor had just delivered when I realized she was staring at me. She continued, "I'm concerned about the infection. We've got the bleeding stopped now and I've ordered IV antibiotics. You can't have anything to eat or drink for a while. We'll start you on IV nutrients. I recommend surgery, a temporary colostomy. You won't get over this infection unless we operate."

"You don't understand," I sputtered, thinking about the time it would take to recover from surgery.

"You don't have much choice." Then she left the room.

Grief stricken by not being able to care for my parents in the way I had expected, I just wanted to get back home as soon as possible. A wave of anxiety hit me when I thought about the burden Robin would be carrying trying to do it all herself. Until I got home, she would have to do all the tasks we shared—shopping, cooking, pill dispensing, taking my parents to doctors' appointments. Her ministry was demanding enough without having to provide for my elderly parents' needs.

When he was done with his office appointments for the day, my hematologist came in to see me. I greeted him with, "I'm not having surgery."

"Don't worry, we can manage the clotting. You have to do this; otherwise, you'll never get over the infection."

"Never?" I said.

"Never. I've alerted a surgeon. He'll be in to see you."

At that moment, Robin arrived. She had fixed supper for my parents and driven ninety minutes to Boston to see me. She reached for my hand. "I wanted to see you in person," she said. "I have bad news."

I squeezed her hand fearing whatever might come next.

"You know, my dad had radiation for the prostate cancer a few days ago. Now he is at home and bleeding profusely. His doctor wants him to come into the hospital tomorrow and since my mother doesn't drive, he needs me to take him. I'm so worried about him." Robin turned her eyes to my doctor.

My hematologist knew that what affected Robin would affect me. He didn't waste time or words reassuring her. He asked Robin how old her father was and then said gently, "At his age prostate cancer will not kill him. The bleeding after radiation treatment is ordinary." Then he turned his eyes to me again and said, "You have a decision to make." Wishing Robin well, he left my room to check on his next patient.

"What decision?" Robin asked.

I explained.

Robin's eyelids lowered and her forehead creased. "I don't know what to tell you." She shook her head. "My dad called me because the doctor wants him in the hospital. He needs me to drive him. I've arranged for someone to come help your parents with their dinner. I'm leaving early tomorrow morning and I may not be back until late." Her shoulders stiffened.

Robin would be anxious about going to her parents' house. Her mother had stopped speaking to her four years earlier without an explanation. During that time her father called, but in the background Robin could hear her mother saying, "I don't want to talk to her, she's too critical. I don't want to see her either."

Outside the window I could see tiny flakes of snow sparkling in the darkness. I began to worry about her driving home on the slippery roads. "I'm safe here. Don't worry about me. Call me when you get home." I gave Robin a kiss. I ached when I let go of her hand. We had not had time to talk about my decision. Yet I knew that was not possible. Alone in my hospital room, I struggled against self-pity.

When Robin returned from her trip to Connecticut, she called me. It was nine o'clock at night. She sounded exhausted. "I cried the whole way home," she said. "My mother forgot she hadn't been speaking to me. We had lunch in the diner and she told a man sitting on the stool beside her that they had been friends for years. He looked at her like he had never seen her before."

Robin's mother had always liked chatting with people in diners. Perhaps this man really was someone she recognized.

"Could it be that the man just didn't remember?"

"I don't think so. In the afternoon, she couldn't find the dog's leash and she couldn't remember if she had walked the dog earlier that day. I was afraid to leave her alone in the house. The house is a mess. She has been hoarding and every room is full of junk. I think she has dementia, and I don't understand why my father hasn't done something. I didn't want to leave her alone, but I had no choice. I fixed her something to eat and left to come back home."

Like someone had just placed heavy bags of sand on my back, I drooped with this additional weight of two more elders to care for. Now our load had just doubled. Instead of two parents to care for, we had four and neither of us had siblings to give us a respite.

Robin continued, "The doctor thinks my father will be released from the hospital tomorrow. I'll have to go back to bring him home. I don't expect to get to Boston to see you. I'm sorry."

"How are my parents holding up?" I asked.

"They're okay. Your dad is feeding the cat and letting the dog out. They are worried about you, of course. They ask me every few minutes if I have heard any news."

"Please don't tell my parents that I might need surgery," I said. When we ended the phone call, I pictured another day without Robin beside me.

The next morning the surgeon came to see me. He stood by my bed and began to explain the surgery he planned to do. "Any questions?"

"No," I said.

He handed me a consent form and I laid it on the tray table without signing it. "But you must." I shook my head no.

"You are risking your life if you don't do this." He frowned. "Don't let fear influence your decision."

I started to sob without restraint. The surgeon scurried out of the room and sent in a nurse. The nurse stood at the doorway. She looked at me and then at the door. "Would you like to talk with a chaplain?" she said.

I shrugged. "Sure." I had used all the skimpy tissues in the box by my bedside and was mopping up tears with the bed sheets when the chaplain arrived.

After he introduced himself, I said, "Got any tissues so I can blow my nose?" He left and returned in a minute with several boxes.

"Tell me why you're crying," he said, pulling up a chair to sit beside the bed.

"I've abandoned my parents and my partner too," I began. "The doctors say I must have surgery." I blew my nose. "Surgery," I continued, "that's a really big decision for someone like me with no clotting. I'll have to have infusions until the incisions heal. If I do get a colostomy, I will have to come back for a second surgery and more infusions of clotting factor."

I blew my nose one more time and then took a deep breath. "I don't know if I am just reacting out of stubbornness. I don't know what to do." My speech was rapid fire—bang, bang, bang.

There was silence for a few seconds. "You can trust yourself to make the right decision." His voice was soft and calm.

"No," I said, "I can't. I don't know what the right decision is anymore."

"Pray or meditate and you will find that you do," he advised.

When the chaplain left, I still did not know if I should sign the consent form for surgery. Yet I no longer believed the decision was urgent. I relaxed and as my panic dispersed, I could think more clearly. I considered waiting until the antibiotics began to work.

Each morning for the next few days I sat cross-legged on the bed, lowering my eyes and paying attention to my breathing. When I opened my eyes after my morning meditation, I would see the surgeon standing at the doorway staring at me. I would smile at him and shake my head no. Then he would walk away. "Why is that surgeon haunting me each day?" I asked one of the nurses.

"He's a very skilled surgeon, and he's at the stage in his career when he has become bored by the routine operations. You're a challenge for him."

"Well, he's not going to take a scalpel to me just to make his life more interesting."

My hematologist came in daily to repeat his opinion, which did not change. I could see him becoming more frustrated as I became more confident.

The nurse came regularly to check the access to the IV line. Now at fifty years of age my veins were not only spidery, they were scarred. The nurse's best option was to stick a vein on the back of my hand or the edge of a thumb. Every few days the site would inflame or swell and the nurse would have to find another spot to stick.

By day five a breakfast tray of clear fat-free broth, gelatin, and black coffee was set in front of me. I savored every sip. I got out of bed several times each day and paced up and down the hall, pushing my IV pole beside me. I walked to regain muscle strength. I walked to release some of the anxiety. I walked so I could pass the final test and move my bowels. Day seven my breakfast tray held soft, solid food. I rejoiced. Grateful for the chaplain's advice, I plopped a spoonful of jelly onto cream of rice cereal and savored the boiled egg.

The morning I was due to be released, I dressed in the clean clothes Robin had brought me. She had only been able to visit me infrequently, and when she had, I worried about her driving two hours in the icy winter nights. I watched the weather reports on the television and cautioned her not to travel when snow was predicted. She ended our telephone conversations with, "I love you."

Robin was on her way to take me home. Because I wasn't wearing a robe and slippers when I walked down the hall, the nurses didn't recognize me.

My hematologist breezed out of the elevator door with his lab coat flapping. He stood beside me, "We have to talk… somewhere private." Then he guided me to a conference room and asked me to sit down. He stared at his hands for a few seconds. When he raised his eyes to look at me, he said, "I'm so sorry. You contracted hepatitis C from all the blood products we gave you this time."

I shrugged. All I cared about at that moment was getting home.

His face showed annoyance that I wasn't taking this seriously enough. He tried again. "Linda, you probably only have fifteen years to live."

# The Consequences of Forgetting

Not long after the doctor told me I had hepatitis C, I remembered the odd symptoms that I had in 1974. I guessed it was the onset of the virus, almost thirty years ago. They didn't know about hepatitis C at that time. Why no one had bothered to test me again was a mystery to me. Now that I knew I had hepatitis C, I believed it was a waste of time to give it much thought. What happened was beyond my control.

We now had four parents to watch over and no siblings to help. By summertime, Robin began making regular trips to Connecticut to check on her parents. I often went with her. The house was so cluttered with boxes, bags, old magazines, and artificial flowers that it was hazardous just to walk the maze without tripping or toppling a heavy pile. Five cats lived in the tiny house along with one large dog. The stench of cat urine permeated the air. Neither of Robin's parents seemed to notice.

Thelma sat in her lounge chair watching television. If we asked what she wanted to eat, she said she wanted a muffin. She got up only to walk awkwardly to the bathroom or to go to bed. Donald did the best he could to keep her clean and fed. It wasn't easy, since Thelma was becoming increasingly angry with anyone who tried to help her. There was very little we could do for them as long as they were still living in the house. Each time we visited, we sneaked some of their junk into the trunk of our car, taking it to a donation center on the way home or dumping it in with our trash.

Robin went with her parents to a doctor's appointment. Thelma had been given a brain scan and the doctor slipped the results of the scan surreptitiously under his desk and into Robin's hand. She glanced at the image and could readily recognize the portions of her mother's brain that had already atrophied. The doctor spoke gently, reassuring Don and Thelma that although there was no cure he would prescribe a medication that might slow the progress of the dementia. He fixed his eyes on Robin and said, "If I were you, I would make an appointment with a lawyer who can draw up the papers for a health care proxy as soon as possible."

The next week Robin and I went to the attorney's office with her parents. Thelma managed to scribble on the lines marked signature. Her fluid elegant script was barely legible now, but the lawyer said it was sufficient. While the secretary was out of the room making multiple copies for Robin and her father, the attorney looked Robin in the eyes. "You'll need to use Medicaid one day, so there are some things you want to do in advance."

Don looked stunned. Like my parents he had never given any thought to the need for long-term nursing care. There would not be enough money to pay for this care without Medicaid.

"What do I need to do?" Don mumbled.

"Trade in your car and buy a new one. You won't have another chance. Put your daughter's name on all of your bank accounts."

Then the lawyer turned to Robin. "Start applying to nursing homes now. Most have long waiting lists. Also, prepay for your parents' funerals from their accounts."

Donald's mouth dropped open.

"I hope to move them both closer to us," Robin replied. "I'll start researching senior housing for my father and nursing homes for my mother near our home."

# *Flapping Fish*

Doctors had made false statements about my life expectancy before. It frightened me less now. I believed I had already survived more than twenty-five years after the hepatitis C virus had entered my system. I brushed aside my hematologist's prediction that I would die in fifteen years. However, like swatting a fly from my dinner plate, the anxiety kept coming back, distracting me. I wondered if this time the doctor was right.

My parents were both healthier and happier than they had been two years earlier, while my physical condition had deteriorated in that time. The fatigue clung like a creeping vine entangling my actions and thoughts. My body was not keeping up with the plan.

In early March I received a call from the Department of Public Health. The woman on the phone said she was verifying that I had hepatitis C. "The state is documenting the number of cases," she explained.

I was startled by the unexpected call. My jaw clenched as I answered, "Yes, that's true." As I put the telephone down, I realized I was shaking. If hepatitis C was being tracked by the state, that meant it was a serious threat to public health.

I had not yet told my parents about the hepatitis C diagnosis. Luckily for me, they were not by the phone when I answered the woman's questions.

Unnerved by the invasion of privacy, surprised the state had my name on a list, I said to Robin, "Perhaps I should learn more about hepatitis C."

Even though I worked in a library, I did my research after I got home, eking out time between caring for my parents and Robin's parents. Truthfully it was not just a matter of limited time; anxiety prevented me from being more methodical in my investigation. The task made my heart beat quicker. Remembering the osprey we had watched in Maine, how it had seized the flapping fish in its claws, and how the fish struggled to survive, I felt a kinship with that doomed fish.

I learned from the Liver Foundation website that there was a scheduled public information forum not far from our home. On a chilly spring evening, Robin went with me to a program on the latest treatment for hepatitis C. We drove forty-five minutes through the back roads in the dark listening to the shrill of spring peepers. Frozen earth was becoming mud.

I shivered as we walked from the parking lot to the education wing of the medical school. Following the maze of signs, we found the correct room. The white walls reflected the stark glare of fluorescent lights. The doctor was setting up a slide projector at the back of the room. His face was hard to see since he was tall and had to stoop to insert the slides. He didn't glance at the people who passed by him.

A few folks were already seated. Others continued to straggle in until there were about fifteen people in the seats, which had been set out in two rows facing the blank white screen. I tried not to stare, but the woman sitting not far from me had stringy hair and wild eyes. She looked to me like she had been, or perhaps still was, a heroin addict. Some people looked healthy, while others had sallow skin and dark circles around their eyes.

Emotionless, the doctor wasted no words. He continued to stand behind all of us at the slide projector even though he held a remote control for advancing the slides. He briefly introduced himself, turned off the lights, and started his carousel slide projector. Click, a slide fell down before the light bulb and appeared on the screen.

"This is a picture of a healthy liver." He described the features of a healthy liver. Click. "And this is a slide of a cirrhotic liver. This part of the liver is essentially dead. The liver has enlarged to compensate. If you have hepatitis C, you will get cirrhosis." Click. "This is a photo of a liver that has cancer. If you get cirrhosis, you will get liver cancer. Then you will die."

My mouth felt dry. I swallowed and looked around in hope of finding something to drink. The other faces of people in the room were blank. I can't be the only one holding back a scream.

The doctor went on. "There is a treatment. It has about a fifty percent cure rate." Then he passed out flyers with more information on pegylated interferon given in combination with Ribavirin. "The treatment uses two medicines that work better together than alone," he explained. "One of the medications is a pill and one must be injected weekly. Patients have to continue to take the two medications for twelve months."

He ended with, "There are some possible side effects with any medication. Suicidal depression, nausea, and extreme fatigue are some of the common side effects. It can cause heart failure if you have a heart condition. But it is your only chance. There are no more cures in the foreseeable future."

I looked at Robin. She looked as overwhelmed as I did. I heard people around us squirming in their chairs. This was a lot to take in all at once—death by liver cancer. Perhaps a cure, perhaps not, disturbing side effects, and the implied pressure that a decision must be made before it was too late.

When the doctor asked for questions, no one in the room spoke. The doctor handed around a sign-up sheet for people to give their information if they were willing to begin treatment. I tucked the brochures into my purse and turned to Robin. "Let's go," I said. "I'm overwhelmed."

As Robin and I left the medical school classroom and walked across the parking lot, images from the slide show of livers flashed in my memory. On the drive home neither of us said anything for several minutes. Finally I said, "What do you think?"

"I don't know," she said.

My mother was in bed, but still awake when we got home. Dad was watching television and gave us a wave as we headed up the stairs to our bedroom. We had gotten into the habit of lowering our voices when we were upstairs. Although my father would never hear us, my mother's ears were sharp. We sat up in bed, since there was no other place to sit on the second floor. I spread the pamphlets out and we began reading.

I took a breath. "Maybe I will be one of the lucky people and I'll have only mild fatigue or loss of appetite. I think I could live through almost anything if it was just a year. I don't want to die now. It would crush my parents and leave you to care for four elders by yourself. It's a fifty-fifty chance, but if the medication is effective, I will be cured." I stared out the window at the moonless dark. "Can I really do weekly injections with my bleeding disorder?"

Robin squeezed my hand. "He said it was your only chance."

"My parents need our care, your parents need our care, and our jobs...Don't we have enough to deal with already?" I whispered. "It will put an even larger burden on you."

Robin shrugged. "We'll work it out, we always do. You should try it. Don't worry."

Grateful for her support, I agreed.

"The first thing I need to do is talk with another doctor, maybe the gastroenterologist I saw when I was in the hospital. I'll call my hematologist tomorrow and ask him to make the referral."

# *Zigzag*

T he hematologist was clear. "This isn't a good treatment for you, but if you want another opinion, I'll ask the gastroenterologist to meet with you."

In a few weeks I sat in the gastroenterologist's office facing her stiff smile. She leaned forward in her chair before I had finished speaking, shaking her head side to side.

"I've read a lot about the treatment and I've decided to try it," I said.

She snapped, "No responsible doctor would allow a patient with a bleeding disorder like yours to do this treatment. It could be deadly for you. I've already spoken to your hematologist and he agrees."

How dare the two doctors make a decision without first talking with me. "But it's my only chance," I pleaded.

"Well, there is a world-famous liver specialist right here in Boston. You can make an appointment with him, but I will tell you right now, he won't agree to treat you either."

Shocked as if by a bolt of electricity, her uncompromising reaction left me breathless. It had taken me a while to get free of my rock-hard denial, but there was no crawling back under that rock now. My parents depended on me. I had promised to take care of them for the rest of their lives. I could not succumb to a fatal virus if there was any chance of a cure.

It was July before I could get an appointment with the famous liver specialist. I was worried that this second doctor would refuse to treat me. I must find a way to convince him that I need this treatment, no matter what. Fear clouded my ability to listen and to think. I did not want to face this alone. I asked Robin to go with me and take notes.

The waiting room was crowded. Robin found two chairs in a corner and waited while I checked in. From behind a glass screen, the receptionist ticked off my name on the computer, and then in a robotic tone of voice she said, "Go to that phone on the table over there and give the person who answers your name, your date of birth, insurance information, and credit card number." It could not have been less friendly or impersonal. I was just a cog in their money machine.

Sitting down beside Robin, I could think of nothing to say. Nervously I flipped through a magazine. We did not wait long before my name was called. I entered the assembly line with Robin. In the first room a nurse asked questions about my history, in the second room an assistant took my vital signs, the third room had a medical student. He asked a different set of questions than the nurse and walked us into a fourth room, saying, "The doctor will be with you in a few minutes."

In the fourth room Robin and I had just sat down when a man entered. His rumpled, white lab coat would no longer button across his bulging stomach. He seemed distracted by the extravagant lunch that was being delivered to his staff lounge, compliments of one of the pharmaceutical companies. The delicious aroma filled the hall.

"I've looked at your lab results," he said as he shuffled papers and glanced at me. "Your viral load is very high. We must start your treatment immediately. Schedule an appointment to come back to see me in a few weeks." Then he tossed the pile of reports on his desk and said a dismissive, "Good day."

"That was surprising," I said to Robin as we drove back to our home. "Wait until I tell my hematologist that this so-called world specialist says I should do the treatment." At last we were making progress.

It was time to tell my parents. I told them as little as possible in an attempt to minimize their fears and reassure them that things would work out fine. I wished I could believe that was true.

At my second appointment with the world-famous gastroenterologist, he surprised me again. Without a word of explanation, he said, "I can't treat you. It's impossible."

"You said it was urgent," I sputtered. "What happened?"

"Well, I talked with your hematologist. He was very convincing," he said. "He told me it was too risky for you."

"You said I had to do this right away!" I could hear the shrill panic in my voice as I glanced at Robin. She had been writing on a notepad, as she had done during the first appointment. "You can't drop me now."

There were several seconds when I stared at him. The doctor glanced at Robin, pen in hand. When he met my eyes, he faltered. "I suppose if you can pass a stress test for your heart, then I will proceed as planned."

He doesn't get it. I don't have a heart problem. I have a bleeding problem. "If this would assure you, I would be happy to do the stress test," I said.

Before the stress test I walked every night after supper. Down the hill to the park, then around two blocks and up the hill. My heart pounded, my breathing became more rapid, but each day it became easier.

The results of the stress test concluded that my heart was strong. Victory did not last long, however. I was in my office at work when the phone rang. "Your doctor is on line two," announced the employee who was transferring the call. How out of the ordinary for him to call me at work.

After I punched the button for the phone line and said, "Hello," I heard my hematologist's voice.

"I won't let you do this treatment," he sputtered as if I was a disobedient child. "I don't care that the stress test was normal. You can't do this."

He was the doctor who had stopped giving me any blood products when HIV was still an unsolved mystery. When I fell and landed on one knee, I was shocked in 1980 when he said, "Go to bed and put ice on it. Until we figure out what is lethal in the blood supply, I won't infuse you." I didn't argue with him then, and later I credited him with saving my life. This time was different.

"I have no other option," I responded. Tears of exasperation poured down my cheeks. I stretched the phone cord to reach the door and turn the lock. The last thing I needed was for an employee to enter my office now. I had kept all my private life trials to myself.

"I've jumped over a lot of barriers. It's my life and my body. Why don't you understand that I need to do this?" By now I was blowing my nose loudly into the phone and choking on my own tears. "I am going to do this treatment with or without your approval," I said.

"All right," he sighed. "But I am going to order the medications for you and I will need you in here every month for blood tests. Just to be clear, this doesn't mean I approve."

On September 11, 2001, my parents sat in front of the television watching the World Trade Center crumble and collapse. When I got home from work that night, they could not find the words to express the horror that the images had left in their minds.

At church that evening Robin held a special service. People talked about how the world would never be secure again. I had difficulty remembering if there had been a time when the world seemed safe to me.

When the doctor prescribed the pegylated interferon and Ribavirin treatments, I believed I had won a battle. In order for the treatment to succeed, it needed to be a year before it would conclude. It would be twelve months before I knew if I had won the war.

Some people reported having only mild side effects from the treatment while others were so disabled they ended treatment prematurely. It was impossible to know how my body would tolerate the medication. I believed I could do this. I had to.

I scheduled an appointment with the nurse who would train me on administering the weekly injections. "The injections do not go into a vein or a muscle," the nurse explained. "They are injected subcutaneously, just under the skin." Then she told me it would take some time for them to process the required health insurance request. "We will schedule you to start treatment in mid-January 2002."

# Hapless Holiday

We had Christmas with Robin's parents and mine for years. I had come to dread the day as Robin's mother, Thelma, became increasingly sour-faced and disagreeable. We had all tried to live up to Thelma's expectations of Christmas, which revolved around the presents. It was never enough for her, not the gifts she received or the gratitude for ones she had given.

Four years ago, after the dinner dishes were washed and put away, we played a game of cards. My father rarely won. When he did, he reacted like a happy child. Jokingly he said, "It's not luck. It's scientific discarding."

Thelma threw the deck of cards on the table. "You cheated."

I watched my dad's smile dissolve into confusion. I was furious at Thelma's accusation and said so.

Thelma abruptly turned to her husband, "Come on, Don, we're leaving." They picked up their belongings and were out the door in minutes. After that, Thelma and her daughter had not seen each other until the day when Robin drove her father to the hospital. Now that we knew she had Alzheimer's, it no longer seemed that her rage was about a lost game of pinochle.

On Christmas Day 2001, Robin's parents were on their way to our house. The sparks of nervous energy between Robin and me had ignited my parents' apprehension. What we all wanted was a peaceful family Christmas. Early in the morning, Robin had removed the gizzards and prepared the stuffing for the turkey. She went upstairs to wrap the gifts she had for her parents and me. The aroma of the turkey roasting in the oven filled every corner of the house as I went downstairs to the kitchen to peel and chop vegetables.

As I entered the kitchen, I froze at the sight of my mother teetering on a step stool and reaching for a serving bowl on the top shelf. My mother, shaking from her Parkinson's disease, fragile as a twig from her osteoporosis, turned and said, "Good morning."

Without thinking, I shrieked, "What do you think you're doing? Get down off that stool now! You will be the death of me." The sound of my voice echoed back. What a horrible thing to say. In my mind I saw myself at four years old, standing on the kitchen counter stretching on tiptoe and reaching up to the top shelf where I knew my mother kept the cookies. When she caught me that day, she probably yelled those words at me.

Mom carefully climbed down, setting the glass bowl on the counter. As if she expected me to thank her, she said, "Don't worry so much, I'm fine." I looked down at her bent and shrunken form. Her white hair sparkled in the sunlight from the window. She smiled with a victorious grin. She was fiercely proud. I had not realized before that she was as defiant as I. Despite myself I smiled at this revelation.

When Mom left the kitchen, I quietly picked up the stool and carried it to the basement, stashing it behind the washing machine.

At ten o'clock, I heard Robin call out, "They're here. I just saw them parking the car in front of the house."

Robin and I went to the sunroom to open our front door. We saw her father, Donald, walking up the steps and her mother behind him, her right foot on the first stair. Helpless we watched as Robin's mother lost her balance, fell back, and landed hard on the paved walkway. Thelma screamed.

"It's all your fault, Don." She glared at Robin's father. Because there was no snow or ice on the walkway, there was nothing else for her to blame. "Get me up!"

Robin and I squeezed our way past Don, who seemed locked in place. Robin's mother was on the ground moaning and barking orders at all of us. "Get me up, you idiots. Just help me get up!"

I looked at Robin. She looked appalled. Thelma had gained weight in the past few years. Somehow the three of us managed to get her to her feet. She was gripping her right arm, accusing us all of being clumsy, thoughtless, and incompetent.

"Just get me inside," she said between her gritted teeth. She had covered up a lot of pain in her lifetime. Raised in an abusive foster home, she had learned to hide her brokenness. This, however, was more than she could bear. Her face betrayed her, agony written in lines across her brow.

"I think we should have you checked out in the emergency room first," Robin said, "just to make sure nothing is broken."

Robin and her father assisted Thelma into the front seat of Robin's car as I went inside to report to my parents. Robin needed me. I did not have the attachment that would cloud Robin's ability to ask the probing questions. I knew how to demand that proper attention to Thelma be given without insulting them. I had long ago understood the unwritten rules of hospitals. If you didn't know the right questions to ask, you would not get the information you needed. If you did not know the correct person to talk with, then you would not receive the best medical care.

"We're taking Thelma to the emergency room," I said putting on my coat and grabbing Robin's. "I don't know how long it will take."

"Of course, dear. We'll be fine here," Mom said.

Reluctant to leave, I hoped my parents would not get into any difficulty when left on their own. I was glad that dinner would not be ready for at least two hours. I decided to drive my own car since I wanted the freedom to go back and forth between home and hospital. The hospital was only two miles from our house, and it would take minutes for me to go check on my parents.

Christmas morning was slow in the ER. They quickly got Thelma settled on a stretcher. It took forty-five minutes, however, before a doctor came to take her history and examine her. He ordered x-rays and some pain medication. It was eleven-thirty when I left Robin and her father to sit with Thelma while I went back home.

My parents were in the sunroom watching for my return. Mom had put the vegetables I had left on the countertop in saucepans. Thinking that I had time enough to serve them their dinner, I said, "I'll cook the vegetables now and take out the turkey from the oven. I'm sure Thelma will be in the ER for a while longer."

My parents nodded soulfully. We had all been through this sudden change in plans. Usually I was the one injured. Mom and Dad stared blankly back at me. I had seen that helpless look on their faces many times.

I set the dinner for my parents on the table. Before I filled my plate, I realized that I should call the ER to find out what was happening. "May I speak with the charge nurse?" I said to the person who answered the telephone.

When the nurse came on the phone, she said, "The doctor is with them now, giving his report. We'll be releasing her soon."

"Releasing her?" I better get back there quickly. I kissed my parents.

"But dear," my mother said, "you haven't eaten yet."

"No time now, Mom. Eat without me." We would have to drive Robin's parents back to Connecticut. There was no choice if the hospital would not keep her overnight. Don couldn't handle Thelma alone. If Robin drove with them in her father's car, she would have no way of getting back home. As I hurried to put on my coat, I said, "I doubt that I'll get back before supper. Can you manage here?"

"Of course, dear," Mom said. She looked dazed. "Drive carefully."

The peaceful family Christmas had shattered like a broken glass ornament. We might not have too many Christmases together left. Regret and sadness prevented me from looking back. I knew my parents would be standing at the window watching me drive my car away.

By the time I reached the hospital, the nurse was in the hallway explaining to Robin. "The arm is broken. We can't put her in a cast. All we can do is put her in a sling and send her home with some pain medication. I've ordered a wheelchair to take her to the car, and the aide will help you get her in."

Robin turned to me and sputtered what I had already realized. "I guess we have to drive them back to their home in Connecticut. Can you take my mother in your car? It's easier for her to get into. I'll drive my father in his car."

The aide pushed and pulled Thelma's hefty, limp body into the car, as if the nurse had whispered, "Make sure she leaves the hospital no matter what it takes." Robin fastened her confused, drugged mother into a seatbelt as I put the key in the ignition. Robin's mother babbled incoherently until I turned on the car radio. She began singing along to one standard Christmas carol after another.

By the time we reached the highway I glanced at her. She was sliding downward in the seat, like jelly on a hot day. I gasped. There was nothing I could do. Still under the seatbelt, her back was now halfway down the seat, her knees buckled and short legs stretched as far as they could go below the glove compartment. She was singing, "Rudolf the Red-Nosed Reindeer had a very shiny nose…"

The singing only magnified the sadness of my parents eating their Christmas dinner alone. I had moved them away from their own home and their old friends, and now I was not there to celebrate Christmas with them.

We arrived at Robin's parents' house at four o'clock. The sun was already going down. The temperature had dropped below freezing. Thelma's pain medications had worn off. With Robin and me encouraging and gently prodding, we lifted Thelma back up to a sitting position and out of the car. We walked slowly to their front door, Robin and I on each side of Thelma, Don in front so that he could unlock the door. When we reached the cement step in front of the door, Thelma looked at the step for a few seconds. Then much to our surprise, she sat down, collapsing just in front of the step. Don turned with horror in his eyes. Robin sat on the cold cement wedging her own leg underneath her mother's body in an attempt to protect her.

"Get me up," Thelma began to wail.

Don stepped toward us. I had seen enough. This was it. None of us could handle this, and it would be foolish to try.

I looked at Don. "Go in the house and call an ambulance," I said firmly.

He hesitated. "But—" he started to protest. He was used to taking orders only from Thelma.

"No," I shook my head, "we can't bring her inside. She's forgotten how to walk up steps. Call an ambulance."

It was obvious to me and to Robin that Don would not be able to handle Thelma by himself even if we could get her inside. He had been able to care for her when her memory loss had made it impossible for her to care for herself. This disaster had tipped the scale. He looked at me in defeat, too exhausted to argue, and turned and walked inside the house.

"The ambulance is on the way," he said. Slumped over with fatigue, he looked hopeless.

Minutes passed. We all shivered. Finally we heard the siren in the distance getting louder. For the second time that day, we entered an emergency room. We waited, huddled in a corner. No one came to check on Thelma. Eventually a nurse came to the waiting room. "The doctor is on the phone. She will speak to you now."

"Hello?" Robin said, baffled by the doctor calling on the telephone, rather than speaking to her in person.

"What do you want me to do?" the doctor said. "I have no reason to keep her here. She'll have to go home."

"She's not going home," Robin argued. "I won't take her. My elderly father cannot take care of her with a broken arm and her Alzheimer's. He is already overloaded with her care. They live two hours away from me. I can't help them with their daily needs. If you won't see her, I'll call her primary care doctor and let him know that she is here."

The primary care doctor agreed readily. "Don't worry. I'll order some tests and go see her tomorrow."

We left the hospital. We dropped Robin's father at his house at seven that evening.

"I can fix my own food," he told Robin.

When we said good-bye, Donald was standing in his kitchen, looking forsaken.

Tired, hungry, and worried about all four of our parents, we drove toward the interstate. We would not be home until nine. It had not been a merry Christmas for any of us.

# Falling Apart

Thelma's doctor ordered enough tests to keep her in the hospital for three days. Then she was admitted to a nursing home. Robin increased her visits to her parents in Connecticut, checking in on her mother and then going to the house. Encouraging her father to discard the clutter, which had accumulated over the past few years, Robin made regular trips to the town dump before coming home.

Two weeks before I was scheduled to begin the hepatitis treatment, I awoke at six in the morning from the hall light flicking on, off, on, off. Mom was trying to get my attention. With Parkinson's disease, her voice was too soft to be heard from a distance. She could no longer climb the stairs. It took me a few seconds to come awake and realize that she must urgently need my help.

I raced down the stairs from my bedroom to the first floor before dawn that cold January morning. As I wondered how my arthritic ankles and knees could allow me to move this quickly, my right leg missed the last step and my foot hit the floor. The impact was hard. I ignored the sound of a bone in my ankle snapping. The pain jolted like lightning up my leg, but I hardly noticed. Lying on the floor, Dad appeared dazed. My mother looked frantic.

"Don't move, Dad," I ordered.

"I'm fine," he said, sounding confused. "I must have fallen out of bed."

"No," Mom said turning to face me. "He stood up and then fell."

I limped to the kitchen phone and dialed the doctor. The on-call physician asked me several questions. Just as I was answering them, Dad wandered into the kitchen and asked Mom to fix him breakfast.

"Whatever it was," said the doctor on the line, "if he is good enough to walk and ask for breakfast, I don't need to see him."

As I let the relief seep in, I began to sense the full force of my ankle pain.

I picked up the phone again, this time to call my own doctor. "I think I broke my ankle," I told my hematologist.

"Impossible," he said. "You'd be in much more pain if you had. Come in and we'll do an x-ray."

Robin carried my clothes downstairs for me and helped me get dressed. She found the plastic boot-cast in the back of the closet. I had worn it several years before when I sprained my ankle. Then I called one of the private caregivers to come over and check on my parents later that morning.

The orthopedist shook his head looking at the x-ray film. "You broke it all right. The fracture is a crack that runs from the ankle toward the fibula. We've got to stop it from crawling up any higher."

"What about starting the interferon injections in two weeks?" I asked.

"There's no reason for you not to, as long as you keep the foot in the boot-cast night and day. Stay in bed except to go to the bathroom. I'll order you crutches. Don't put any weight on that leg until you come back for another x-ray in six weeks."

"I can't," I stammered. "My parents live with us, and I can't make it up and down stairs with a crutch without injuring my elbows and shoulders."

"I don't want you to use the stairs for six weeks anyway," he said. "I'll order you a Canadian crutch. They have hand grips. That'll take the weight off your shoulders and elbows."

It was noon when I got back home. The only way to take care of myself was to move my parents out of our house. I picked up the telephone and called the newly constructed assisted living center in our town. It was just a few blocks from our house, and they had only been open for a few years. They were not filled to capacity."

"We'd love to have your parents stay with us for as long as it takes for you to recover," the woman said. "We have a furnished room available now."

The cost seemed outrageous. There were added charges that were not covered by the basic monthly fee. My parents' small savings would be depleted in less than two years. There was no choice, however. At least they would be safe while I healed.

By later that same day, Robin and one of the home health aides packed my parents' belongings and settled them into their new housing at the assisted living center. I lay on what had been my mother's bed. My wish to care for my parents at home had come crashing down when my leg missed that last step. Defeated by my vulnerability, I kissed them good-bye when they were ready to leave.

"We'll be fine," Mom said giving my hand a squeeze. "I'll call you when we get settled in."

The house was oddly quiet. It had been three years since I been able to get rest. I wanted nothing more than to hibernate like a black bear for the next six weeks until my ankle healed. I pulled the covers up, submerging myself into the darkness.

The only way I could communicate with my parents was over the telephone. Within a day or two my mother burbled on the telephone, "I'm taking tai chi and going to lectures and trying to keep your father from eating too many cookies at the afternoon teas. We go out for our morning walk to the pond, when the weather is good enough. Everyone is so nice here."

"Really?" I said. I wasn't surprised that my mother enjoyed the socialization and stimulation. "How's Dad?"

"You know him. He's happy if he has a book to read."

What I knew was that he was happy as long as he had her navigating.

Mom said, "We're better off having some independence."

A van transported residents to their medical appointments and a local grocery store. The van also took regular field trips. Dad enthusiastically told me that they had all gotten into the van one day and gone to a local bookstore. In spite of their enthusiasm, I could not shake off my guilt.

As scheduled, I began dutifully taking the medication. The Ribavirin was a pill, but the interferon had to be injected into the skin once a week. The only suitable place I could reach was my thigh. Each injection left a four-inch, inflamed red blotch. It wasn't a bruise, but a reaction to the interferon. In a few weeks I began to grimace at the thought of using this same area for another injection.

The worst side effects from the interferon were in the three or four days after the injection. I would just begin to get back a bit of strength when I was due for another dose. I was relieved that my parents could not see me now. It was agony watching Robin struggle to cook, clean, grocery shop, visit my parents, and keep tabs on her parents, while still working.

"Can I fix you anything to eat?" she would say as she put a frozen dinner in the oven for herself.

Nauseated, I said, "No, thanks." I sucked on another hard candy and considered it my dinner.

At the end of six weeks, Robin drove me to Boston to have the ankle x-rayed again. The orthopedic surgeon stared at the plastic black and gray images of my ankle. "It's healed well. Now you need physical therapy so you can gently begin to put weight back on that foot. I'll write up the orders."

Three days each week the therapist drove to our house. She stood beside me as I gently began to put a little weight on the injured leg. I was still wearing the boot-cast and using crutches. Each week the exercises increased my ability to bear weight on the leg. Anemic from the Ribavirin, it seemed to take the effort of an Olympic champion to stay focused and complete each set of daily exercises.

The hematologist demanded I come in for blood tests once a month. Robin drove me to his office, where I had learned to anticipate the doctor's frown. Each visit he asked if I was ready to stop. Each visit I said, "Not yet."

By the time I could walk without the crutches, I was ready to sleep in my own bed.

"Do you want your parents to move back here now?" Robin asked as I climbed up the stairs for the first time in ten weeks.

"No," I said with a firmness that startled me. "I can't do it. I'll call about returning the rented hospital bed." I had sacrificed my health for their happiness and comfort. Whether they were truly happier being more independent or whether they were just saying that to relieve my guilt, it didn't matter. I needed to take care of myself or I would surely die before they did.

# *Everything Changes*

When I was able to drive again, I began to visit my parents regularly. It seemed to me that my father should have a birthday party. He was going to be ninety in March. I alerted relatives and secured a private dining room in the assisted living facility for the celebration. When the cake was put in front of him, Dad repeated over and over, "I'm ninety years old. I'm an old man!" His eyes were wide and questioning. He shook his head from side to side.

"Yes," the family and friends around the table agreed. There was no denying it.

Dad didn't seem happy to have lived nine decades, just surprised.

I was astonished that I was still alive too. I awoke in the morning drained of energy before the day began. I gave myself the injections of interferon each Friday, so that by Tuesday I could make it into work. The side effects of nausea and fatigue worsened, as the course of treatment progressed.

In a daze, I was exhausted physically and emotionally. My sense of smell was overly sensitive; household-cleaning products made me wretch. Lozenges had no effect on the incessant dry cough. The annoying headache became my constant companion.

Each time I showered, I watched the swirl of hair from my scalp cluster around my toes and rinse down the drain. I avoided mirrors that would remind me of how exhausted I looked.

The doctor prescribed a medication for my nausea and suggested that I put the canned supplement in a blender with ice to make it easier to swallow. I could actually drink it without gagging, but I lacked a desire to eat. I sipped it down with no enjoyment. Until that time I had used food to cheer me up. Now I simply ate to keep from starving. Soon my clothes were loose and baggy.

Sick as I felt, I had to continue working. If I didn't show up, I would lose my health insurance. I dragged myself to work four days each week, sitting at my desk accomplishing little. It was misery. I was unable to focus on the job. I continued to argue with the doctor after he looked at each month's test results and tried again to persuade me to stop.

At the assisted living center, Mom collapsed at the breakfast table one morning. They put her in an ambulance and called me. I rushed to the emergency room. She was alert and flushed. It took forty-five minutes to get her in an exam room. When her vital signs were taken, they told me she had an elevated blood pressure. In the next six weeks she had several similar incidents, and each time I dropped what I was doing and raced to the hospital only to be told that her blood pressure was extremely high.

"The assisted living isn't a nursing home," the director informed me. "If someone requires medical attention, we call an ambulance."

"What about the nurse you told me was on duty?"

"She just distributes the medications," was the curt reply.

I sighed. I expected the nurse should at least take a resident's blood pressure and notify a resident's primary care physician if it spiked. The frequent ambulance trips to the emergency room were a strain on my mother, my father, and me.

In July, my doctor put his fist down hard on his desk. "I can't allow you to continue. Your platelets are at a dangerously low level. If you had an emergency, I would not be able to save your life."

"Have I gone through this for nothing?" I moaned. I knew that for the treatment to be effective I needed to continue it for twelve months. It had been only six, but it had seemed like an eternity.

My hematologist was done with listening to me. "No more. I can't allow you to continue, end of discussion. Go get your final labs drawn and go home."

I was too weak to protest anymore. I believed myself doomed to certain death. I had broken my promise to myself, and my promise to my parents. My career was in jeopardy due to my illnesses. I had led Robin down a bottomless well of caregiving. In a daze, I was exhausted.

Late in the afternoon, I walked down the empty hallway to the lab. No one was in the waiting room, but I heard a rustle of paper coming from an office down the hall. I waited. In a few minutes a young man came walking out of the office. He looked startled to see one more patient waiting.

"Come in," he said.

"I'm really a hard stick," I said. "I've been stuck so many times in the last six months it will be difficult for you to find a vein."

"Do not worry," he said in what sounded like a Jamaican patois. "I am an expert at this."

I've heard that one before. To my amazement he put on the tourniquet, effortlessly stuck me on the first try, and filled the vile with a sample of my blood.

"Wow," I said. "You really are an expert!"

His laugh was deep and resonant. He winked. "I tell you now. I lied. This was my first time."

I walked down the hallway toward the elevator shaking my head. Had he lied the first time or the second? I would never know. He had spun my head around. To have an unexpected success at the end of a prolonged failure amused me. Lighten up, I said to myself. Then I thought about the forty pounds I had lost and the hair that had filled my brush and comb and decided grimly that I had already done that.

# Picking Up the Pieces

When I looked into the mirror, I saw my pale face still had deep, gray circles below my eyes. It would take time to bring my red blood cell count up, and until it did, I was anemic. My platelets were at an all-time low. I covered up bruises that appeared on my arms and legs with clothing as best I could, given the hot weather of summer. With a force that surprised me, the depression I had kept at bay for the past six months hit me full force. I sank into a hole of emptiness, not wanting to get out of bed in the morning, not caring if I lived or died. The only thing that stood between me and suicide was the thought of what that would do to Robin. At Robin's urging, I called a psychologist and made an appointment.

"You need some antidepressant medication," she told me. "I have a colleague who can write a prescription for you."

Within an hour after taking the first pill, I rushed into the bathroom retching. I vomited the antidepressants into the toilet bowl, tossed the bottle of pills in, and flushed. When I told Robin what I had done, I said, "I'd feel better if I could just eat my favorite comfort foods again." Weary to my core I wanted to get into bed and stay under the sheets forever.

"Of course I'm depressed," I told Robin. "My attempt to cure the hepatitis C failed spectacularly."

"I'm worried about you," she said.

I wanted to withdraw from the world around me. Instead I hobbled back to work and resumed my job. We could not live on Robin's salary alone.

I also wanted to visit my parents more frequently, now that I was no longer treating the hepatitis C and making routine visits to my hematologist. There was no time to be sorry for myself, so I struggled to keep going.

By the end of June, I had used all my paid leave for the previous fiscal year. However, effective July 1, I had a new bank of vacation time and medical leave available. Instead of taking time off for vacation, I increased my visits to my parents. Mom seemed to sense my depression.

She tried to console me with happy stories of their days in assisted living. "Every morning when it isn't raining, we walk to the town pond."

I was pleased they were able to resume walking together. However, in order to get to the pond, they had to cross a busy street. I shuddered each time I saw one of the other residents of the center riding his wheelchair. Since there were no curb cuts on the sidewalk, he operated his chair as if it was a bicycle traveling on the street, hugging the curb. He seemed unaware of the vehicles dodging or coming to an abrupt stop just feet away from hitting him.

"We've made friends here. We eat all of our meals in the dining room," Mom said. "We were interviewed this afternoon. The article about us will be in this week's newsletter." She sounded pleased. "I'm going to pick up some extra copies at the front desk when it comes out. Maybe we'll mail them to some of our friends."

Dad chimed in, "Yes, I showed the woman the ship's log I kept when I was in the navy. She was mighty impressed." The log was one of the few things that he had kept in the move from their Springfield home. During the Second World War Dad saw both the Atlantic Ocean and the Pacific. It had been a long time since I saw my father looking proud.

Even though they had van transportation to medical appointments, if there were recommendations from the doctor or changes in medication, I wanted to hear them firsthand. I took time off from work to drive them myself. Control might be slipping away, still I could not let go entirely.

Mom surprised me one day when she asked the neurologist, "I've heard that some Parkinson's patients have hallucinations. Should I expect that?"

Calmly he replied, "You might have some hallucinations eventually, but Parkinson's patients usually see things that are friendly, not frightening."

This seemed somehow to relax my mother who leaned back in her chair and nodded. I wondered if she had started to see things already that she doubted were real. I flashed back to a snowy day when my parents were still living with us. Mom had insisted she had seen a snowy owl sitting on a tree branch.

"There's no owl out there," Robin said, but Mom insisted there was. At the time I thought it was my mother's failing eyesight. Perhaps it had really been a hallucination.

My father didn't need hallucinations to delight in the imaginary. He still took comfort in fantasy, often preferring it to reality. Driving my father to a doctor's appointment one day, Dad glanced up at a Victorian-style building in the center of town. Dad shook his head and said, "Hogwarts."

"What?"

"Hogwarts," he said pointing to the building, as if I had not heard him.

Relieved that he didn't call me a Muggle, I smiled. At least he still believes in magic. I wished that I could.

During this time Robin was visiting her parents in Connecticut weekly. Since his retirement, Don had been working at a local burger restaurant. He arrived at his station on the grill at five in the morning several days each week. It had been a welcome escape from the house when Thelma's memory problems increased and she became angrier. He relished mentoring the young cooks and servers who called him "Dad."

With Thelma now in a nursing home, Robin's father conceded that he could no longer take care of the elderly dog himself. Don took the dog to be euthanized. After that he decided the cats would have the same fate. They had never adjusted to being pets and had remained semiferal. Thelma had found them behind shopping malls or in the woods and brought them meowing and scratching indoors. The five cats had long ago shifted to spaces in closets and rarely came out except to eat. Few had adapted to using a litter box. The smell of cat urine invaded every room of the house.

"I need to get started on finding senior housing for my father," Robin said. "I've already put my mother's name on wait lists for two nursing homes. There's no telling when she might make it to the top of the list."

The director of the senior housing in our town told Robin, "It will be ten years before we could offer your father an apartment. Doesn't matter that you live here. He lives in Connecticut. We need to take care of town residents first."

"He's eighty-four years old now. That won't work," Robin said.

Robin and I went to two nearby towns to look at their senior housing apartments. We picked up the application forms at each office.

Robin completed as much as she could, and then we drove to Connecticut to get her father to fill in the gaps and sign each form. When that was done, Robin suggested, "Let's go visit Mom together."

Donald hesitated. "All right, I guess."

Thelma recognized us when we came in her room. She could no longer find words to describe her thoughts or emotions. She didn't know where she was or why. There were eight wings to the facility, and Thelma was in a wing with other residents with dementia. The doors had alarms that went off at the slightest touch. Thelma was considered an escape risk. She wore an ankle bracelet, which would set off an alarm if she tried to go out one of the doors. A red welt appeared under the bracelet where it had irritated her skin. The nursing aides had done nothing to ease the discomfort.

"This place feels like a prison," Robin whispered under her breath. "There seems to be no personal attention, no compassion, and my mother looks so lost. I sure hope we can get her out of here and close to us soon."

Donald was eager to leave quickly, and there seemed to be little we could do if we stayed longer. We said our good-byes to Thelma and returned to the house to continue to sort through the clutter that still overwhelmed each room.

Boxes and plastic bags filled rooms, closets, and the two-car garage. We never knew what might be in a bag or box. We discovered that a trash bag might hold yarn, or old purses, or plastic flowers. It was a distressful legacy for Thelma to leave for her daughter.

# Slip Sliding Away

On a Wednesday afternoon in early August 2002, I was at work when I picked up a memo from Town Hall. I stared at it in my hand. I could see the printed letters on the piece of paper clearly, but I had no idea what the letters meant. For some odd reason the words were beyond my comprehension. They might as well have been written in another language.

I carried the memo to the assistant director and sheepishly asked her to tell me what the memo said. She looked at me with concern, and then she read the memo aloud to me.

Wandering back to my office I decided to telephone my hematologist to report that I had lost my ability to read.

"It doesn't sound too serious to me," he said.

Thursday I prepared to return to work despite the building headache. Probably just tension. I was angry that the board of trustees accused the assistant director of making errors. Believing the accusations to be unfounded, my anger spiked. She doesn't deserve this. The trustees should be praising her for doing a fabulous job while I was too sick to get to work. I was sure my blood pressure was rising.

By afternoon the reverberating pain in my head motivated me to call the doctor again. "Call me if it gets worse," he said.

On Friday morning, I stood in front of my closet. What am I doing here? Oh yes, trying to pick out clothes to wear. What am I doing here? Clothes. The repetitive question and answer in my head sounded like a skip in a record, when music played from a disc on a turntable. Round and round my only thoughts were, What am I doing here? Need to get dressed. Go to work.

The meeting to discuss the future of the English-as-a-second-language program was scheduled for that morning. I believed I had to be there to support the program.

As I drove to work, the streetlights hurt my eyes. I squinted attempting to focus. I gripped the steering wheel and was grateful that I lived less than two miles from the library. What is wrong with me? When I pulled into a parking space in the staff lot, I wondered if I would be capable of backing my car out at the end of the day.

At lunch a friend called, "I'm next door at a church meeting with Robin. She said you have a bad headache. Would you like me to come over and do some Reiki?"

"Could you come over and drive me home?"

Sounding surprised, she said, "Of course."

It was late afternoon before Robin came home. I called the doctor again. By that time my hematologist had left for the day. "Do you think it could be a migraine?" I asked the on-call physician.

"I'll call the pharmacy and order some medication for you," he said.

I lay in bed until morning, not able to sleep. By the next morning the throbbing had become pounding, like noise blaring in my ear. When I reached for the phone, I couldn't remember how to use it. I asked Robin to dial the number for me. This time the on-call doctor responded, "Get to the hospital."

By then, it was Saturday. Robin drove. Like a deflating balloon, I collapsed in the front seat. Robin clicked the seatbelt across my chest. I kept my head down and eyelids closed tight against the brutal light.

The risk of having a bleed in my brain had terrified me for most of my adult life. Once I began to meet other people who had no fibrinogen, I realized it was common for one of us to have an intracranial hemorrhage. Still, when it happened to me at age fifty-three, I did not recognize it. Since my blood does not form a clot, I didn't bleed faster than other people. From a cut or a scrape, bleeding would begin slowly like a leak in a faucet, but it would not stop.

It was an hour's drive to the hospital in Boston. Robin drove while our dog Penny lay in the backseat napping.

Robin drove to the hospital entrance. She flagged an assistant who brought out a wheelchair. As Robin parked in a shady spot and walked Penny, the aide pushed me down the long hallway to the observation unit. Regina, a nurse who had frequently cared for me when I needed an infusion, took one look at me and asked, "Do you know where you are?"

I tried to figure out what Regina had just asked me. Regina paged the IV nurse to respond stat. By the time Robin settled Penny in the car and made her way to my side, Regina had also paged my hematologist for instructions. "Her doctor has a wedding to go to today, but he would kill me if I didn't let him know," she told Robin.

When the doctor returned the page, Regina reported, we're shipping you to the hospital that specializes in neurosurgery. An ambulance will take you there. It was impossible for me to grasp what she was saying, but I sensed her urgency and saw the terror in Robin's eyes.

I had no sense of time. From inside the ambulance the siren seemed to be coming from far away. The wail annoyed me. Can't somebody make it stop?

As they rolled the stretcher into the hospital, I had the sensation of being a helium balloon set free to drift in and out of rooms and hallways. The walls were glass, and faces floated into my view and asked me questions: "Do you know what day it is?" "Do you know who the current president is?"

I wondered silently why I would care about either of these.

My hematologist's face came into my view. Relief engulfed me.

"You've had an intracranial hemorrhage. I told you it was dangerous for your platelets to drop so low from the interferon treatments," he said. Then he softened, "The MRI results look good. You probably won't need surgery. I expect you to make at least a ninety percent recovery."

I nodded not sure of what he meant, unable to find words to respond.

He went on, "I don't have privileges in this hospital, but I have friends on staff and I'll keep in touch through them."

I have no idea how long I was in the recovery room. I was unaware of people coming and going into the room or the infusions that were given. When urgent voices talked about failed attempts to start a new IV line, I tuned in momentarily and then drifted out of consciousness again.

By the time I was well enough to be moved to a semiprivate room on the surgical floor, I was fully conscious. I understood what people were saying to me, but I was unable to remember how to speak. I took stock of the damage to my body. A large tube was inserted into the right side of my groin leading to my femoral artery. I examined the other bandages and scars created by the IV technicians and interns. Collateral damage. Now I wanted to get out of the line of fire. I wanted to go home.

Years ago I had learned that the first step to release from the hospital is to get up and walk. I looked over the bandages and tubing and decided that, even if I could not talk, I might be able to take a stroll. A new patient was admitted to the bed opposite my own. She had just come out of the recovery room and was still groggy. Her fiancé was holding her hand and speaking softly to her in Spanish. She looked abandoned when he left.

I was relieved that she didn't speak English because neither did I at that time. We used body language and pointing to communicate, and we both seemed to understand each other well. By the next day, she was strong enough to walk with me. Arm in arm down the hospital hallway we shuffled. By the third walk of the day, I was uttering "trees" and "birds" as we gazed out the dayroom window. She was repeating each word in English and both of us were smiling at our little victories. When she went home, another woman was put in the room with me.

When the menu for the following day was distributed each morning, I requested a serving of chocolate mousse at each lunch and dinner. I would have ordered it for breakfast if it had been an option. I could not get enough of it to satisfy my sweet tooth.

The doctor had promised me that I would be released before the Labor Day weekend. After checking the lab results on Friday, however, he decided that it would be safer if I had one more infusion of clotting factor early the next week. My disappointment was profound.

I had a long cry before I telephoned Robin. "I'm desperate to get out of here," I said.

"Perhaps it's for the best if you stay a few more days." I was instantly furious. Doesn't she want me home as much as I want to go home?

On Saturday, I announced to my roommate that I wanted to shampoo my hair. At least that would help to cheer me up and make this extended hospitalization bearable. Since entering the hospital two weeks before, my hair had compacted into a greasy mass that smelled like a wet dog. It was a holiday weekend, and the nursing staff was sparse. I knew that they would not be able to help me or even notice what I was doing.

When taking a sponge bath, I had been warned not to get the bandages that were over the line in the femoral artery wet. I knew I could not stand under the shower or the water would run down my torso and over my thighs. Carefully I maneuvered the plastic chair in the walk-in shower to the outermost edge. This was challenging because I was also dragging the IV pole with me. I wanted to wet my hair, but not my body. I arranged the shampoo where I could reach it easily and placed as many extra towels as I could find on another chair just outside the shower. I had to leave the shower door open so that the IV pole would be in a dry place.

Smugly I undressed, sat in the shower chair, and covered my bandaged leg with a plastic bag. I tilted my head back and turned on the water. I was lost in the sheer bliss of suds, giving myself a scalp massage when I realized that the water had poured out of the open shower door and was now flooding the hospital room. I left the reverie of my spa, turned off the water flow, toweled off, and shuffled my way back to bed while pushing my IV pole through the puddles. My legs and bandages were dry.

"Steroid head," muttered my hematologist, when he learned what I had done. It was true. My unquenchable hunger for sweets, my volatile emotions, and my driving need to keep active were all side effects of the corticosteroids.

Tuesday morning, I paced the hallway waiting until noon before the last infusion was set up to run. With that complete, the catheter inserted into my femoral artery could be removed. This procedure required a doctor. The resident physician was paged. I waited impatiently for him to arrive. When he struggled to peel away the layers of tape covering the wound, his movements were awkward and tentative. I tried not to react when he commented that it was more difficult than usual because the tubing had been improperly inserted.

With help I managed to get dressed, and by late afternoon that day, I was back home. Sitting at our dining room table, I turned to Robin and asked, "Pass me the hippopotamus."

"The what?" Robin looked worried.

I pointed, "You know, that yellow thing."

"You mean the banana?" Her eyebrows lifted up. The look I saw in her eyes was fear. In the thirty years we had lived together, she had seen me recover from many injuries, but nothing quite like this.

At my follow-up appointment with the neurologist he said, "Your symptoms were atypical. We couldn't find anything in the journals about patients with a fibrinogen deficiency who had a hemorrhagic stroke. "

"Then you didn't look very hard," I scoffed. "There are several documented cases already." He had no idea he was dealing with a woman who had been in communication for years online with approximately a dozen people who also had little or no fibrinogen.

He stared at the file on his desk and shuffled his papers. "I expect what you are going to get back in brain function will occur in the next year," he mumbled.

Although most of my language had returned, there were gaps when I tried to come up with certain words, especially numbers and the names of people, common objects, days of the week, and months in the year. I still could not decode printed words. The next week I began going to a speech therapist, putting names to line drawings of fruit and common objects three days each week. The printed words took longer to decode than the drawings. I realized that it would be a long time before I could work again. My sick leave and vacation time were completely used up.

As I was considering my options, the town offered an early retirement deal to employees who were at the top of the pay scale. Awed by the serendipity of this offer at a time when I needed it desperately, I asked Robin to pick up the application and help me complete the paperwork for Town Hall.

"There are two options," Robin explained from the directions for filling out the retirement forms. "You can take more money each month and leave nothing to your beneficiary, or you can take less money and the remainder of your retirement funds will go to the person you name."

"I'll take less money now. I don't expect to live that long and I want you to have the benefit," I said quickly.

"Nope," she said, "I think you should take the larger amount. You should be able to do whatever you want no matter how long you live. Anyway, I'm betting you will live longer than predicted."

We argued back and forth briefly before I gave in.

Robin dropped the completed application off to Town Hall. Within a week I retired. I was fifty-three years of age. My income would drop radically, but I could still hang on to my health insurance. First, I could get the sleep my body craved. As soon as I was able, I could visit my parents often. I would have more time to help Robin with her parents.

The woman who had been the assistant librarian was again made acting library director while I had been hospitalized. When she called me to see how I was, she said, "Of course we will be planning a retirement party for you. So many people will want to be at that party. I'll invite everyone you have worked with."

After thirty years as a librarian I had worked for three public libraries and the state library agency. I had been active in professional organizations, spoken at conferences, and facilitated planning workshops.

I requested that they postpone my retirement party until December when I hoped to be stronger.

"Is there anything special you want at your party?" the children's librarian asked when she dropped by my house with a large potted azalea.

"Yes," I said, "I'd like everyone to wear a name tag because I'm afraid I will not be able to remember the names of some of my colleagues."

# *Fractured*

The hemorrhagic stroke had not affected my ability to move my arms or legs. I soon slipped into the role of homemaking, grocery shopping, cleaning the house, and cooking meals. Grateful to be active and busy, I was relieved to be useful again.

In early October, I went to church one Sunday morning. After the service I lingered while talking to friends. It was almost noon when I turned the key on our back door. I could hear the telephone ringing. My fingers fumbled. These days, that meant bad news more often than good. As I feared, it was the assisted living center.

"Thank goodness I reached you. Your mother is in the emergency room at the hospital," the voice said.

"What happened?" I asked, guilt sitting heavy on my chest. I should have come home earlier. They needed me and I was not here.

"Your mother fell. The aide tried to help her up but she couldn't stand, so we called the ambulance. We've been trying to reach you to let you know."

I hung up the phone and slammed the back door behind me. The priority now was for me to get to the hospital.

Entering the hospital emergency room, I glanced behind the nurses' station. Listed by room number, last names were written on a whiteboard with the patient's room number. Asking no one's permission, I walked straight to room number four.

Mom was picking at bits of food from the lunch tray. When she saw me, her face relaxed with a smile.

"I'm fine," she said. "I fell, then your father fell too, trying to help me up. We had a good laugh as we lay on the floor. Neither of us could reach the emergency cord on the wall."

It didn't seem funny to me.

She was struggling to get a spoonful of applesauce in her mouth. Her hand shook and I wondered if she had taken her Parkinson's medications that morning. "Can I help you with that?"

"The doctor is coming back after he reads the x-ray," she said.

"When did you fall?" I asked as I scooped up a spoonful of applesauce for her.

"We were getting ready to go to breakfast."

"You mean to tell me that you and Dad missed breakfast and no one noticed or came to check on you until three hours later?"

"The housekeeper came to make up the beds about eleven. She found us."

What good is assisted living if they don't notice when two people who are always at breakfast together don't show up? I knew better than to say this out loud. Mom didn't need my anger or frustration now. She needed me to get that spoonful of applesauce into her mouth.

When the doctor arrived, he said, "You're lucky. No broken hip. You can go any time you want."

Mom looked at me with her I-told-you-so face. I helped her get dressed and rolled her walker over to the bed. She winced when she took a few steps. The nurse offered to take her in a wheelchair to the front door while I pulled up the car.

"Good idea," I said before Mom could decline the offer.

Back in the assisted living center, Dad was sitting in his recliner. His forehead was creased. He didn't even have a book in his hands. Had he been staring out the window brooding? He looked unsteady when he rose to greet us. He must be hurting from lying on the floor for so long. He leaned down to kiss mother gently on the top of her head.

Mom looked exhausted. I got her a glass of water and her morning pills, then settled her in bed. "I hope the pain pills the nurse gave you help. Try to get some rest," I said as I kissed her good-bye.

At the door, I looked back to see my father picking up one of his books. Now that she was back, I knew my father would be snoring in the recliner before I walked to my car.

Two hours later my phone rang again. "Your mother's back in the hospital. The ambulance just left."

Dashing into her room in the ER, I saw Mom could not hide the pain this time. It was displayed in the tightness of her face.

"I got up to go to the bathroom and fell again," she said looking confused. This time Dad had pulled the cord hanging on the wall to get help.

"The hip is broken," the doctor said when he came into the room. "It probably cracked when she fell the first time. Now it's fractured."

I was angry with the doctor and furious at myself for not recognizing that a woman almost ninety with osteoporosis could fall and not break a bone. I did the best I could to compose myself.

"We can operate and replace the hip. There's some risks with surgery for people your age," the doctor said to Mom. "But I don't think you want to live with this pain."

Mom did not appear to be listening to the possibility of stroke or heart failure. She patted my extended hand, saying, "Do the operation."

The surgery took hours. I paced the hall waiting to hear news. I imagined my father alone and worrying. When the doctor came to talk with me, he said he was pleased with the results. The anesthesia was wearing off slowly. She had been given a bed and I went to see her there.

Caressing her forehead, I pulled a chair close to her bedside so I could hold her hand.

Her eyes searched mine for answers. She whispered, "You always seem to know what I need. How do you know so much?"

"Don't try to talk, Mom."

Of course I knew. A single event had disrupted my life so often that catastrophe was one of the few things I could come to depend upon. Only compassion could make it better.

Within minutes, Mom closed her eyes and drifted off to sleep.

I sat beside her bed, sniffling, and then rose quietly to go see my father.

"In a few days," the doctor said, "she'll go to a rehabilitation center to learn to walk again."

I remembered Logan's warning when he was keeping watch on them in their own home: "If you fall, you will break a hip. If you break a hip, you will go to a nursing home." She was going to rehabilitation. That sounded more optimistic than a nursing home.

My father insisted on visiting her every day when Mom was in the hospital and after when she was transported to the rehab center. I picked him up and drove him to the facility, bringing him back to the assisted living center after an hour. He looked like a lost puppy whenever she was not by his side.

"You know, if your mother dies, I will have no reason to live," he told me.

He had said this before many times. It brought a lump of sorrow to my stomach. It might be a comfort for him, not to me though. Now I wondered if he had a suicide plan worked out, or if he thought he would die just because he wished it.

While driving my father from the assisted living center to visit Mom, we passed by my home. Dad's face showed no sign of recognition. I gripped the steering wheel tighter as I thought of how my plans to care for my parents in my home had failed. I wondered if I should offer to bring him home for a meal with Robin and me. If I did, would he recognize it as the place he had lived for three years? What had been his bedroom had been turned back into a living room. His sitting room was now a sunroom again. Momentarily I thought about offering to move him back to live with us. To reconfigure the first floor of our home would take away time from visiting my mother and transporting my father. Besides I wasn't sure I had the strength or energy it would require of me. I clung to the hope that my mother would return to the assisted living center soon, and both of my parents could be together again.

I attended the biweekly care plan meetings with the doctor and the nursing staff. Before each meeting I asked Mom if she had any questions or concerns, making notes on a scrap pad. She wouldn't ask questions herself, but I would on her behalf. My mother sat attentively at the table in her wheelchair. She was making good progress, the nurse reported. She's gaining strength.

Mom chatted with the staff, made friends with her roommate, and welcomed the visitors who came on the van from the assisted living center to see her. "Soon I'll be out of here and back with all of you," she told them.

She was using a walker, promenading daily, up and down the hallway with a physical therapist holding onto a belt tied to her waist. Her steps were slow and tentative. Not long ago they had been quick and sure.

My mother didn't seem amazed at reaching the age of ninety the way my father had been. The starkness of her birthday celebration in November was unlike the one I had given Dad the previous March. I carried in a bouquet of flowers and a freshly made strawberry shortcake. Robin, my father, and I sat around the table. I forced myself to make pleasant conversation in the small room at the end of the hall where the unused or broken wheelchairs, other assistive devices, and computers were strewn around in a jumble of metal and leather. Our out-of-tune singing made the party even more maudlin. After the joyless birthday party, Robin and I drove my father back to the assisted living center.

Dad said, "I think she's doing quite well. Don't you?"

Inhaling, I waited a few seconds trying to decide if I should give an honest answer. I opted for the answer he wanted to hear. "Yes, Dad, I do."

*Part 3*

# *All I Want for Christmas*

The week before Christmas the social worker at the rehab center called and said, "Your mother is being moved today into the permanent residence section. She has improved as much as we expect her to. Come in and sign the paperwork."

Stunned, I'd had my fill of surprises. I called the doctor and asked, "Why? They said she was in rehabilitation to learn to walk again."

"She had a stroke in surgery. A serious one," the doctor stated flatly.

Nothing about a stroke had been mentioned in the regular assessment meetings, and there was no indication that they planned to move her to the permanent wing of the facility. I knew that was the code for the nursing home section. Protest would be futile. She had stopped making improvement and the facility could no longer bill Medicare. The bottom line was written in red ink. Why now? Why the week before Christmas?

"Why can't she go back to assisted living?" I asked the social worker.

"She can't regain her ability to walk again, and she needs help just to get to the bathroom, so the assisted living center will not take her back."

That afternoon, they shifted my mother into the other wing of the facility. I went in to sign the paperwork and help move her meager belongings into her new room. She was placed in a bed beside another resident. Four residents shared the single bathroom. My mother's bed was positioned in front of the window. Mom cheerfully exclaimed when she noticed the bird feeder just outside the window. She had not comprehended what the decision to move her to long-term care meant. I did not understand that all physical therapy for Mom would cease that day.

After she was settled, I went to visit my father. He was sitting by the window waiting for me. I glanced at his hands and noticed how long his fingernails had become. My time with Mom had deprived him of my care.

"Here, Dad, let me clip those nails for you before we go see Mom."

Nail clippers in hand, I pulled up a chair beside him. Snipping the first few nails I began, "Mom has been moved today, to the permanent wing."

"Oh?" he looked confused.

I snipped two more fingernails. "I'll show you where she is now." Snip, snip.

He looked at me with his clear blue eyes and I saw tears filling his lower eyelids.

I took his other hand in mine and began to clip more nails.

Since we had moved them from their house in Springfield three years before, my father had no attachment to where he lived. All he cared about was being with his wife.

Did he leave his room at all now that he was alone? I couldn't even be sure he remembered to go down to the dining room for breakfast or dinner. His visits to Mom were the only time of the day that he seemed to come alive.

What my father wanted for Christmas was to be by his wife's side. "Would you like me to call and see if they have space in the assisted living center next door to the nursing home?"

"Yes," he said without hesitation, as I scooped up the nail clippings.

While my father was keeping my mother company, I walked across the parking lot to check out the small assisted living building. It had no dining room, no activities, not even a common room. People who lived here were expected to walk next door to the nursing home if they wanted these amenities. They had several vacant single rooms and there was no waiting list.

The day before Christmas Eve, Robin and I packed up my father's belongings and moved him. Each time we had moved him, his belongings had to be reduced as his living space diminished. Items he found familiar disappeared. I stacked three of his favorite books on the end table beside his recliner. His chair was all we could squeeze into the room. He would no longer have a private bathroom where he could leave his toothbrush or towels. He didn't seem able to pay attention when I showed him where the showers were. I wondered if anyone would help him find the correct hallway to the bathroom. He asked only which door he would go out to visit Mom. He would no longer have to wait for one of us to pick him up and drive him to the nursing home. That was all he cared about.

Robin and I ate Christmas dinner in the nursing home dining room. Don drove up from Connecticut to join us. We tried to keep smiling, but our hearts were filled with sadness at the losses we had faced in 2002.

Each morning, Dad trudged across the parking lot through the snow and ice from his room in assisted living to the nursing home. In his puffy thermal coat and gray wool fedora, and carrying his cane, he arrived by Mom's side in time to have breakfast with her.

He sat by her whether she was in bed or sitting in her wheelchair. Mostly they spent their time together in silence, but when my mother requested it, Dad would read aloud or describe the birds he saw at the feeder outside the window.

When I arrived in the afternoon, Dad had already been there for hours. He went to the events in the program room with Mom and read the newspaper when she needed a rest. He ate his lunch and dinner with her. Mom persuaded him to leave before sundown, and he did so reluctantly, returning to his single room to sleep.

On a bitter cold February morning I arrived at the nursing home. When I sat down, Mom blurted out, "Your father left here last night in the blizzard and forgot his coat, hat, and gloves."

Dad was sitting next to her holding her hand. "It wasn't so bad," he said.

Mom shook her head. "It was freezing out there. What if you fell in a snowdrift?"

My father shrugged. I jumped to my feet and went straight to the director's office. "How could the staff let a ninety-year-old man leave in a snowstorm without a coat or hat?"

"We were understaffed that day due to the storm," he said. Then he turned back to look at the reports on his desk avoiding eye contact with me.

"Did anyone at the assisted living center notice him when he came in covered in snow? Did anyone help him into a warm shower or guide him to bed?"

"I have no idea," the director muttered.

He looked annoyed.

"This isn't assisted living. This is neglect." I turned my back on him and left his office, not expecting a reply." There was none.

When I started my car to go home, I sobbed.

I went to visit my mother in the nursing home almost daily. My mother, determined to do what she could for herself, used her feet to move her wheelchair. Together we strolled down the hallway. None of us wanted to talk in her room where the foul-mouthed roommate would eavesdrop and interject her insults.

We stopped at the billboard, which posted the menu for the week and the activities scheduled.

"I go to everything," my mother said, "except the manicure days." Mom had never used nail polish. "I get my haircut at the salon here once a month and so does your father."

Mom told me about her day. "I had a shower this morning. They get me in with a lift. It's exhausting. After that I went back to bed and had a nap until it was lunch time."

Searching for a way to keep the conversation going, I said, "What did you have for lunch?"

"I chose the tuna sandwich. I didn't want the cheese."

"What did you do after lunch?" I said in an attempt to sound sincerely interested.

"This afternoon they had a musician in the dayroom. She was pretty good."

These were the only things in her day. It made me deeply sad. Mother still seemed to enjoy what was left in her life, and my father enjoyed being with her. It was not what I had hoped to provide for them. I decided that having them where I could see them every day had to be enough. As difficult as it was for me to witness, I would be with them to the end.

On a recommendation from a friend, I visited my mother at different times of the day and evening. By making my visits unpredictable, I got to know the staff on different shifts. I became aware that staff decreased significantly in the evening hours and increased in the mornings and afternoons, except on Saturday and Sunday.

Each day held another unpleasant surprise. My parents' primary care doctor did not have privileges in the nursing home. Furthermore, like the assisted living center, they shipped any patient in physical distress off to the hospital emergency ward. Mom's blood pressure continued to be erratic. I believed that she was having transient ischemic attacks, yet no doctor made a diagnosis. From our house, I would hear the ambulance siren just a few minutes before our home telephone rang. "We just sent your mother to the hospital," the voice would say. I pulled on a coat and ran for the car, arriving so quickly that she was often still on the stretcher in the hallway.

Sometimes it was more than an hour while I stood holding her hand. By the time a nurse came to take Mom's vital signs, my mother was already more coherent and the symptoms were beginning to disappear. Then an ambulance would transport her back to the nursing home. Dad was sitting beside her empty bed each time. Too worried about her to eat, he sat silently with his hands folded in his lap, staring out the window. When Mom was rolled into the room, his face would break into a smile.

I wondered what awful things my mother's roommate had been saying to Dad while we were out of the room. Each time my father walked into the room, the woman in the next bed began a running monologue of insults: "That's the ugliest man I've ever seen." She seemed to get some perverse satisfaction by calling him stupid or nasty. My father either didn't hear her or pretended not to, but my mother could hear her and her jaw would tighten.

I spoke with the director and requested that my mother be moved to another room. The director refused. "We can't let people choose their own rooms. It would be chaos."

I wanted to tell the director that the institution was already disorganized, inadequately staffed, and poorly managed. It was apparent, however, that arguing would get me nowhere.

Many of the staff came from Brazil. English was their second language, and they too had been victims of insults. They gave my mother special attention whenever they had a free moment. Mom asked that they teach her a few words in their native tongue and they were delighted. One day I dropped in to see my mother who greeted me with, "Bom dia!"

When spring arrived, one of these nursing assistants planted a vegetable garden behind the nursing home. Glowing with appreciation, mother told me, "Gloria took me out in my wheelchair to her garden. She gets here every day before work to weed and water. She gives the cook here some of what she grows and takes the rest home for her children." It must have reminded my mother of the squash and tomatoes she had grown in her own vegetable garden patch.

Children were still very much on my mother's mind. She loved to see them in the common room when they came to the nursing home to visit their grandparents. When she began telling me about a little boy named Willy who came to visit his grandmother and liked to play tricks, I wondered why I had never seen this child on my visits to Mom. The next time she told me about Willy, she said, "I saw Willy again last night. He likes to hide under my bed."

I remembered the neurologist talking to my mother about pleasant hallucinations. Willy was a comfort for her almost every evening after my father left her bedside. I chose not to tell her that he wasn't real. If he gave my mother a smile, it didn't matter to me.

# Now We Are Six

Robin's father, Donald, continued to work, making breakfast at the fast-food restaurant. Some days he would go to see Thelma by himself. Often he would wait for us to arrive. He did not like to see the faces of people he thought of as old.

During the summer, Robin completed the applications for senior housing for her father and a nursing home for her mother nearby to us. We waited to see which one of them would move first.

Every time Robin visited her parents, she continued to empty the house of junk. Her parents' mattresses were on the floor in their bedroom. Robin stepped carefully around the beds and clutter as she cleaned out the dressers and closets. She discovered dollar bills not only hidden in purses and clothing, but also tucked into the back of drawers. After she found five dollars in one spot and ten dollars in another, she began to check more carefully.

Thelma had squirreled away the cash for years. Robin stopped at her father's bank at the end of each foray, depositing the found money into his account. In all she found over $3,000 from her mother's hiding places.

Donald was accepted to senior housing just a few miles from our home at the end of the summer. Once he was relocated with some of the furniture and his personal belongings, Robin arranged for a resale company to pick up and carry away the remaining items. Thelma had filled the kitchen with Styrofoam coffee cups from fast-food restaurants. She had strewn boxes of new or used small appliances, artificial flowers, holiday ornaments, and bric-a-brac over every floor in every room of the house. Piles drifted like dunes, making it impossible to vacuum any carpet.

Five undomesticated cats competing for space had made a disaster area under the mounds of bags and boxes. The hardwood floors in the living room were stained. Don agreed to hire a company to strip the floors and coat them with fresh polyurethane. Soon there was a "For Sale" sign on the front lawn.

When the house was sold, I drove with Robin to the signing. Unlike my parents, Don and Thelma had lived in several homes during the past fifty years. They had stayed in one house for a few years until Thelma had become dissatisfied, or Don changed his job. Their moves had become so frequent that Robin finally refused to go home to help them on moving day. The signing was just a business transaction for him.

What Don would miss the most was not his house but the young people at the fast-food restaurant who called him Dad. He had loved their stories of school, advising them on matters of the heart, and rejoicing at their graduations or engagements. When he told them he would be leaving to live near his daughter, they awarded him a plaque, holding a picture of him in his working clothes, inscribed with "Employee of the Century."

Even after he moved to be closer to us, Don continued to drive to Connecticut to visit "my other kids." He would stop in at the fast-food restaurant to have a hamburger and returning with news of who was now engaged to be married and who would be graduating from high school in the spring.

Don made an easy transition to senior housing. He was able to do his own grocery shopping and laundry. We had him over at least once a week for dinner. The rest of the week, he heated a frozen dinner in the microwave. Robin selected new doctors for her father and went to the initial appointments. Six years younger than my parents, Don's health was excellent.

When the weather was warm, we would find him sunning himself in a lawn chair, chatting with one of the neighbors.

Two months after Don moved, a nursing home just down the street from his apartment notified Robin they had a space available for her mother. Robin went to finalize the paperwork. From the exterior it was a large Victorian house, once a single-family home. Inside, the rooms were small and cramped. When Robin saw the space that would be her mother's room, she panicked. It had five beds stuffed into what must have been a back porch.

Robin exclaimed, "I can't put my mother in this place. She spent the first seven years of her life in an orphanage—a place she hated more than the abusive foster home where she spent the next nine years of her childhood. She'll think she is back there again."

What looked horrible to Robin, however, suited Thelma fine. Her bed was in a room with four other residents, not far from the side door and the dining room. The five women were all in various stages of dementia and responded to one another as old long-lost friends. The staff treated the residents as if they would their own family members.

Thelma seemed cheerful and relaxed whenever we visited her. It was sad for us to see her unable to remember much, but she smiled when we came to visit. Often we only held her hand in silence or nodded in agreement when she babbled nonsense.

In the autumn Robin got a call from the senior housing manager. "I'm just calling to let you know your father fell on his way back from the laundry room. He's okay. Nothing major."

"It was just a little fall," Don insisted when she called him. "I tripped on a piece of the walkway that had heaved up from the frost last winter. One of my neighbors got me up on my feet again. He was a blabbermouth to tell the manager about it. I don't need anything more than a few aspirin."

"You mean the manager didn't know you fell?"

Robin drove to Donald's apartment with some aspirin. Then she stormed into the manager's office to lodge her complaint about the walkway that needed repair.

"This is just an apartment complex for seniors," the manager responded. "We don't have a big budget."

"Don't you see this is a safety issue?"

"There's nothing I can do about it," the manager replied.

Exasperated, Robin left. Now that all four of our parents were in need of assistance, they (and we) were at the mercy of institutions.

# To Everything There Is a Season

At the nursing home on March 15, Mom and I were the only ones to mark Dad's ninety-first birthday by sharing a meal in the dining room. There was nothing special about the meal, no cake with candles, no presents, no wishes. All of Dad's wishes had been used up. The genie's bottle was empty.

Dirty snow piles still sat frozen solid around the parking lot. I worried about how beaten-down Dad looked by the bitter cold he encountered walking back and forth to visit Mom. When he was a younger man, he would go out after work each day in March, to chip away at the piles of snow and distribute them onto the black asphalt of the driveway. Then he stood back and puffed on his pipe as the piles of snow shrank into puddles. This year the spring equinox brought no relief. It was late in April before the buds on tree branches began to appear.

At sundown Wednesday, May 14, I walked with my father back to his room. "I got a jury notice, Dad," I said. "I won't be visiting you and Mom tomorrow."

He didn't respond. He used a cane instead of the walking stick he had taken on his many hikes through woodland trails. Prior to my mother's admission to the nursing home, he had been walking three miles each day. For months now his only exercise was the few hundred feet from his room in assisted living to my mother's bedside. His legs were stiff from sitting most of the day.

The bareness of his room—a bed, end table, and closet— looked like a cell in a monastery. "I don't know where I am anymore," he said. His eyes searched for something familiar and not finding anything. There was nothing to remind him of home. Three moves in four years left him bewildered and morose. For the first time in his life he couldn't make sense of his surroundings.

I kissed him gently on his cheek. "Good-night, Dad. I hope I don't get chosen. If I do, it may be a few days before I see you again."

Dad nodded and stared at the floor.

The next morning, I reported to the county courthouse. Opening my knitting bag, I sat in the waiting room where others watched television or read. I gripped my needles and looped stitches with a fury. At other times in my life I would have welcomed the opportunity to serve on a jury. Now I resented the time away from my parents. A man in uniform called my name from a list. Several of us rose and followed him out of the waiting room and into the hall. "Put all of your personal belongings into one of the lockers. All purses, books, electronic devices, and that knitting too, ma'am."

"But—" I started to say. When I saw the glare he gave me, I realized I shouldn't argue.

We filed in one at a time and filled the three rows of chairs set up for jurors. Not one of us was excused. The judge, a woman at least ten years younger than I, explained we would hear a civil case brought against the city. It was a matter before the housing court.

I fidgeted in my chair, and my mind drifted back to my mother in the nursing home and my father's despair. When the judge had finished giving us instructions, she allowed us a short break, just enough time to get a cup of coffee or go to the restroom. In the hall, one of the other jurors asked people if we had been sent a jury notice before and, if so, had we asked for a deferral? One by one we answered yes on both points.

"I knew it," he exclaimed. "That's why we're here. They aren't going to let us get away this time. The best we can hope for is that this won't take long."

When I had received the first notice, I was still in the hospital recovering from the hemorrhagic stroke. They didn't care why I had asked for a delay. I was just a number that had popped up on some computer screen. I was tagged as a person who had shirked my civic duty.

When the break ended, we were led back to the jury room, walking in single file. When the first lawyer stood, detailing the way the city failed to provide residents of public housing with basic services, I shook my head sadly at the negligence.

The nursing home and the assisted living center where my parents now resided were both managed by the town. With all I had witnessed with the attitudes of the nursing home director and the lack of concern given to my father at the assisted living center, my heart was solidly with the people living in public housing. I was hardly impartial. I rolled my eyes at each accusation from the lawyer representing the tenants until the judge warned me to stop.

When we were released for a lunch break, the judge announced that we were not to leave the building. We could purchase a sandwich from the cafeteria. I went to the restroom. In the mirror, I saw my cheeks were flushed, just the way my mother's looked when her blood pressure shot up.

The following day I was back at the courthouse. At least it's Friday and I can see my parents tomorrow, I thought.

Saturday morning the telephone rang before dawn. I struggled to come awake and croak, "Hello?" into the phone.

"This is Dr. Stanley. Your father was taken by ambulance to the hospital. He was found lying on the floor this morning. He had a heart attack sometime in the middle of the night. He has massive damage to his heart. His vital organs are shutting down. He won't live more than a day or two at most."

I yanked on a pair of jeans and a turtleneck jersey and raced to the car, giving no thought to breakfast. I felt the beat of my heart thumping against my breastbone. In a daze I found the intensive care unit. Outside the doorway of each room a monitor displayed red lines on a graph registering the heart rhythm of the patient inside. An alarm went off in one room and I jumped. I took a breath, trying to prepare myself. When I reached my father's room, I entered tentatively, not knowing what to expect.

Dad was sitting up in bed watching the pieces of equipment strewn across the room. Everything blinked or beeped. I stood beside my father's bed reaching out for his hand. There was no space in the room for even a chair.

Dad greeted me saying, "I'm fine. How's your mother?" Slowly he explained, as if I didn't know, "I'm usually at the nursing home to sit with her by now. Please go visit her."

"I'll call Robin and she'll check on Mom for us and let her know why you're not with her today," I said with the calm authoritative voice my mother had often used in times of catastrophe.

I glanced at the snaking cords tangled around the small room. Tentacles attached him to the monitoring machines. I wondered if anyone had explained to him that he would not recover. I gulped back tears and couldn't force myself to blurt out the words that came to my mind. Dad, you're not fine. You're about to die. Instead I reassured him that everything was as it should be.

I understood the confusion on my father's face. Sixty years ago he had spent a few days in sickbay with meningitis when he was in the navy. He only remembered that it had earned him the luxury of fresh orange juice. He had responded as if it was a joke when others had believed him near death. He hadn't been afraid for himself. In the past few years, he had dreaded that my mother would die before him. He hadn't imagined that he would leave us first.

A nurse came in to draw a blood sample. I leaped to get out of her way and caught my foot on one of the cords, lunging toward the opposite wall. The impact of my head hitting the wall made a resounding thud.

"You hit that wall so hard with your head," said the nurse, "you should go to the emergency room and check to make sure you didn't get a concussion."

"I suppose," I hesitated, reluctant to leave my father's room. I glanced at Dad. He seemed unaware of what had just happened to me. I didn't want to alarm him. My eyes shot up to the monitor. How much time did I have before he died? How could I leave him now? This could be serious though. I gently touched my forehead. A head injury was not something I could afford to ignore. I should get an infusion of cryoprecipitate. The ER was just down the hall. They had treated me before. My records would be on file. Maybe I could get this done quickly.

"I've got to leave for a little while, Dad," I said patting him on his shoulder. "I'll be back as soon as I can."

The nurse in the ER bragged he had been a medic in the army. "I can start an IV on anyone."

I gave him a half-hearted smile.

He jammed the butterfly needle into my arm and missed the vein. I gritted my teeth and said nothing. He stabbed a second needle into my wrist and missed that vein. Sure he could get an IV started on anyone given enough tries, I thought. I'd give him one more chance and then demand another nurse. On his third try he connected with a vein on the back of my hand. The doctor on duty ordered the pretreatment of steroids and antihistamine to suppress my allergic reactions to the blood products. In two hours the infusion was completed and the doctor released me.

When I returned to my father's hospital room in intensive care, the nurse said, "Does he have a living will or a health care directive?"

"Yes," I said, thankful for her question. I was not able to think clearly. My panic was rising. The steroids I had just been given in the ER were making me jittery while the antihistamine was making me fuzzy-headed.

Within minutes Dad was removed of all entanglements, medications were discontinued, orders for further tests cancelled. He was transported to a large private room. There was a comfortable chair by the bed, and a window overlooked the city. Late afternoon light began to fade. By eight o'clock the city lights flickered on like stars. I pulled the chair in the room close to my father's bed.

"I need to go to the bathroom," he said. "Help me."

I rang the call button. It took several minutes for a nurse to appear at the doorway. "How are you doing, Mr. Wright?"

"I'm fine," Dad told the nurse. "I just need to go to the bathroom."

The nurse took out a plastic urinal from the bedside table.

"I can't do this lying down," my father said. "I need to stand up."

The nurse looked doubtful, but at my father's insistence the nurse helped him to stand up, braced him, and held the urinal in position. Nothing happened. "Just let me walk to the bathroom," Dad begged. The nurse shook his head no, then settled him back into the bed.

My father was unaware that his kidneys had shut down. He turned to me and asked, "What do we do now?"

The nurse skittered out the door.

Throughout the night I sat by his bed. At a loss for things to talk about I sang, "We Belong to a Mutual Admiration Society, My Baby and Me." I remembered walking with my father, singing this tune at the top of our lungs. Dad didn't respond to my singing. From the look on my father's face, I knew it didn't spark a memory for him.

I sank back in the chair, wishing desperately that I could help comfort him. He had sat with me when pain kept me awake all night. He read me stories and stroked my forehead. If only I had some of his favorite books with me I could read to him now.

After several minutes of silence, Dad began to recite verse. Many I had not heard him quote before. His mother had been a schoolteacher and she had instilled a love of poetry in her youngest child. He had stashed in his memory long passages from the Bible, from the plays of Shakespeare, and his favorite poems. About two o'clock in the morning Dad looked me in the eye and said, "This is just like being born."

I gasped. My father had an astonishing memory, but was it possible he could remember his own birth or was he talking metaphorically? He looked pleased to have made this discovery. Dad was approaching death with the same wonder and curiosity he had for life.

As my father turned inward, my sense of myself came clearer into my consciousness. I needed to find some energy. I couldn't recall how long it had been since I had eaten. Was my last meal the previous morning? No, I had left the house without breakfast after the telephone call. I got up from my chair and walked down the deserted hallway. There were no nurses in sight. I hunted for the little room where the hospitals I had been in kept a supply of tea bags and crackers. I had no idea where to look in this hospital and there was no one to ask.

Returning to my father's room, I saw he had managed to wriggle out of his hospital gown, and, to my amazement, he had thrown off the sheets. He looked as naked as a newborn. I could not remember ever seeing him without clothes. He had been a modest man, closing the bathroom door whenever he bathed or went to the toilet. Now his nakedness seemed appropriate. He had no shame and I had no embarrassment. His body was bloated with fluid, skin stretched taught around his torso like an overinflated balloon.

Hunger, lack of sleep, and overwhelming sorrow had depleted my reserves. I stared at his blue eyes a long time, knowing I would never see them again.

No one had suggested hospice or palliative care. I rang the call button.

"Oh, my," the nurse said when she entered and saw my father lying naked on the bed. "I'll get him back in some pajamas and change the bed linens."

I had an urge to say, "Just let him be, he's dying and if he wants to leave this world the way he came in, let him," but I didn't.

"I'm exhausted," I mumbled.

"You need to get some sleep. Go home, there really is no reason for you to stay now. I'll get him a sedative." I hesitated. She added, "We have a volunteer that will sit here while you are gone."

Soon Robin would be getting up, putting the finishing touches on her sermon, and leaving for church.

As I stood up to leave, Dad called out my mother's name. "Daisy," he pleaded. He no longer recognized me as his only child. All he wanted in the end was to hold his wife's hand one more time.

Tears streamed down my cheeks as I shuffled down the hallway to the elevator. I left the hospital and drove, thankful that home was less than a mile away. Robin was dressing for church. I gave her a kiss and collapsed into bed, sleeping fitfully for six hours.

When I awoke, I had something to eat and returned to the hospital. Dad lay unconscious, eyes closed. He was wearing clean pajamas. Under the bed linens neatly folded over him, I saw his chest rising and falling as he tried to pull oxygen into his lungs. He had not given in yet. Tears ran down my cheeks as I watched him struggle for breath.

His heart still pumped. It had pumped out love and compassion for his entire life. My father lost four loved ones, including his mother, two sisters, and a brother-in-law before his graduation from high school. He had been clear. He didn't want to endure any more grief. He had dreaded that my mother or I would die before him.

I held his hand and spoke to him softly. I told him how thankful I was that I had him as my father. Each time I had told him that when I was a child, he had not been able to accept my gratitude. He would counter my appreciation with, "I am the one who is lucky." He would not hear me then and he could not hear me now.

He was expending all of his strength in pulling in breath and letting it out. I withdrew and took up a seat beside him again. By six o'clock Robin came to encourage me to come home before dark. I spoke to the nurse and told her I was leaving and requested that she call me if there was any change.

The next morning my alarm woke me early. I called the courthouse and reported to the judge that my father was dying. She mumbled her sympathy and released me from serving out the remainder of my time on the jury.

Monday was Robin's day off. At breakfast she said, "I'll buy the groceries, then go to visit your mother. I want you to take some breaks today. Promise me you'll eat some lunch."

"Okay," I said flatly. A part of me wanted to be there beside my father all day, and a part of me wondered if there was any point to that.

I went back to the hospital, sitting in the chair beside Dad. The words I spoke aloud fell in the empty air, never reaching his ears. I stared out the window of my father's hospital room. Flowers were beginning to blossom outdoors. My father would never witness his favorite season of the year again.

At five o'clock Robin came to encourage me to go out for dinner. We left. While I was gone, Dad took his last breath. He had lived one more day than the doctor had predicted, although the last two days he lay unconscious.

"His body is still in the room," the nurse said. "Go down and see him."

There on the bed was his stiff, lifeless body. It bore little resemblance to the father I loved.

"They did a nice job cleaning him up," Robin said.

Cleaning him up from what? I didn't ask. Life is messy and apparently so is death. I told the nurse at the front desk which funeral director to contact and left to tell my mother.

# *Memorial*

The nursing home was emptied of social workers, activity directors, and visitors, as the echo of my footsteps followed me down the hallway. None of the red call-button lights above each door blinked as the residents slept. The only sounds were forced laughs on situation comedies from a few televisions left on. Some residents had trouble sleeping in the quiet darkness.

Mom sat up in bed staring out of the window at the rising moon. As I walked toward her, she didn't look surprised. She extended her hand as I sat down beside her. I took it and gently stroked her bony fingers. Her hand was no longer rough from gardening and dishwashing. Her skin, as thin and smooth as fine silk, made each knuckle visible.

She waited for me to state what she already knew.

I took a breath and exhaled, "Dad died, Mom."

Believing it would make it even more painful for her, I didn't tell her that his last words were spent calling her name in desperation. I chose to hold the secret of Dad's struggle to stay alive for three days and how before he slipped into unconsciousness he had observed moment by moment the process of dying.

We sat in silence. I felt the tremor of her hand in mine. True to her stoic nature, my mother refused to cry in my presence. Mom looked like a wilting hibiscus collapsing into itself. I had seldom seen her cry—not when I was in the hospital, not when she herself was in pain.

The rare exception was on the few visits we had made to her birthplace in Nova Scotia when I was a child. My mother would cry each time we said good-bye to her sister, Zula. She would wait though, until we were in the car and my father had started to drive away before the tears would come.

"I'll never see her again," Mom would say, blowing her nose. In fact my mother did see her elder sister many times as we visited Canada. Still, each time we departed Nova Scotia, it was my mother's belief that Zula would die before we returned. Despite my aunt's failing health, she lived to be ninety-three.

After I left my mother's bedside, perhaps she would allow herself to cry tonight. I said, "You will see him again."

"Think so?" she said, looking confused.

She had never believed in a heaven or hell, and that was not my implication. I imagined that she would sense her husband's presence for the rest of her days. In the past sixty-five years he had been with her every day and every night except for the time he had been in the navy.

Mom already had vivid dreams she confused with reality. She had startled me one day when she announced, "I had a long talk with Byron last night." Byron was the brother who had stayed at home to tend the farm until his arteries clogged and he could no longer remember enough to live alone. He had died twenty years before.

Tonight, my mother looked as vacant as the hallways outside her door. I stood up, leaned over, kissed her, and said good-night.

Back at home, I pulled out my mother's tattered address book. The telephone numbers and addresses of family members and friends were written with my mother's airy scrawl. The names that were added later showed the shaking hand of a woman with Parkinson's disease. The last entries were printed in my father's precise lettering. At least one entry on each page had been crossed out. That person had died and so their address was no longer needed.

As I flipped through the address book, I made notes. The closest family members and friends would require a telephone call. Others I could mail cards and notes to. Setting the address book down, I heard my father's voice saying, as he had often done when he kissed me good-night, "Tomorrow will be a better day." Later in his life, he changed this phrase to say it would be another day, not a better one, just another day. I put down the address book and went to bed.

By noon on Tuesday I had called a dozen people, setting off a family telephone tree. As people expressed their sorrow, I repeated, "We won't have a funeral or a memorial service. My mother doesn't want that."

Mom hated funerals. When I had brought up the subject years earlier, she announced that she wouldn't want a funeral for herself or for my father should he die before her. When I was still a child, my mother insisted that she and Dad donate their bodies to Harvard Medical School.

"I don't want you to have to spend any money for a cemetery plot or coffin," my mother proclaimed. "Harvard will pay for the transportation of our bodies and the cremation when they are done. You can put our ashes in the medical school cemetery and it won't cost a thing. Besides," she added, "we've an obligation to medical science."

Dad, I thought, would find it amusing that in death he would be going to a prestigious university. His unfulfilled desire to go to college would now be granted.

Thinking about my own wishes, I wanted some sort of memorial. If not a public one, at least one that would celebrate my father's life. I asked each friend and family member to send me a story or a memory of my father.

I could not explain the sense of detachment, the widening gap that came between my father and me when I became a teenager. He and I had walked hand in hand through the park of childhood. In my adolescence, there was nothing I could do to make him smile anymore. He sat silently at our dinner table while my mother and I chattered away. I thought he had left me, not physically but emotionally.

When I was in high school, friends of mine came to our house to talk to my father. It galled me to see Dad sitting with his pile of books beside his chair and my friend Marlene sitting cross-legged on the floor in front of him as if he were a guru. I believed he had shut me out by not including me in these conversations. Why would he not talk with me about the books he was reading or the ideas he was exploring? Resentful, I became angry with him beyond reason. I began to think of him as foolish.

Compared to my sensible mother, who reacted quickly and with confidence, he seemed slow and dim-witted. I stopped turning to him for his opinions or advice. Worse, I stopped listening to him. During the past four years I had been given a second chance. Unfortunately by then his interests had been acutely reduced.

In a few days the sympathy cards and notes from relatives and friends began to arrive in our mailbox. One at a time I opened each. His nephew's memories were of my father in his early twenties. Childhood friends of mine remembered my father in his forties. Many of my parents' newer friends sent stories of their Wednesday walks together.

Remarkable to me was the similarity of these memories. The way my father would pick up a stone from the ground and give it his full attention, his wonder for all things small, whether it was a child, a spider, or a chipmunk, had made a profound effect on many people. Some of the people who wrote had been raised in abusive families with unpredictable and unreliable parents. My father had changed their lives by his concern and respect when they had no one else who valued them.

The letters kept coming in the mail until I was overwhelmed by the number I had received. There was little difference between who my father was in his twenties, and his nineties. His beliefs were most clear from his actions. I had known and understood him far better than I imagined.

# *Clouds*

Each day following my father's death, I drove to the nursing home to sit with my mother. In an attempt to partially fill the gap my father left in her day, I increased the time I spent by her side. Following her lead, I didn't cry in her presence, but each day when I left the nursing home and got in my car, I had trouble seeing through the tears dribbling down my face.

Mom no longer used her feet to inch her wheelchair down the hallway. She lacked the energy or desire for this small bit of exercise. Our attempts at conversation were stiff and awkward. Too many unshared emotions blocked our words. Her friends from the assisted living center had stopped visiting after she had been moved to the nursing home. I assumed these ambulatory seniors did not want to consider that they might be the next ones to end their lives in this institution. Now I was her only consistent visitor, her only connection to life outside.

On warm sunny days I pushed her wheelchair to the veranda at the front door of the nursing home. That summer, big, fluffy cumulus clouds sliding across the azure sky enthralled my mother. "European clouds," Mom would say. "They look like the ones May Sarton described." Some book, I did not know which, had left a lasting impression on her. Her mind seemed to be adrift with the clouds.

Desperate for the time to mourn for the death of my father, I asked my mother one afternoon if she would mind if I left for a two-week vacation. I ached to smell salt air and watch the tide ease in and out.

"You should go," she said firmly. "I'll be fine."

One of my cousins in Canada had mentioned vacationing on Grand Manan Island off the coast of New Brunswick. It sounded like an ideal way to get some peace and relaxation. "All I want to do is sit on the beach and watch the puffins offshore." I told Robin when she asked where we should go.

Without further discussion, Robin made reservations for pet-friendly lodging. She found an ocean-front cottage on Grand Manan. She needed the time away too. Her mother was comfortable in her new nursing home. Her father still drove his own car. He could do his own grocery shopping, check on Thelma, or drive back to Connecticut for a visit.

We filled the car with our suitcases and dog food. Our first day of travel took seven hours of driving time. This didn't include the frequent stops we made for Penny. Her years of seizure medication had left her with weakened kidneys. We were all weary when we arrived at the Resort in St. Andrews. No one was playing tennis or swimming in the outdoor pool. Most guests had gone inside for dinner.

Robin pulled into a parking space and went to check in. I leashed Penny, taking her for a quick walk, then picked up a suitcase and headed to the front door when I saw Robin coming back with a key in her hand. "Take the elevator up to the third floor," she said. "Here's the key and room number. I'll be there in a minute after I collect the dog's bed and food."

Penny tugged on the leash encouraging me to get moving. I entered the lobby, turned into the alcove where I was told to look for the elevator, and pushed the button. A large dog that looked like a Labrador retriever came from nowhere, growling and lunging at Penny. Without thinking, I stepped between the attacker and Penny, who looked paralyzed. She quivered behind my legs. Penny had frequently played with dogs much larger than she, tumbling and wrestling. This dog wasn't in the mood to play.

My shouting brought a staff member who led the attacker away. By the time the elevator door opened, I was shaking. Penny was not fond of elevators, but she licked my chin when I stooped to pat her. The door closed. I pushed the button for the third floor.

When Robin came in with the dog food and the portable crate, I was on the in-house phone asking to speak with someone in management. I explained what had just happened, and the man on the phone said, "Oh, that's my dog. Did your poor little doggie get hurt?"

I didn't like his tone. "No and, luckily, neither did I."

I persisted trying to describe how we had been cornered and savagely assaulted. It had taken two humans to intervene. He gave no apology.

"How can we get out safely when our dog needs to leave?" I asked with as much condescension as I could.

"Well, my dog is never on a leash. When I'm here, he roams the grounds and people really like him. Guess you'll just have to get out when you don't see him around."

"When are you not here?" I asked.

"I'm about to leave now, but I'll be back tomorrow early."

I slammed the phone down. Incredibly lucky that I had not gotten bitten or bruised in the fray, I decided we might be better off to check out extra early the next morning.

Before sunrise we packed and scrambled to load the car. We could take our time driving to Black's Harbour where we were meeting the ferry. Penny had never been comfortable in a boat. Although she was too large for a lap dog, when we had taken whale-watching tours from Maine, she had spent the time nervously sitting on one of us with her legs trembling. The vet had given us some tranquilizer pills in case the ferry ride proved stressful. We stood by the dock waiting for the ferry to arrive on a beautiful sunny summer day. Our car was parked in a line of cars that would soon board the ferry. Penny suspected nothing. She had never been in a car, inside a ship.

Once the ferry pulled in, the passengers, both those walking off the plank and those driving off, disembarked. There was a brief wait while fresh supplies were added to the snack bar and the cleaning staff had a chance to prepare for the next trip. The metal ramp clanked and shook as we drove aboard ship. Penny began to whine.

When we entered, we were directed to park in a tight row of vehicles, including campers, trailers, and passenger cars. The air was thick with exhaust fumes and brine. Orders from the crew rebounded against the metal surfaces all around the hold. "Pull up, more, more, more! Okay, shut off your engine!"

As the cars were secured with chocks, the banging reverberated and the crew's voices grew louder to compensate. Penny trembled. We sat in the car, uttering soothing words to Penny, hopeful that the tranquilizer we had given her would work, until there was an announcement that all passengers must leave the car deck. We left Penny perched on the narrow space between the rear window and the back seats. She looked at us with her huge brown eyes as if to say, "Don't go." We gave her a last scratch behind her ears, and then we climbed the metal stairs going above deck.

Once the ship pulled away from the dock, the regular commuters to the island went directly to the snack bar to purchase beer and pretzels. I stood leaning over the deck as I had watched my father do on our many ferry rides from Bar Harbor, Maine, to Yarmouth, Nova Scotia. Dad would stand outdoors in even the most inclement weather watching the waves, seabirds, and flotsam for the entire voyage. He held that perch even on the day the ferry was rocked by a tropical storm. That day my mother and I sat inside with our feet tucked up under us and watched the cylindrical trash buckets, heavily weighted with sand, tip over and roll freely across the lounge.

I shivered and began to weep at the memory of my father and his love for the sea. A gray fog wrapped around the ship so tightly that I could see only the waves as they rippled along the edges of the ship. The deck was slippery with moisture. Now that I had allowed myself to think about my own memories of my father, my tears merged with the salty cold droplets of fog.

When Robin persuaded me to go into the snack bar in hope of a cup of tea or something more substantial than a few pretzels, we saw that every seat was taken. There was no tea and no snacks other than candy bars and potato chips. By the time we finally pulled into the port at Grand Manan, we were among the first to stand in line leading to the deck where the cars were parked.

Penny was eagerly wagging her tail when she caught sight of us coming down the metal steps. When we opened the car door, we saw that Penny had thrown up on our suitcases. There was nothing we could do but sit in the smelly car until the gate opened and we were instructed to start the engine. Robin drove onto dry land, my eyes too red and puffy from crying to see clearly.

It was not hard to find the cottage since the island was only twenty-one miles long and eleven miles wide. We assured ourselves that the fog would lift soon. Between our cottage and the Bay of Fundy was a narrow strip of grass. We cleaned the suitcases before lugging them indoors. I put away clothes and kitchen supplies while Robin took Penny for a quick walk.

The cottage door burst open. Robin held our thirty-pound dog in her arms. She kicked the door shut behind her and lowered Penny to the floor. Breathless she said, "A dog ran at Penny, teeth bared. It came right at her. The only way I could protect her from being mauled was to pick her up and yell as firmly as I could at the dog."

"Not again," I said. "Not twice in two days."

"I'm going to the office to complain," Robin said as I bent over to pet Penny.

The manager told Robin it was a neighbor's dog, let out to roam as it pleased. "There's nothing I can do about it," he said, shrugging.

The fog was getting thicker, encasing us into a shrinking space with no view of the beyond. One of my mother's beloved clouds had come to earth. Each day we would put Penny in the car, drive to one end of the island that was advertised as having a scenic view, and stare at the fog. We awoke the next day with the hope that the fog would lift. Day after day the dreary haze blocked our view of whales and porpoises just offshore.

I could no longer tell myself that my father had lived a good life, or that at ninety-one years of age his death did not seem unusual. That was what I had told friends and family when they expressed their sympathy. The misty gloom of the weather mirrored my state of mind. I grieved Dad's death in a way I had not allowed myself to do while I was caring for my mother. I relived his last few days of life. I heard his voice calling out for my mother, in a frightened cry as I turned to leave his hospital room. "Daisy," he had pleaded. "Daisy!" That was the last time I would ever hear his voice.

My mother would have no visitors while I was on vacation. Selfishly I had abandoned her, retreating to a place she could not find me. Tormented by thoughts of my mother missing me, my father gone, I could neither sleep nor eat.

In a few days, when I was hungry, my stomach hurt. When I ate, nausea replaced the pain. Worried that I might be having an intestinal bleed, I investigated and found that there was no local hospital, only a clinic incapable of offering me help. For emergencies a helicopter transported people to the mainland, but that was impossible in the fog. That news only heightened my worries. Claustrophobic, trapped by the wall of fog, the dream of a stress-free vacation had turned into a nightmare.

When we heard that the weather was not predicted to turn sunny until after our planned departure date, we packed up our car, forfeiting the rest of our payment for the cottage, and took the next ferry back to Black's Harbour.

"Let's get out of here and drive until we find a place to spend our last few days of vacation in Maine," I said.

Without any discussion we abruptly left. The cottage owner told us it was unusual for the fog to settle in for that long. He hoped we would return. Not likely, I thought bitterly.

We passed easily through customs into Maine and took the slow shore road down the coast looking for signs on pet-friendly motels or cottages that read "Vacancy." Just before sundown we spotted one and pulled in. It was a roadside motel with no view of the ocean. The next day we drove home.

After we left the island, my stomach calmed down, but my nose was now so inflamed from sobbing that each morning I awoke with a nosebleed. It took longer each day to get the blood to stop pouring down my nose until one day just before Labor Day weekend, I could not get the bleeding to stop. I called the doctor. Robin drove me to Boston for an infusion of cryoprecipitate.

"I'm going to keep you in the hospital overnight," my doctor said. "I'll have a specialist pack your nose."

Hospitals were never a good place to get rest, contrary to what most people thought. When the ear, nose, and throat specialist arrived at my bedside, he looked perturbed at being called back to the hospital on a Friday evening before a holiday weekend. With a rough hand he forced his scope up my nose and announced, "The bleeding is coming from so high up, I can't see it."

He stepped back from the bed and asked the nurse to gather the supplies he needed to pack the nose. When the nurse left, he said, "I think you have a herpes virus." Then he added in a lowered voice, "Don't tell anyone that, they'll think I'm crazy, but I see more and more patients with herpes these days."

Oh great, just what I need, a crazy man poking up my nose. "Really?" I said, trying to sound interested in his findings.

"You should take L-lysine if you want to prevent another flare up."

The nurse returned with a metal tray of supplies and the doctor began poking the absorbent stuffing up my nose. He pushed it as high up as he could until I had a piercing headache. My nostril was stretched out to a size twice the width of the other nostril.

"Here's my card," he said tossing it on the bedside table. "Call my office and schedule an appointment for me to take out the packing in a few days." He turned and left without saying good-bye. Now he could get started on his holiday weekend.

I groaned, not able to sleep. I forced myself not to cry. Crying seemed hazardous to my health. Once I had begun to cry on our trip to Grand Manan, the backlog of tears began to spill out and I could not seem to stop.

Robin went to visit my mother while I was in the hospital, trying to reassure her that I would be back soon.

On the day the nasal packing was removed, Robin drove me to the doctor's office. She sat in the waiting room with me. I flipped through the magazines with impatience. A nurse called my name and led me to an examination room. Tapping my fingers on the arm of the reclining chair, I hoped the doctor would be gentler removing the packing than he was inserting it. The door of the room opened quickly. The doctor glanced in my direction, picked up a pair of tweezers and said, "Let's get this out." With one swift tug he ripped the plug from my nose and left the room as rapidly as he had entered.

I stood up and tottered back to the waiting room, making my way back to Robin. It was as if all the blood in my head emptied when the doctor pulled the packing out of my nose.

"That was fast," Robin said.

The next thing I knew I was on the floor and people were trying to help me up. For the first time in my life, I had fainted. None of the doctor's staff came over to see if I was all right; no one alerted a nurse or the doctor. Was the staff so unconcerned because this happened to patients here on a regular basis? When I began to feel less shaky, Robin held my arm and walked me back to our car in the parking garage.

I told her, "If I have another nosebleed, I won't be coming back to this doctor."

# *Empty Spaces*

On my first visit back to the nursing home after my vacation, my mother's roommate greeted me with, "Your mother cried every night when you were gone." The roommate sounded smug. This jab cut me deeply. Like my father, I pretended I had not heard her.

The postcards I had mailed from Canada were taped to the wall behind Mom's bed now. She wasn't there. I found her sitting in the activity room staring at the wall. Her face crinkled into a toothless smile when she saw me enter. She quickly closed her mouth and covered it with her hand. I kissed her and sat down in a chair beside her. "What happened to your partial plate?" I asked.

"It may have been thrown out by mistake. No one can find it." I found it difficult to understand her because she continued to cover her mouth with her hand in embarrassment.

"I'm so sorry," I said. She had a few teeth of her own, but several teeth had been extracted long ago. She had new partial dentures made after my parents moved in with us. The original ones had become so loose they fell down when she talked or ate. It had taken me weeks to persuade her to get fitted for new dentures. "These have lasted me for fifty years," she said at the time. "I don't need new ones."

"Can you bring me my old plate?" she asked now.

I had not kept the old set. "I don't have them anymore."

She nodded. Despondent, she didn't chide me the way she might have not too long ago. I was scolding myself for leaving her so soon after my father's death. My suspicion was that her roommate had thrown her dentures in the trash. There was no proof of course, so I kept this thought to myself.

"Would you like to go and sit outdoors for a while with me?"

She gave an apathetic nod and I wheeled her chair out to the front patio deck. Her life was empty without my father. Conversation was hard. I didn't want to tell her about my vacation or that I myself had cried every night for the past two weeks. Mom didn't want to speak about her grief. She had played the role of the strong one for so long that she didn't seem to know how to reveal her vulnerability.

After an hour I wheeled her back inside to her room. The aide put down the supper tray on my mother's bedside table. There was a cold chicken sandwich, a plastic cup of canned fruit, a cup of hot water, a carton of milk, and a tea bag. I looked at my mother, realizing that she could no longer chew a sandwich or peel the lid off the canned fruit. "I'd like the tea," she said.

"How have you been managing when I wasn't here?"

"I'm not very hungry," she said.

I dipped the tea bag in the cup of hot water, removing it quickly, since she liked her tea weak, and poured in some milk. Handing the cup to her I said, "Are you able to eat anything they bring you?"

She hesitated. "I have a good breakfast. Sometimes scrambled eggs, sometimes oatmeal." She took a sip of tea. "At noon I go to the dining room. They like to serve the supper trays in the room." Her sly answer left me wondering how much food she was able to swallow.

I looked at her more carefully now. She had been skinny before. It was hard to tell with her in the wheelchair how much weight she had lost.

"How about some of this mixed fruit?" I said, pulling off the foil top and filling a spoon with a chunk of peach.

Mom opened her mouth obediently. I made a mental note to talk to the dietitian tomorrow and explain that my mother needed soft food now that her teeth were missing. Exasperated that there seemed to be no aides available to assist my mother at mealtime, I realized that I should be sure to visit her every day at lunch and dinnertime.

By October it had become too chilly outside to sit comfortably. I often spent my time with Mom in the activity room. Mom went to the activity room only when I visited her. We would sit in a corner by the window together. One day I brought my knitting with me. When I pulled the yarn out of my bag, my mother's face saddened.

"I used to knit," she sighed.

I tucked the yarn back in my bag, zipping it shut. Her abilities were unraveling. It was hard for her to accept the losses.

When the activities director wandered over to us and asked, "Would you like a manicure?" My mother shook her head no.

"What other activities do you have scheduled?" I asked.

"I just take what I can get at no cost," she said. "Around the holidays, we have groups that want to come in and sing carols. Some churches provide religious services. Other than that, not much."

I glanced at my mother who looked disinterested.

"Would it be possible for me to teach a weekly class here for the residents on bird identification?" I saw Mom sit up a bit straighter in her chair.

"We'd love to have that!" she said, "Which day is best for you? Our calendar is wide open."

"How 'bout Tuesday afternoons?" I suggested.

"Fine with me," I said, glancing at my mother who was now listening with interest. She knew more about birds than I did. I hoped she could add comments of her own at these classes.

Each week I picked a common bird, one that I knew would be coming to the feeders outside the nursing home windows. I would print out photos or drawings of the bird from my computer. Then I made a list of facts about the species. Some weeks I found a native folk tale I could tell.

It wasn't long before I began to see the images of blue jays, chickadees, and cardinals stuck on the bulletin boards in residents' rooms. My mother kept every page in her drawer, perhaps so they would not go missing the way her dentures had. She wouldn't speak up in class because she was still too embarrassed about her missing teeth, but the classes gave us something to talk about.

November was the month when my parents had married. It was also the month of Mom's birthday. Just before her ninety-first birthday, my cousin Bill drove from Connecticut to visit my mother. My cousin had been diagnosed with a rare and fatal condition a few years earlier and travel was not as easy as it had once been for him. Mom was happy to see him and his wife. Since I did not know they were coming, I didn't happen to be there when they arrived.

Bill telephoned me after the visit, his voice apologetic. He explained, "When we said good-bye, your mother stood and then fell to the floor. I didn't know she could not stand up anymore. The aides helped her back into her chair. I'm afraid she may have been injured."

When I drove to the nursing home to see how she was, I saw that the only bruise was to her pride. She looked chagrined. I was taken aback each time her memory failed her, since most of the time she seemed clearheaded. One day she said to me, I think I will go out today and take the bus to the city. I realized why she would be confused. She had been active and independent for more than eighty years. Why wouldn't she occasionally forget that she had become weak and incapable of escaping the nursing home?

Also understandable to me was that my mother occasionally forgot that Dad had died. I made it a point not to correct her at these times. A little denial wasn't so bad. I had pretended not to hear one winter day when she said she saw my father out her window shoveling snow.

When the winter ended and I began to take my mother outside in her wheelchair to sit in the sun, Mom turned to me one warm afternoon. "Your father should come outside and sit with us," she said. "It's too nice a day for him to be indoors."

Dad had died more than a year ago and still he lived in her thoughts and heart. Tears popped up in my eyes and I struggled to regain some composure. This time I was unprepared.

Mom stared at me in regret. "I'm sorry," she said. "I should really stop playing that game."

Game? Was it really a game or had she forgotten that Dad had died more than a year ago? I couldn't tell. If it gave her any comfort to remember Dad as if he was still alive, I didn't want her to stop.

When I went to visit Robin's mother, Thelma, in the nursing home just down the street from my mother's residence, it was different. Her Alzheimer's disease had progressed. She could remember little now. She recognized my face, I doubted that she remembered my name, but she would greet me with a big smile. I would hold her hand, but she was becoming less and less verbal.

My mother was still capable of carrying on a conversation. I could see, however, that her love of life was diminishing month by month. It seemed to me that Thelma was happier than my mother. Mom lived in a state of disharmony with her memories, unable to reconcile her current abilities with those of the first eighty-nine years of her life.

# Love and Marriage

Following my father's retirement, my parents spent most of their time together. Their tenderness to each other had expanded in the past fifty-five years. They would sit, watching television or listening to music, then turn toward one another signaling their awareness of the other's presence with a wave of a hand. There was no need for words.

"We never had a harsh word between us," my father told the woman who interviewed him when they were in the assisted living center. At that time Dad was eighty-nine, and I was glad he had forgotten the harsh words that had once troubled him.

As a child living in a small house with only my parents and myself, I had overheard mother's angry accusations and seen my father retreat into a sullen silence. Their disagreements were infrequent. I had witnessed only a few. The one I remembered most vividly was the day my mother had criticized Dad for not washing the wooden stairs leading from the basement to the hatchway before he had painted them. She called him stupid—a word she had never used with me. After that, she stormed into their bedroom and slammed the door. I tiptoed down to the basement where I found my father looking dejected.

"I'm afraid your mother doesn't love me anymore," he said. At eight years old my stomach tightened. I attempted unsuccessfully to console him. I climbed the stairs slowly and discovered that the door to my parents' bedroom was open again.

I found Mom in the kitchen shelling peas. When she saw me, she grunted, "Any fool knows you wash a surface before you paint it. Your father has no commonsense." I could say nothing to soften her annoyance. It shocked me that something as trivial could make my mother furious.

How they resolved their differences was a mystery to me. It would take me a long time to realize that these events meant little. Their disputes were not irreparable. Their angry words didn't bring physical injury. They loved each other and respected each other. I vowed that I would not say hurtful things to the person I loved. I would not become entangled in petty disagreements.

Once Robin and I began to live together in 1974, I broke that promise to myself time and time again. My childhood memories had sparked the fire of inadequacy, fueling the flames of resentment. Robin and I had resolved many small disagreements, but after ten years of living together, our anger at each other became intractable.

In the early 1980s I was active in the local chapter of the National Hemophilia Foundation. Before we understood what was happening, people with hemophilia and other bleeding disorders began to die from a mysterious disruption in their immune system. One after another, people I had come to respect and friends I could rely upon for understanding became sick. Many died almost immediately; others clung to life while researchers struggled to find out what was happening. Like myself, many understood we were vulnerable. In addition, not only could we become terminally ill, but we might face discrimination by medical professionals, employers, and even family members.

Most of us had reached a time in our lives when treatment options proved effective. Our disorder interfered with our daily lives much less than ever before. Many of us used clotting factors derived from blood on a routine basis. We didn't have to wait until a joint swelled to twice its size before being infused. Doctors recommended that if we thought there might be internal bleeding, we infuse quickly with whatever clotting factor our own bodies did not produce. Patients kept supplies of clotting factor in their homes, infused themselves, and rarely needed to be hospitalized.

We had more freedom to work or play without the consequences of a hemorrhage. Now blood might be poison. We had been betrayed. Our hopes for a long and healthy life were crushed against an invisible, unidentified, untreatable, and unpreventable evil.

I was incensed that Robin did not understand my terror. She was angry with me, although I had no idea why. What right did she have to be angry with me? Our fury ate away inside us like a corrosive acid. By 1984, I believed I could not tolerate living with her any longer. I couldn't live with her, yet I couldn't imagine life without her.

Looking back on that time it seems unbelievable that we had lived together in a platonic relationship for ten years, each of us looking for a man to marry. Locked into the cultural definitions, which said a person was either straight or gay, we tried to find a man we wanted to spend the rest of our lives with. While many of our coworkers and friends thought we were a lesbian couple, we believed otherwise.

We sought the advice of our minister, who said, "Have you thought about couple's counseling? I can recommend someone."

Even our minister thought we were a couple. The counselor thought we were a couple too. In the first session with the counselor, she asked if we had given up on our relationship and wanted to separate or was our goal to remain together. The question did not hang in the air long before we each said we preferred to stay together.

Eventually in the sessions with the counselor, Robin revealed what made her angry with me. "She doesn't expect to live long," she said. "I want her to live to be eighty at least, but she can't even imagine that."

Astonished, I said, "You're angry that I have given up hope?"

Her words unlocked something inside me. I wanted to kiss her, embrace her, and transform our relationship. In the next several counseling sessions, it became clear it was what both of us desired.

When I told my parents that Robin and I were more than good friends, Mom's initial reaction was, "Don't tell anyone. It's dangerous." It was reasonable to be afraid. It hadn't been that long since being gay was a felony. It was labeled an illness in the *Diagnostic and Statistical Manual of Mental Disorders* until 1974. People who were suspected of being gay or bisexual risked imprisonment, institutionalization, and physical attacks.

Robin's mother had reacted more strongly screaming, "I can't love you anymore." Robin's internal torment eased when her father said, "I don't agree, but I'll always love you." Their initial reactions faded quickly from their minds, if not from ours. Within a month we resumed celebrating holidays and summer picnics all together: Robin and I, Thelma and Donald, Daisy and Horace.

In January 1989 we had been together for fifteen years. We did not have the option of being legally married. Although the state did not recognize our love, our church did. In a Service of Holy Union at the Unitarian Universalist Church, we publicly exchanged our vows. We walked singly up the side aisles of the sanctuary, and when the service ended, we shyly kissed each other and walked hand in hand down the center aisle together.

The guests were all friends. We invited no family members. We doubted they would attend.

That spring we put down an offer to purchase our first house. When we went to sign the agreement at the attorney's office, he said, "There are two ways to co-own a house; one is to own it as if one of you is a tenant, which I recommend for you. The other is to own it jointly, but surely you don't like each other that much." He chuckled.

"Actually we do," Robin and I said almost at the same moment.

"Oh," was the lawyer's only reply. He rolled his eyes and moved on with his other questions.

Parents, friends, even the attorney knew our truth.

Within two days of the first anniversary of my father's death, the Massachusetts Supreme Judicial Court ruled that it was unconstitutional to allow only opposite-sex couples to marry.

We were among those who cheered the ruling; however, there were many who did not. The State Legislature drafted an amendment to the Massachusetts Constitution that would reverse the court's decision and enable marriage discrimination. Our local State Representative was outspoken in her belief that marriage should only be between a man and a woman. She gained interviews on the Boston television stations and newspapers.

One of the board members of the church where Robin was the minister declared, "We need to talk with her in person. She is our State Representative after all. My father was involved in local politics for years. I'll set up an appointment in the Representative's office at the State House. Who'll go with me?"

Eight of us were available on the day of our appointment with the State Representative. When we arrived, we filled up the small anteroom while the secretary scurried inside to announce our arrival. We sat for several minutes before the secretary came back out to say that the Representative had not realized we would be such a large group and she believed she had been ambushed. The woman who had made the appointment spoke up saying, "I was the one who called you and I explained that there would be several of us. We've driven more than an hour to get here."

Again the secretary disappeared behind the closed door. We sat for several minutes, uncomfortably shifting in our chairs, making note of the luxurious suite, wondering if the door would open for us to go in or if we would be dismissed.

When the secretary returned, she led us to a conference room, inviting us to sit at the table. The Representative entered. Her face was tight, ready for conflict. Robin spoke first.

"Thank you for seeing us today. These are members of our congregation and we would like an opportunity to speak with you."

The Representative nodded, her posture began to soften.

Robin continued, "Will you permit us to introduce ourselves to you?"

Nodding again, the Representative eased back in her seat just a bit.

The first person to speak gave her name and then proceeded to say, "You know my father, he's been a Town Selectman. I'm aware of the good work you have done to protect foster children and women. My wife and I had a service of Holy Union in our church. She and I have been together for ten years now, and we would like to make our commitment to each other legal by being married."

The Representative smiled when she was thanked, but her lips tightened when she heard the woman mention having a wife.

Next came a man who said his name and explained he was a member of the church, and he and his wife had been married for almost twenty years. "I'm here today because I believe marriage is important and should not be denied to any two people who love each other."

One church member explained that Robin had married her and her husband a year earlier. The comments went clockwise around the table. The Representative's face looked impassive. Robin's turn came.

She said, "I know you from the committee we both serve on for protective services to abused women. Linda and I have been together almost thirty years now. We love each other. We have provided shelter for Linda's parents when they became unable to care for themselves and now we provide care for my parents too. We're a family."

The Representative knew that Robin and I lived together. I had been open with the Board of Library Trustees at the time I was interviewing for the position of town library director. I was next in line to speak, but the State Representative shifted her eyes past me to the person on my left.

"Excuse me," I quipped, "even though Robin is my spouse, I don't allow her to speak for me."

The Representative chuckled and before she realized what she was implying, she said, "I don't let my husband speak for me either."

People around the table nodded in agreement. I saw a flush of embarrassment on the Representative's cheeks. For a brief second she had recognized our commonality. I shook the Representative's hand as we left her office, smiling at my small victory.

Our appointment with the Representative made little difference to her. The Representative did not change her vote. She did, however, stop releasing statements to the press on this issue.

When the vote was taken at the statehouse, the constitutional amendment failed. Within days, the broadcast media began reporting stories about marriages between same-sex couples. Like us many had been unrecognized as couples even though they had been partners for thirty years or more.

When we discussed our plans for a wedding, I said to Robin, "My mother is too fragile. I can't bring myself to have a wedding now."

There was the problem of transporting her—fragile and debilitated. More of a concern to me was that Mom was grieving for the love of her life. It was as if she was drowning, sinking under slowly, rising temporarily, before becoming submerged in sorrow again. She was paying the inevitable price for loving deeply and long. I both wanted her there to celebrate with us and aware that, if she was present, my attention would be fully drawn to her sorrow and not to my joy.

"Let's set a date in the fall, invite everyone, family, friends, coworkers," I suggested.

Robin replied, "My mother can't leave her nursing home. Her dementia is in the final stages. I think my father would like to have a part in our ceremony though."

"I'll ask my cousin Bill if he would consider taking a role in the service." Bill had been a United Church of Christ minister until his illness forced him to retire. "I hope he's well enough to attend."

We set the date for our wedding early in September on the thirtieth anniversary of the day we had begun living together.

Robin and I began sending out invitations to our wedding. Robin asked a ministerial colleague to officiate and talked to a bagpiper about which tune to select instead of the traditional wedding march. The piping would honor both Robin's Scottish ancestors and my own Nova Scotian roots.

# Till Death Do Us Part

In mid-July a bed opened up in the nursing home. I requested that my mother be moved to that vacancy so she would not have to endure her verbally abusive roommate any longer. It was a smaller room, with only two beds, nearer to the nurses' station and activities room. My request was granted, and I moved my mother's few clothes and personal items to the other room. I introduced myself and my mother to the woman who lived in the room. Although she looked close to Mom's age, she did not look as if she belonged here. She sat primly in the chair by the window, introducing herself as Margaret and smiling politely.

Margaret watched like a curious bird as I filled up the dresser drawers with socks and tattered underwear, T-shirts, elastic waist pants, and sweaters. Mom had forbidden me from purchasing her any new clothing. Her frugality would not allow this. Each item of Mom's clothing was labeled with my mother's name. Margaret, on the other hand, dressed for style rather than comfort. The shirtwaist dress and high-heeled shoes she wore made her look more like a visitor than a resident.

Several items of Mom's clothing were missing from her closet. Even though the required black indelible ink had withstood the hot water cycle and industrial dryers in the laundry room, there were items with no name marked on them. Some of these items were obviously not my mother's size. This was another sign of the nursing home's disregard for the dignity of people in their care. Exasperated, I tossed the odd clothing into a pile to return to the laundry room. I asked the staff to locate Mom's missing items.

My mother and her new roommate appeared to have little in common on the surface, but Margaret graciously welcomed Mom.

Mom was spending more time in her room. Bouts of aspiration pneumonia were coming frequently now that her ability to swallow was compromised by her Parkinson's disease and her missing teeth.

On a hot and muggy afternoon in early August, I entered Mom's room to find a nurse attempting to find a vein on my mother's arm. A bottle of IV antibiotics hung from a metal pole beside the bed. The nurse had failed once already, and she looked shaken by having to make a second stab at the tiny woman who lay in front of her. Mom glanced up at me, tension wrinkling her brow, her free hand curled tightly in a fist.

I knew that my mother's tension had contracted her already small veins, automatically pulling them deep under her skin in a defensive action. I had learned relaxation techniques, finding them to be more successful than the moist hot compresses some nurses used to bring my veins up to the surface. I asked the nurse to wait a few minutes before trying again. She said, "Gladly," putting down the syringe she had been about to unwrap from the sterile package.

I gently stroked my mother's arm, kissed her forehead, and then said, "Mom, I want you to do something for me."

"Okay," she said, but the tone of her voice sounded doubtful.

I placed one of my hands gently on Mom's stomach, barely touching the surface, just below her rib cage. "Now take a deep breath, Mom. One that is so deep you will raise up your belly until it pushes on my hand, then let your breath out slowly."

She looked at me as if I was from another planet, but she did as I asked.

"Good," I said. It was a labored breath, but I felt it raise and lower her stomach a bit. "Again," I said softly.

The nurse watched intently as I continued to coach my mother in her deep breathing until I gave a slight nod in her direction, then she located a vein and inserted the butterfly needle in one quick successful move.

"In!" the nurse exclaimed with relief. "I couldn't have done this without you." She began rapidly searching for something in her bag. "I want to give you a gift, but all I have is my scissors. Please take them." Then she loaded up her supplies and said good-bye before I had time to protest the unusual present.

My mother appeared exhausted. The IV fluids were flowing from the bottle hanging from the poll down the tubing and into Mom's body. My mother turned to me and whispered, "I don't want to do that again. No more."

"If that's what you want, Mom, of course."

I sat by her side until she drifted off to sleep. When I got home, I told Robin what my mother had said. "Do you think she understands that if she doesn't get the antibiotics, she will die?" I asked her. "Would you be willing to go visit her tomorrow and find out if she understands what it means?"

The next day Robin confirmed that my mother did understand her decision.

Mom was well for three weeks before the next pneumonia began. In the last week of August swelling from edema trapped the gold wedding band she had worn on her left hand for sixty-four years. The finger was turning blue, the ring cutting off circulation. I reported this to the nurse, who said, "When this happens, we call the town fire department. They can cut the ring off."

"You mean this happens on a regular basis? Why didn't anyone suggest that I take the ring off before?"

The nurse shrugged as if she hadn't given that option any thought.

In minutes two uniformed firemen with bulging utility belts around their waists clunked into the room. Their tall, heavy frames towered over my mother in her bed.

"Where's the ring?" one of the firemen said. My mother raised her shaking hand.

One fireman pulled a metal cutter from his belt and, more gently than I would have thought possible, held her swollen hand and slipped the cutter around the ring. With a snip he cut the gold band apart without injuring Mom's skin. I felt a shiver creeping up my spine as the fireman spread the ring further apart and removed it from her finger. What a horrible thing for my mother to endure in the last days of her life. Her husband dead, the symbol of her marriage cut off. I struggled to gulp down my emotions. Mom seemed detached from the procedure as if she had not noticed what was going on around her.

After the firemen left, I picked up the ring and held it in my hand. It had worn down to a thin, almost weightless band, less than half the width of the bands Robin and I would exchange in a few days. I stuffed it in my pocket—why, I was not sure. Perhaps it was as a reminder to me of the price of love.

It was only a few days later when one afternoon my mother reached out for my hand, her expression serious. "I'm dying," she whispered as if it was a secret she needed to tell me. I detected a hint of surprise in her voice. At some level she had always known she would die, but to know something and to fully comprehend are two different things.

I wiped the tears from my cheeks and nodded, "I know."

"You do?" she said as if it shocked her. She gazed directly into my eyes. "Take care of yourself," she said. Her final wish was for me. She might have had some lingering doubts that I would be able to care for myself. I realized that there was reason for her concern. I had given up taking care of myself to take care of her and my father.

"I will," I said sniffling.

We sat in silence for several minutes before she drifted off to sleep. We had just had our last conversation. As I walked down the hallway heading toward the door, a nurse stopped me. She said, "We'll let you know if there is any change in her breathing." Then she paused, "When I call you, get here as quickly as you can, so you can see her one last time."

The phone rang before sunrise the next morning. I threw on my jeans and a shirt and sped to the nursing home. My mother, unconscious now, lay breathing so shallowly I was not sure if she was still alive. I sat beside her in the darkened room and picked up her hand. It was warm to the touch. She gave my hand a gentle squeeze and then her grip relaxed. The essence of her was gone, only a shell remained.

For several minutes I could not bear to remove my hand from hers. I didn't want to let go. Like my mother I had always held on to the belief that she would somehow manage to escape death or at least delay it until after I died. I had not contemplated outliving her.

When I arrived back home, Robin said, "Our wedding is in two days. Don't you think we should postpone it?"

My mother's last words to me lingered in my ears: "Take care of yourself."

I had made taking care of myself secondary when I began taking care of my parents. When I did take care of myself, it had frequently been too little or too late. I had lost ground I would never regain. I had stopped physical therapy prematurely; the left shoulder was now permanently frozen. I had ceased a daily yoga and meditation practice, which had previously helped me maintain my health. The diverticulitis that had perforated my large intestine could recur at any time. Aphasia after the hemorrhagic stroke still hampered my ability to read text.

My parents would not need me ever again; Robin's mother was safe and secure; and Robin's father was looking forward to doing a reading at our wedding.

"No," I said. "I don't want to postpone the wedding."

# *Wedding Day*

Robin chose a wine red dress and I picked out a dress of soft blue-green. Wedding dresses or tuxedoes were not our style. Besides, this event was also a celebration of thirty years together and a renewal of the vows we had made fifteen years earlier in another Unitarian Universalist Church.

The bagpiper arrived early. We hid him in one of the church classrooms in the basement. Then we went up the stairs to help the church custodian, who was also a wedding guest, set up the folding tables. The guests who arrived early helped. Robin and I unfolded the white linen tablecloths and tossed a sprinkling of gold hearts on each table.

Don had purchased a suit and tie for the occasion. He had also paid for the food and drink for the reception. He sat in a chair memorizing the reading we had asked him to do. My father, I thought, would never have looked as comfortable in a suit and tie as Robin's Dad did. How I wished that my father was doing a reading today, perhaps one of his favorite sonnets.

It was as if my brain was caught in a tide pool, trapped in an outpouring of joy and swirling loss. My mother's recent death. Robin's mother unable to remember the names of her husband

and daughter. My knees felt wobbly. I wondered if I could get through this day of extreme emotions.

The reception would be in the space by the accessible door. Most people avoided the steep granite steps at the front of the church, choosing instead to enter through this door. For the minister who would marry us and for my cousin Bill, the accessible door was a necessity. Since my adolescence I had found stairs difficult to navigate. I was proud that people in wheelchairs and walkers could now enter our church in dignity. The congregation had cared enough to pay for the accommodation that required removing a window and cutting a hole in the granite wall.

The caterer placed the three-tiered wedding cake decorated with fresh autumn flowers on the center table. Someone carried the matching flower arrangements to the sanctuary. Nervous energy kept me moving, stopping only to make adjustments to the place settings and greeting people as they entered.

A few of the people who had traveled the farthest distance had spent the night before in a local hotel. A friend whose husband shot the photos for college sports events had volunteered to bring his professional camera, although he admitted that portrait shots were not his strength. The couple lived in Maine. We had spent many a vacation day exploring the coast together.

My cousin Carolyn and her husband arrived. They had driven from Connecticut. Still there was no sign of my cousin Bill and his family. While I paced anxiously awaiting Bill's arrival, our friend took photographs of Robin, her father, the minister. Then the photographer took photos of the uncut cake and the flower arrangements in the sanctuary. I could not stay still long enough for him to get a photo of me.

Five minutes before we were scheduled to begin, Bill, using his rolling walker, came through the door. I sighed in relief until I noticed Bill's wife and two daughters looking worried as they came through the door just behind him. Bill had lost weight. His walk was shaky even with the walker's assistance. Had I asked too much of him to participate in the ceremony? Bill gave me a grin and announced he would not use the walker inside. I saw his wife and daughters exchange concerned glances. Bill and his family proceeded slowly into the sanctuary. They were the last to arrive.

I nodded to Robin. "Ready?" I said.

"Ready," she replied and went down the stairs to let the bagpiper know it was time to begin.

From deep below us, sounding faint and far away, we could hear the wail of the pipes moving slowly toward the stairs. With each step the piper took, the resonant music grew louder and stronger. Robin and I stood at the top of the stairs, just out of view of the people seated in the church. We heard the muffled conversations in the church grow quiet, the curiosity of people drawn to the approaching music. It captured my mood, sounding half like a sorrowful cry and half like a dance. This, I thought, was what love was truly about—joy intertwined with tears, making the twist and turns of life into a strong rope that held us together.

Robin and I took up our pace behind the bagpiper, entering the sanctuary as the guests stood. Sunlight streamed through the stained-glass windows created by a student of Louis Comfort Tiffany. We lit the three candles together for our parents who could not be there to witness our marriage. When my cousin Bill stood, he told of being present at my parents' wedding sixty-five years earlier.

Robin and I renewed the vows we had made to each other fifteen years before. We slipped a gold wedding band on each other's finger and kissed. Then the minister announced, "By the power vested in me by the Commonwealth of Massachusetts, I pronounce you married."

Spontaneous whoops of joy rose from the wedding guests. The thunderous applause brought tears to my eyes. Guests stood clapping, as we paraded behind the bagpiper and out into the reception hall.

My relationship with Robin had become stronger during the past five years. We had given up time with each other to dedicate our available minutes and hours to nurture our parents. We had become a team with a unified goal, and I doubted either of us could have achieved what we did without the other's full support and assistance. Instead of weakening our relationship, the challenges had strengthened it.

Marriage, the legal acknowledgment of our commitment to each other, was to use the cliché, like frosting on the cake.

# *Waves of Care*

The month after our wedding, my cousin Bill died. Before his death, he had left instructions for his own memorial service. He planned the details himself, including the hymns he wanted us to sing. His memorial service was held in the church he had served as minister. Friends, family, and members of the congregation filled the sanctuary to capacity. They told stories of how Bill's life had enriched them. Together we celebrated their lives and acknowledged that we would miss him. My tears flowed freely as I grieved.

My parents didn't want a funeral or memorial service for themselves. They both avoided funerals whenever they could. I had missed not being able to share stories of Dad with my mother. Instead Mom played the "game" that he was still alive. Whether the pretense was due to her hallucinations or was intentional, it prevented me from expressing my own emotions.

When my father's ashes returned from Harvard Medical School, I sent them to the US Navy for a burial at sea. My mother's ashes were sprinkled in a place where Indian Pipes sprouted under the shade of a woodland forest. From that spot, you can hear the lapping waves on the shore of Maine.

On the day that would have been my parents' sixty-fifth wedding anniversary, Robin, her father, and I drove to the Unitarian Universalist Society in Springfield. It was the church where they had been members for years. We shared soup, sandwiches, cookies, and stories around the table. I brought with me photograph albums of my parents. It comforted me to hear their stories and watch people exclaim, "I remember that day," if they spotted a photo they recognized.

For ninety-one years Daisy and Horace had lived well, loved deeply, and put their beliefs into action. It was time for me to let go of my regrets.

The rambling nursing home, which seemed more like a refuge than an institution to Thelma, closed. The owner could not afford to make the necessary renovations. Thelma was moved to a newer, more accessible facility. When we went to visit, she was uncommunicative and lay with her head on whatever table she had in front of her. Visits became even more painful. Two months later there was no stopping her rapid decline.

Robin received a call from the nursing home in late December 2004. Thelma was plummeting nearer to death. Conferring with Thelma's doctor led Robin to conclude that sending her mother to the hospital would only prolong her dying. The doctor didn't hesitate to tell her, "You're making the right decision."

Robin hastily gathered up a collection of music that had previously set her mother to singing. She included Christmas carols and Judy Garland belting out "Somewhere over the Rainbow." She played the music all night as she sat curled up in a chair beside her mother's bed. The doctor had assured Robin her mother's death would be a swift and painless end. Finally, she decided to come home for a while. Only a short time later, the phone rang, and the activities director from the nursing home told Robin her mother had died.

Cape Cod was Thelma's favorite place in the entire world. Robin managed to find someone who'd put a small boat into the water in a Cape Cod bay. Donald, Robin, and I carried Thelma's ashes in a biodegradable container. Without ceremony the container floated away from us succumbing to the tides. Giving Thelma's remains back to Cape Cod gave Robin some solace.

In 2006, Robin was ready to search for another congregation to serve. The urge to move on was so great that Robin was willing to resettle in any location. It terrified me to leave my hematologist of thirty years. I expected that it would not be easy to find a doctor who had any understanding of my rare bleeding disorder. I swallowed my anxiety and proclaimed, "Search for the church that suits you best, and I will be by your side."

It turned out that the right church was in Florida, where our marriage license was not recognized. I shuddered when I thought of the time before we were married when Robin had been denied the right to see me in the emergency room.

By April 2007, we were planning our move. Don had been coming to our house more frequently for dinner and traveling to Connecticut less often since Thelma's death. We asked Don if he would come with us. He was greatly relieved when we told him we hoped he would live with us now.

We sold our house, packed our household belongings and the items from Don's apartment, and found a new place in Florida, all in the space of three weeks. We filled the car with enough supplies to last until our furniture was delivered to our new address.

Once we moved, I became a pastor's spouse in earnest. The church was large enough and active enough to demand most of Robin's time. She relished the opportunity to use her abilities fully. I spent my days with Don shopping, cooking, and going to the senior center for programs.

In October, as the church year was gaining steam, Don fell in the bathroom. Robin was at a planning retreat that day. I called the ambulance and sat with Don in the emergency room. The x-rays showed that he had broken the second vertebra in his neck. Metal rods attached to a halo were screwed into his skull. The contraption seemed designed to create more discomfort than assistance. Even though he lived with us, Robin could only manage to help him with nightly routines. I hired, trained, and paid caregivers who assisted him with bathing.

The doctor explained that the halo needed to be left in place because, at Don's age, the fracture would never fully heal. A year later a second specialist gave a contradictory opinion, and the halo was removed without catastrophe. Although he was relieved to be free of the metal contraption, his energy was never again the same. He spent most of his days doing crossword puzzles or searching the internet.

In 2010, a mysterious illness required Don to be hospitalized. After he underwent a series of tests, a nurse convinced him he would die if he didn't allow them to insert a feeding tube. Robin dashed to the hospital when Don told her he wanted to let them insert the tube. There was nothing she could say to dissuade him. She knew from the research she'd done during her mother's last years that once a feeding tube is inserted, doctors rarely want it removed.

In went the tube, and because we'd never be able to manage the many times a day it needed to be flushed and his new limitations, Don went to a nursing home. He never recovered enough to come home, the feeding tube remained in place, and respiratory issues eventually sent him to the hospital again. This time hospice was brought in, and Don struggled to breathe for seven weeks.

When Robin visited, he would nod, occasionally take her hand, and seemed to listen to the few topics she could muster to share with him. One day she went in and his bed was empty. The staff didn't seem to know where he was. Robin went from desk to desk sure that he'd died and no one had called her. But he'd only been moved to a new room. Even though Robin had been visiting every day, the staff didn't seem ready to apologize for failing to notify her.

In July 2012, when Robin sat with her father, she noticed blue nail beds. She'd only been home a few minutes when a nurse called to let her know Don had died. She could only offer small thanks that Don had been released from forty-nine days of suffering, striving to get enough air into his lungs. "How his chest must have hurt," she wailed, "how many hours must he have lain there waiting for some release to come."

My fear that I would not find another hematologist who could treat my rare form of hemophilia was unfounded. After we moved to Florida, advances in the standard of care for people without fibrinogen radically improved, and my new doctor encouraged me to switch to a virus-free factor. The insertion of a port-a-cath has made intravenous access obsolete. I currently receive infusions on a routine basis. These advances in medical care make my life easier than ever before.

In 2016, I used a medication that eradicated the hepatitis C virus from my system. The damage done to my liver by the virus has not yet been determined. I live with the uncertainty.

I began this memoir when Robin and I spent a month in a cottage facing the Gulf of Mexico on the hidden coast of Florida.

Robin was intent on her artwork as I outlined my memories. From the deck, we watched pelicans plunging into chopping waves, beak first, scooping up fish and salty water. The fish they captured in their large throat pouches beneath the waves of turbulence sustained them and their newborn chicks. The chicks would reach deep into the throats of their caregivers. The act nourished both the lives of the young and the old.

Today the waters were calm, the ripples gentle. Tomorrow might bring hazardous tides or heavy winds. It didn't matter in the end. What matters is the care we continue to give and receive during our lifetime.

# Gratitude

Thanks to many other writers who advised me and encouraged me. A few of these writers are Bonnie Armstrong, Barbara Beaird, Roberta Burton, Susan Cerulean, Carla Cramer, Jenny Crowley, Cheryl DAmbrosio, Patty Daniels, Shirley Dunn-Perry, Adrian Fogelin, Kate Kerr, Laura Newton, James Nobel, Nancy O'Farrell, Judy Ray, Louise Rill, Jane Ruberg, Mary Jane Ryals, Marianne Ryan, Eileen Sperl Hawkins, and apologies to those whose names I have inadvertently left out.

I am deeply indebted to two editors, Heather Whitaker and Sandra Wendel. These women each did far more than correct what I had written. They also helped me each step along the path to publication.

Thank you to Cheryl J. McDowell for letting me use the title of one of her poems, "Pair Ants," and for helping me to experience high school through her eyes.

Because my life journey required medical assistance, I thank hematologists Murray Bern, MD, and Janice Lawson, MD, for their compassionate care.

# About the Author

Linda Wright is a member of the Tallahassee Writers Association and a former student at the Osher Lifelong Learning Institute. She was also one of the editors and contributors to *Life Lessons: Writings from the Osher Lifelong Learning Institute at The Florida State University*, published in 2010.

She is a retired librarian and long-range planning consultant for libraries and library organizations. She worked for one school library, four public libraries, and the Commonwealth of Massachusetts Board of Library Commissioners.

As a person with a rare genetic bleeding disorder, Linda has served as a past president of the New England Hemophilia Association and a regional board member of the National Hemophilia Foundation. She has been a writing coach and editor for My Girls Blood, an international organization dedicated to sharing the lives of girls and women with bleeding disorders.

Her short stories have been published in *Chicken Soup for the Soul: O Canada: 101 Heartwarming and Inspiring Stories by and for Canadians* and *Persimmon Tree*, an online magazine of the arts by women over sixty.

Her interests include mindfulness meditation, adoption of shelter animals, and knitting. She and her spouse live in Tallahassee, Florida.

# Contact the author:

## My Turn: When Caregiving Roles Reverse

Paperback: 978-1-945505-33-1
Kindle: 978-1-945505-34-8

www.GraywoodPress.com

Made in the USA
Columbia, SC
19 November 2018